AN INVITATION TO THE READER

Although it is unlikely that the roads you walk and cycle on these tours will change much with time, some road signs, landmarks, and other items can. If you find that such changes have occurred on these routes, please let the author know, so that corrections may be made in future editions. Other comments and suggestions are also welcome.

Address all correspondence to
janvi@gzguide.net

IMPORTANT NOTE

The world is a dynamic place. Hotels change ownership, restaurants hike their prices, museums alter their opening hours, and buses and trains change their routes. And all of this can occur in the several months after our authors have visited, inspected, and written about, these hotels, restaurants, museums and transportation services. Though we have made valiant efforts to keep all our information fresh and up-to-date, at least a few changes are likely to occur in the periods before a revised edition of this guidebook is published. So users of this guide are forewarned that some small details in this book may have changed. Please also note that we have no responsibility or liability for any inaccurate, errors, omissions, or for inconvenience, loss, damage, or expenses suffered by anyone as a result of the assertions in this guide.

Discover Guangzhou, 1st Edition, 2018
Written by Janvi Chow
Editors: Ron Eng, Mike Roy
Illustrator: Suru Yang (杨粟儒)
Cover & layout design: Francis Zheng (郑燕玲)
Illustration revised & supplemented by Francis Zheng

ISBN-13: 978-0-6483896-0-6
ISBN-10: 0-6483896-0-X

All rights reserved © 2018 Janvi Chow
Published by Janvi Tours Publishing
Published in Adelaide, Australia

No part of this publication may be reproduced, stored in a retrieval system or transmitted in any from or by any means, electronic, mechanical, photocopying, recording, or otherwise without the written permission of publisher, except by a reviewer, who may quote a brief passages.

Additional and supplement information, new maps, updates and corrections are available at www.gzguide.net

ACKNOWLEDGMENTS

Researching and writing this book has been a long time ambition for me because I want to share my passion and knowledge of the City of Guangzhou for the enjoyment and benefit of others. Preparing this book has been time consuming, a task made more difficult for me because I am not skilled or fluent with the English language. I would like to give special thanks to several people who made this book possible.

A very special thanks to Uncle Ray whom I met during my working holiday in New Zealand. In 2011, while he came for a vacation in China, he gave me valuable advice and brilliant inspiration with respect to the future prospect of my job. That has enabled me to find my passion in life. Without Uncle Ray's constant encouragement, it would not have been possible for me to bring about this work which I am passionate in. I truly have no idea where this book would be without his guidance.

Thanks to my friend Ron Eng for helping with the editing, proof reading and the unlimited support rendered. My pursuit of this project is very much aided by his generous help.

I would also like to express my gratitude to Mike for helping me to edit the first two chapters. I am indebted to him for providing me with his extensive personal and professional guidance to improve the write-ups. I met Mike when he went backpacking around China, and read stories about his adventures and encounters at www.threeruleride.com.

I would also like to thank Diana Lin and her uncle Trevor Hilton for translating the supplement information and editing at the last minute to help me get the book finished on time. Diana is a passionate Chinese teacher and you may visit her page at lingobridge.net.

I am also eternally grateful to my parents who have never given me any stress and financial burden in this prolonged process of book writing.

Finally, thanks to many anonymous people for their useful suggestions.

FOREWORD

Janvi was born and raised in Guangzhou. He started Janvi Tours over 6 years ago. Janvi Tour is a platform that engages people to learn and understand Guangzhou through unique cultural activities "off the beaten paths". He creates fun learning experiences that help travelers understand Guangzhou and people's life. To learn more about his Guangzhou private off-the-beaten-path tours, please visit his website at www.gzguide.net

During his years as a private tour guide, he has noticed that more and more tourists are interested in learning more about sightseeing, food, culture and history in Guangzhou; yet, there is no guidebook on the subject in details. For that very reason, he has spent most of the last five years putting this book together. He was motivated by a desire to share the joys of exploration and to help travelers from all over the world experience Guangzhou's unique food and culture. One day the idea struck him, he should write a book of Guangzhou in English to make this possible for the ever-growing number of visitors coming to his city. And so ***Discover Guangzhou*** was born.

He has never had financial sponsorship for his book and he would never contact a restaurant and ask them for a freebie -- lives simpler that way, all the recommendations are his favorite restaurants and snack bars. There are many ways to see cities, but for anyone desiring a sense of the history and character of an urban place, slow, self-powered exploration on foot or bike will offer up the best opportunities for insight. A stained glass window on arcade house, a flea market at the end of a narrow alley, the ancient buildings in the village, encounters with the locals who live and work there -- these are just a few of the rewards of walking and biking tours.

Travelers won't be able to traverse the entire greater metro area in a day, or even in a weekend. Use these tours to explore Guangzhou in small, detailed doses by following the itineraries. You will be rewarded with a deeper understanding of this City's unique blend of culture, architecture and food.

He wrote this book because exploring the City is a personal passion of him. This book is not perfect, but he hopes people find it helpful when they get the opportunity to visit Guangzhou. The purpose of this book is to prove that walking and biking in Guangzhou can be immensely rewarding, opening traveler's eyes to hidden pockets of the City that are otherwise all too easy to miss. These walks reflect the many faces of Guangzhou, and he hopes the discoveries travelers make as their explore the vibrant neighborhoods of this fascinating City will encourage traveler's to dust off their sneakers.

CONTENTS

I HOW TO USE THIS GUIDE — 6
How To Use This Book — 7

II INTRODUCING GUANGZHOU — 12
Travel Weather — 13
A Brief History — 16
Local Custom and Culture — 18
Lingnan Architecture — 22
Lingnan Arts — 23
Annual Events — 28

III EXPLORE GUANGZHOU — 43
WALKING TRAILS — 44
  Map of Walking Tour Areas — 45
  Plan of the city of Canton — 46
  Sai Kwan — 47
  Shamian Island — 61
  Changdi --The West Bund — 69
  Haizhu Square — 82
  Xi Men Kou — 93
  Beijing Road — 104
  Dongshan — 122
  African Town — 130
  Shek Pai Urban Village — 134
  Shiweitang Railway Station — 138
  Julong Ancient Village — 142
  Huangpu — 148
  Lung Dou Mei — 157
BIKE TRAILS — 163
  Map of Bike Tour Areas — 164
  Ersha Island — 165
  Changzhou Island — 172
  Dawen Agricultural Village — 180

IV SURVIVAL GUIDE — 183
Mosques in Guangzhou — 184
Getting Around — 186
Tips, Secrets & Tricks — 188

V INDEX — 195

HOW TO USE THIS GUIDE

Help you navigate the book
and understand the essential neighborhood map.

How To Use This Book

Narrowing down all of Guangzhou city to 13 walks and 3 cycle routes was quite a challenge, use this book as a guide to areas around Guangzhou but venture out on your own to discover the countless pleasures and experiences the City has to offer. Before starting your journey, be sure to wear comfortable walking shoes and if you are biking, check that your bicycle is in good condition. Each adventure should take between one and four hours to complete. In order to avoid potential disappointment, double-check opening hours for museums, parks, markets and restaurants before you set out. All starting points for the walks and bike routes in this book can be reached by public transportation; the introduction to each route explains procedures to follow. The subway is the easiest and generally fastest way to get around town. You can purchase a Metro Card at Seven-eleven and metro stations, valid on metros, buses, taxis and ferries. When you take the bus, check the map at the bus stop, or on the bus for where you should get off. Or you can always ask the driver as you board by pointing at the Chinese characters from the book.

The routes described in this book follow a course starting with the old city and extends into the City's outer boroughs, which makes it easy to add one route onto another should you want to extend your trip. After checking out contents in this book, continue exploring on your own, there is far more to see than any one or two routes could possible contain.

Before you get started on your tour, take a moment to acquaint yourself with Guangzhou's brief history, culture and festivals (Chapter II), but also learn some travel tips in this City (Chapter IV). This will help you put the many places you will be visiting into their proper culture and historical perspective.

Map Legend

 Metro Station

 Metro Exit

 Point of Interest

 Restaurant

 Bike Rental Spot

 Halal Food

 Ferry

 Toilet

 House Numbering (Help you identify the direction on the maps)

These symbols give you the vital information for each listing

 Address

 Subway

 Bus Stop

 Business Hour

 Price

 Telephone Number

 Reference Page

 Recommendation of Must-try Food

HOW TO USE THIS GUIDE

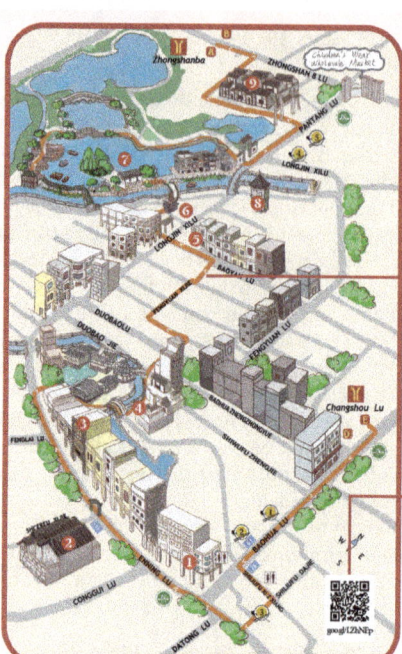

Itinerary Map
A map of the neighborhood showing the locations of the key sites, subway stations, local restaurants and main streets.

Route
Colored solid lines with arrows linking the key site.

QR code & Hyperlink
The QR code & Hyperlink will direct you to the corresponding routes on Google Maps. Entering the URL to your browser's address bar or using the App in your smart phone to scan the QR code and the device will make suggestions accordingly.

Quotes
Quotes and references from other journals and books about Guangzhou, including the title, year of publication, page number and author.

Itinerary Descriptions
These briefly describe practical information about the key sites and give instructions on finding the next site on the tour. Page references direct you to full descriptions of the key sites on the following pages.

Tips

Tips following the itinerary map provides insider information on key sites, extra places to see, and ideas for adapting the tours to suit your interests.

stage in the park every Tuesday, Thursday, and Saturday afternoon.
Take a walk round the **Liswan Lake Park** (; page 56), visit the traditional southern Chinese garden with artificial rocks in the pond with goldfish, exit at the east gate of the park. There is a **Literature Pagoda** (; page 51) on the other side of the Longjin Bridge. A traditional ceremony will be held on the 3rd of March of the Chinese Lunar calendar every year. People who come here will meet the four born stars of wisdom of China on that day.
Just ahead of PANTANG LU, there is the **Renwei Temple** (; page 51). If you come here during the Pai Tai Festival, you will see the Lion Dance at the Renwei Temple Bazaar. Finish your trip at metro line # 8 Zhongshanba station.

Tips:
1. If you feel energetic take 2 stops to Xicun Metro Station Exit D from Zhongshanba metro station, visit **Dui ShanYuan Garden** (page 56).
2. Pat Wo Wui Kun only opened during forenoon 9:00–12:00 everyday.
3. Lychee Bay has classic Cantonese Opera performance everyday from 2 pm to 5 pm. It's free of charge, the opera troupe is mainly composed of retired people in Liwan District of Guangzhou. As a amateur opera troupe to promote and support the development of the Cantonese opera in Guangzhou. There's a basket placed in front of the stage for donations, ideal for audiences that wish to donate as well as offer encouragement and support.
4. While walking along BAOHUA LU, be aware of pricing fraud at clothing stores. A lot of shops place a cheap price tag in front of the shop front or above the products to provoke people to buy but the actual prices are higher than the price tags shown, than what you pay. If this situation occurs, you can refuse to pay or dial 12358 to the Guangzhou Price Bureau to complain, however this is always an unsuccessful effort in this unenforceable law-sanction country.

Points of Interest

Lychee Bay (荔枝湾)
Lychee Bay is located in the Pantang region, west of Liwan District of Guangzhou, this is in the vicinity of the time-honored Sai Kwan City, along the banks of the Pearl River. This romantic attraction is home to celebrities of different dynasties and a showcase of Lingnan Culture such as Sai Kwan Resident Community, Miss Sai Kwan, Five Treasures of Sai Kwan, Sai Kwan Delicacies, and Cantonese Opera. More than 2000 years ago, Lu Jia, the notable chancellor in western Han dynasty, embarked on a diplomatic visit to the state of Yue. When he went by and stopped, he ordered his fellows to plant the litchis and dig up the lotus pond. This is the story about how Litchi Bay got its name. Liwan District carried out an overall environmental improvement project in 2009 and 2010 to beautify the area for the Asian Games. After sewage treatment of the Litchi Bay, the stream, neighboring buildings, and streets were restored to their former historic features.

Key Sites Descriptions

Following the order of the tour, these provide a detailed description and highlights for each site, plus address, website, phone number, entrance fee, days closed, and nearest subway station.

for 60 years after the 1950s, now it has become a nice quiet Zengbu Park in Guangzhou's old industrial area.
There are two 24 meters high circular limekiln towers near the garden; they are the remains of a calcium carbide factory from the 1970s, this area was also the first industrial area in Guangzhou in 1931.

Where to Eat

Refer to these lists for a selection of local restaurants and food stores along the tour.

Menus

Provide a greater variety of featured food menus both with Chinese and English, includes vegetarian dishes.

Where to Eat

Shun Kee Dessert Store (顺记冰室)

Shunji is an old brand name for ice cream in Guangzhou. In Shunji all the ice creams are made the old ancient way by hand mixing a powder to form a slurry to serve people the most delicious ice cream. The most famous ice cream here is the coconut ice cream which is made from the meat of a fresh coconut. This wonderful ice cream has a strong fresh coconut smell and has a distinct flavor. Many honored guests and monarch from abroad have tasted this ice cream and take delight in talking about it.

Menus		
芒果雪糕	Mango Ice Cream
椰子雪糕	Coconut Ice Cream
榴梿雪糕	Durian Ice Cream
红豆冰	Red Bean Ice
红豆雪糕	Red Bean Ice Cream
西关蛋糕仔	Egg Puffs
椰子和芒果雪糕	Coconut and Mango Ice Cream

No.36 Baohua Road, Liwan District (宝华路 36 号)   7:30-23:30

Chan Tim Kee Fish Skin Store (陈添记)

This shop has a history of three generations and has been located in a small narrow alley since 1978. They have inside and outside tables, but most of locals enjoy eating at street side tables, to view the old buildings full of Guangzhou tradition. This shop only sell three items: Smooth and Crispy Fish Skin ¥25(Main ingredients: Peanut kernels, green onion, ginger, Chili, caraway, celery, Soy sauce sesame, etc.), Sampan Congee ¥7 (Main ingredients: pork slices, fried peanuts, sliced fried egg, cut deep-fried dough sticks), and Steamed Rice Rolls ¥3.

Menus		
艇仔粥	Sampan Congee
蒸肠粉	Steamed Rice Rolls
鱼 皮	Cold and Dressed with Sauce Crispy Fish Skin with Peanuts

At the end of an alley beside No.61 Baohua Road   9:00-22:00

In Guangzhou, the translations street names are not the same as in Shanghai. Sometimes, you may find the street name is written in Pinyin, but it may also be fully translated into English (such as in Whampoa village). The confusing English street names are and have long been a headache for foreign nationals traveling and living in Guangzhou. The Guangzhou government has promised to address the issue, but their efforts are still far from satisfactory. Text on road signs appears both in Chinese characters and in uppercase Pinyin, (which is the official system to transcribe Chinese characters into Latin script in China). To make matters more complicated – or adventurous – you may well have to spend time searching around for those street nameplates which hang behind the pillars or are hidden elsewhere. Once you find the sign, the following information should help you to decode it:

There're 4 directions on the road sigh

Chinese	Pinyin	English
东	DONG	East
西	XI	West
南	NAN	South
北	BEI	North

The most common street names

Chinese	Pinyin	English
马路 / 路	MALU/LU	Road
街	JIE	Street
巷	XIANG	Lane
大街	DAJIE	Main Street
大道	DADAO	Avenue
中路	ZHONGLU	Road Middle
东路 / 街	DONGLU/JIE	Road/Street East
西路 / 街	XILU/JIE	Road/Street West
南路 / 街	NANLU/JIE	Road/Street South
北路 / 街	BEILU/JIE	Road/Street North
上街	SHANGJIE	Upper Street
下街	XIAJIE	Lower Street

HOW TO USE THIS GUIDE

INTRODUCING GUANGZHOU

Everything you need to understand the city quickly: weather, history, culture, architectures, arts and festivals and celebrations

Travel Weather

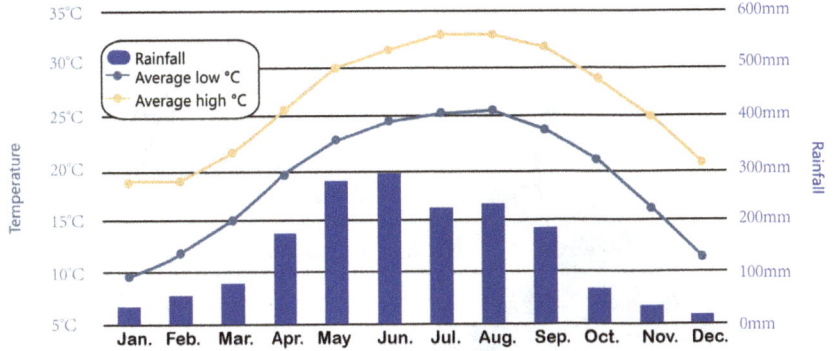

The average temperature and precipitation for Guangzhou

Situated in a subtropical zone and sitting practically right atop the Tropic of Cancer, Guangzhou has a typical subtropical marine monsoon climate. The annual average temperature in Guangzhou is 20 °C to 22 °C (68 °F to 71.6 °F) and the difference of average temperature is small. Spring there is wet and rainy. Summer is hot and sometimes brings typhoons. Autumn is cool and windy while winter is not very cold. The area's climate, with year-round warmth and consistent rainfall is conducive to the growth of plants. It provides particularly excellent conditions for evergreen trees, which decorate Guangzhou throughout all four seasons and lend it the nickname 'Flower City'. Rains fall predominantly between April and June, while the August and September heat may result in typhoons. The heat and humidity at this time of year may prove exhausting for tourists. The intense summer sunlight can cause sunburn very quickly, so tourists should come prepared to prevent it. Temperatures from October to December are moderate, making the autumn the best time for a visit.

Spring

Spring comes to Guangzhou in February and lasts through March. The temperature rises gradually, but drizzly weather is not uncommon. Because it is chilly early and late but warm during the middle of the day, spring travelers will most likely need a sweater to stay comfortable. You'd better take your sweater and light clothes in this season. The spring China Import and Export Fair (also known as the Canton Fair) is usually held from April to May. The Official Flower of Guangzhou, the Kapok, comes into bloom all over the city in spring.

Summer

Guangzhou's summer, which lasts from April to September, is relatively long. The hottest months (Average high temperature for August standing at 36 °C, with an average relative humidity is 82%) are in July and August. There will likely be occasional typhoons and afternoon thunderstorms in summer, so visitors should carry an umbrella when going out. In the summer season, trips to cool

spots like Chime Long Water Park are very popular. In addition to getting some relief from the summer heat, you can also enjoy the fun and excitement of the swimming and water activities.

Autumn

Autumn days in Guangzhou, from October to mid-December, tend to be sunny but cool. The bright, clear skies make this the best time to come. All an autumn visitor will feel comfortable in light clothing such as long-sleeved shirts or T-shirts, with one or two thin coats or sweaters for the morning and evening hours. There always many visitors from every corner of the globe in this season, especially during the National Day Holiday. Meanwhile, the autumn China Import and Export Fair (Canton Fair) will be held from October to September.

Winter

Guangzhou in winter is a sea of flowers. Winter in Guangzhou normally lasts from late December until mid-February, when it can get quite cold (Average low temperature for January standing at 10 °C, with an average relative humidity is 70%), but due to the city's low latitude, it seldom snows. Sweaters and thick jackets are enough for this season. It's the best travel time to Guangzhou in the year.

Notices for traveling

- The rainy season in Guangzhou is from April to June. Do not forget to bring rain gear when you pack for your trip. But everything that's necessary (umbrellas, jackets, sandal, etc.) can be bought easily there in Guangzhou.
- July, August, and September are prime Typhoon season in Guangzhou, so it's better not to visit during the summer. If you do find yourself traveling in and around Guangzhou at this time of year, make sure to check the latest weather forecasts frequently.
- For those who are allergic to pollen, it's suggested that one wears a mask and takes an anti-allergen before going out.

A flooded road in Guangzhou after typhoon Ewiniar.

The Season of Flowers and Locations

Plants	Season	Best place to enjoy flowers
Plum Blossom	Jan.	The rose fragrant snow park, Conghua Streams river
Peach Blossom	Feb.	Taohuajian of Mt. Baiyun
Magnolia Denudata		Taohuajian of Mt. Baiyun, Martyrs' Park
Rape Flower	Mar.	Shimen forest park, Biyinwan of Mt. Baiyun
kapok		Lingyuan West Rd, Haizhu bridge near metro station, Sun Yat-sen Memorial Hall
Powder Palace Bauhinia		Renmin North Rd, Bailing Rd, Baiyuan Rd, Huaqiao New Village, South China Agricultural University, Yuexiu Park, Luhu, Guangdong University of Foreign Studies
Mucuna birdwoodiana		Minglun Hall of Panyu Xuegong
Azalea		Martyrs' Park, Sun Yat-Sen University, South China Agricultural University, South China Botanical Garden.
Powder Palace Bauhinia	April	Renmin North Rd, Bailing Rd, Baiyuan Rd, Huaqiao New Village, South China Agricultural University, Yuexiu Park, Luhu, Guangdong University of Foreign Studies
Mucuna birdwoodiana		South China Botanical Garden.
Saraca dives		South China Botanical Garden, Nanhai God Temple.
Cherry Blossom		Jiaomen Greenway, Huanglushan Forest Park, Guangdong University of Foreign Studies.
Flame Tree	May	Liurong Rd, Guangxiao Rd, Chaotian Rd, People's Park
Rose		Yuntai Garden, Baomo Garden
Orchid		Orchid nursery
Sunflower		Yuntai Garden, Mingzhu building of Mt. Baiyun
Frangipani		Yuntai Garden
Lotus	June / July / Aug.	Liwanhu Park, Baomo Garden, Liuhuahu Park, Sanshui Lotus World
Chrysanthemum	Nov.	Culture Park, South China Normal University
Chorisia speciosa		Sun Yat-sen University
Plum Blossom	Dec.	The Luo Gang Fragrant Snow Park, Conghua Streams river
Metasequoia Red		South China Botanical Garden, Guangzhou Zoo, Luhu Park, Dafu Forest Park.

Travel Weather

A Brief History

By 214 B.C., Guangdong, Guangxi, and northern Vietnam were subjugated and annexed into the Qin empire. Guangzhou was established in 214 B.C. to serve as a base for the Qin Empire's, the town was known as Panyu.

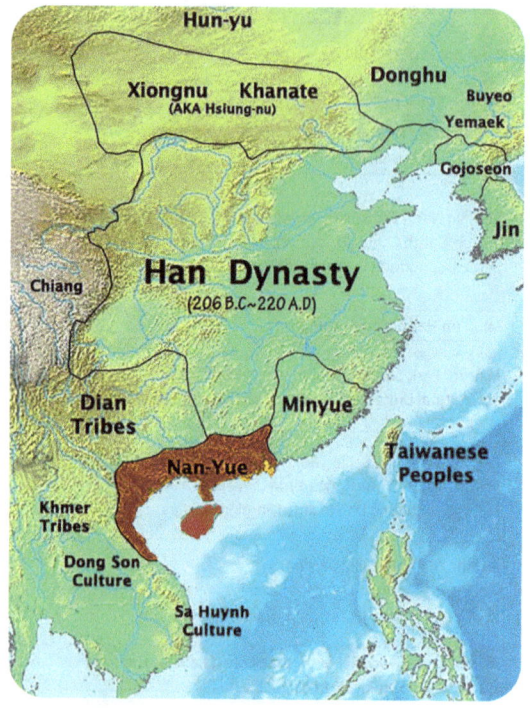

The territory of Nan-yue Kingdom

Zhaotuo took over Nanhai Prefecture in the early Han dynasty, which absorbed the surrounding area. Then the Nanyue Kingdom was established and expanded into the city. The city has been continuously occupied since that time. Panyu was expanded when it became the capital of the Nan-yue Kingdom in 206 B.C. The name of the city was changed a couple of times over the dynasties coming after Qin, and finalized into current name in 1918.

Guangzhou is one of the ancient capitals that has the longest history, the biggest trading port that received oriental and occidental culture. Since ancient days Lingnan was far from the reach of emperors, receiving less of the influence of orthodox politics and culture. As it is on the sea coast, it has a tradition of trading with foreign countries.

Guangzhou was part of the "Maritime Silk Road" that linked southern China with India, South-East Asia, the Middle East, and Africa. As a result of its links with the Middle East, a mosque was established in the city in 627, and a small Muslim community continues to live in Guangzhou to this day. Additionally, the sixth patriarch of Zen Buddhism named Huineng was born in Guangdong Province and taught the famous Platform Sutra in Guangzhou city. As a result, Guangzhou has retained a strong connection with this school of Buddhism, and the monastery where the sixth patriarch studied is considered a local treasure. The first Protestant missionary in China, Robert Morrison, entered Guangzhou in 1807. This started the spread of Christianity in the country.

As a major sea port, Guangzhou's history is full of color. In 786 the city was sacked by the Persians and Arabian. In 1711 the British East India Company established a trading post here. In 1757, the government designated the city as the only port allowed business transactions with foreign nations, trade was restricted to Guangzhou and the foreign merchants were restricted to Thirteen-Trades Monopoly. This continued until the 1842, signing of the Treaty of Nanking, when four other ports were added. Losing the exclusive privilege pushed Guangzhou to become more industrialized later.

Guangzhou is always the center of international trade and economic cooperation in South China. As the host city of the 2010 Asian Games, Guangzhou has sped up its modernization and stands today as an important economical, national and international transportation hub as well as a jewel for the world's finest gourmets!

Have you ever heard Canton?

Historically, the city is called "Canton" by westerners, but the city was never officially named as Canton. Canton is Wade-Giles Romanization of Cantonese dialect "Kwang Dung".

In the Song dynasty, Pearl River Delta region and its east were formally named as Kwang Nam Dung Lou, literally mean vast south east region, which became abbreviated as Kwang Dung.

In the Ming dynasty, the Portuguese were the first Europeans to arrive Pearl River Delta doing trade with China. The name Canton originally came from a Portuguese language rendering of Cantão. After British came it was adopted by the British colonial authorities.

Standard language was set to be Mandarin in 1949 by People's Republic of China. Guǎng Zhōu is exactly the Romanization of the city's name in Mandarin Chinese.

Why the city changed the English name to Guangzhou? I think one of the reasons is the current Chinese governments go through great lengths to erase all forms of colonial influence in the country.

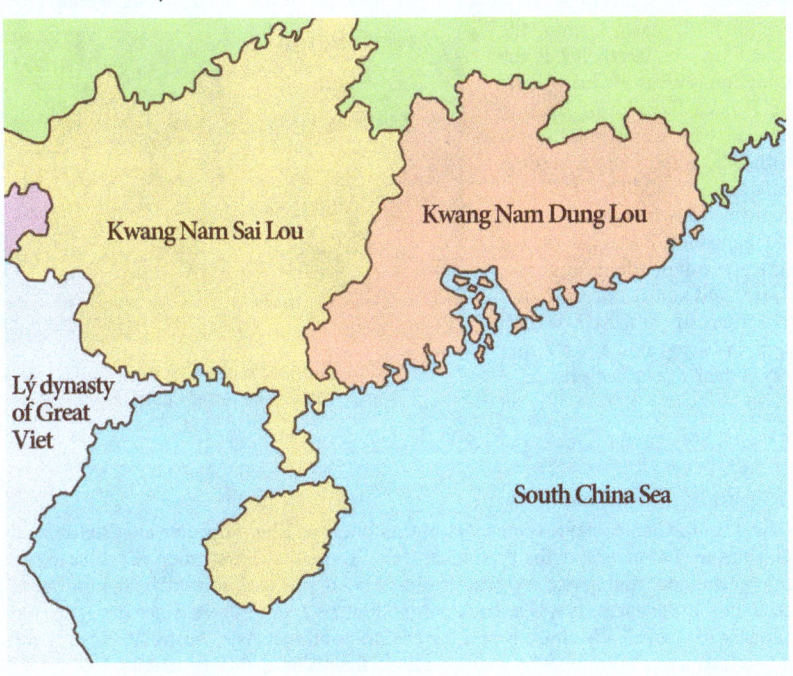

Local Custom and Culture

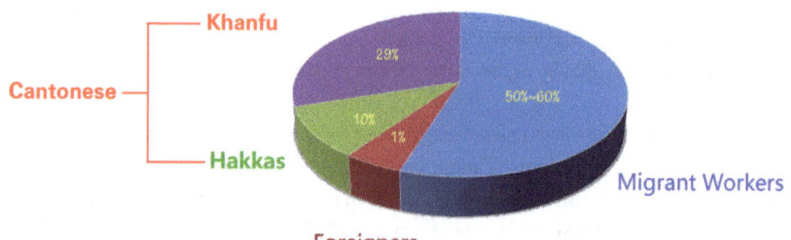

Guangzhou's population composition

Apart from the Khanfu Clan, the Hakka Clan also lives in Guangzhou. To escape warfare and famine, large flows of Han people from Central Plains had been moving to Guangdong Province since the Jin Dynasty, forming the Hakka Clan who largely live in the mountainous areas of Guangdong. The Hakka have their unique language, which originated in the Central Plains and adapted in south Guangdong. In addition, the Chaoshan region, which is located in east Guangdong, it also has its own relatively independent language, culture, and social norms. Nowadays, there are at least 2,000,000 Hakka in Guangzhou and the majority of them live in Zengcheng.

Traditional Hakka dwelling house in Zengcheng District

The Spirit of Cantonese

The Khanfu Clan is often seen as typical Cantonese as Khanfu people are Cantonese living in Guangzhou and the rest of the Pearl River Delta. They are the first group of people to become rich in Guangdong and have the characteristics of being practical, shrewd, bold, innovative, and open to new experiences, as well as having a good intellect for business. Since the Tang Dynasty, Cantonese have been adventurous and traveled to Southeast Asia, Australia, North America, and South America to conduct business and build their homes, thereby making Guangdong the province that has the largest number of Chinese living abroad (there are 45,000,000 Chinese living abroad now and 70% of them are Cantonese). Hakka are accepted and pursue harmony.

Eating Habits & Food Culture

Khanfu people enjoy "drinking tea", which actually means having dim sum. When greeting each other in the morning, they often say, "Have you had any tea?". Cantonese value eating and spend lots of time, say, a few hours, on each meal. Those who "drink tea" in restaurants are middle-aged or elderly Cantonese. Young people and businessmen do not indulge frequently, not because of the cost but because "drinking tea" takes too much time.

When someone pours tea into your cup, tea etiquette requires you to lightly tap the table top a few times with your fingers in order to respectfully thank them. This etiquette is believed to have been passed down from Emperor Qianlong.

An important part of Cantonese life style and culture is about drinking soup. Which Cantonese soup varies depending on purpose, and the season. For example: removing moisture in early summer, reducing heat in midsummer, and nourishing the body in autumn and winter. Cantonese soups are very rich in content. For example, local people enjoy soups combined with duck and wax gourd, to reduce the temperature in the hot summer days, while in winter, they prefer soups with the coix seed and pig stomach to warm their stomachs. Cantonese people tend to prefer a casserole dish with a delicate texture as a soup container. Crock-pots are also popular for slowly simmering soup to extract most of the flavors from the ingredients. This process can take three hours, while making a soup stew can take four hours. The main attraction is the liquid in the pot, the solids are usually thrown away unless they are expensive ingredients such as abalone or snake. Cantonese have always believed that snake meat can treat illnesses, plus it is nutritious and keeps out the cold in winter. Snake's blood and bile is considered a male aphrodisiac among Asian men young and old.

In the eyes of some outsiders, the Cantonese people seem to make a big fuss about soup. But their passion for soup is deeply routed in Cantonese culture and history.

Many Chinese herbal medicines serve as must-have ingredients in Cantonese daily life. Climatic and geographical factors play an important role in the formation of Cantonese eating habits, which gradually developed over time when Cantonese tried to adapt to nature. Chinese believe that medicine and food are of the same source. These principles are still widely practiced even illiterate people can name a number of "prescriptions" for various ailments: spirits made with tiger penis or sheep testicles for virility; or tiger bones for strong bones and muscles. It is generally accepted that health is better maintained through diet than medicine.

Cantonese cuisine is bland and focuses on the original taste of the ingredients as well as their nutrition. Most Cantonese are very familiar with the nature of various foods, whether a certain food is "hot", "cold", "mild," or "nurturing for lungs" is common knowledge.

Cantonese also like rice porridge, which comes in various categories and unique taste. They pay special attention to the ingredients and heating when preparing porridge, often simmering the mixture until rice and water blend in perfect harmony.

Local people learn which kind of tea to drink for which condition from childhood. Herbal tea is a drink made purely from Chinese medicinal herbs by people from Guangdong, Hong Kong, and Macao in accordance with local weather and environmental conditions. The tradition has been a major component of Lingnan culture and influenced by other occasions such as, Cantonese opera or Cantonese cuisine, and even Cantonese dialects. The popularity of herbal tea might largely be attributed to the warm and humid climate of the Lingnan area, which is thought to be the cause of the body's internal heat according to traditional Chinese medical thought. Guided by Chinese medical healthcare theory, Chinese Medicinal Tea has been developed throughout the long course of disease prevention and healthcare studies. Medicinal tea has antipyretic and antitoxic effects, while quenching thirst and dissipating heat and humidity from the body through consumption. Herbal tea can eliminate summer heat from the human body and cure sore throats caused by winter dryness. Drinking herbal tea is a long cherished tradition in the Lingnan culture, which covers Guangdong, Guangxi, Fujian, and Taiwan provinces, with Guangdong as its core area.

Cantonese cuisine is bland and focuses on the original taste of the ingredients as well as their nutrition. Most Cantonese are very familiar with the nature of various foods, whether a certain food is "hot", "cold", "mild," or "nurturing for lungs" is common knowledge.

Cantonese also like rice porridge, which comes in various categories and unique taste. They pay special attention to the ingredients and heating when preparing porridge, often simmering the mixture until rice and water blend in perfect harmony.

Cantonese love having Sweet Water, which does not simply mean water with sugar in it, but rather, desserts that can be easily prepared. Usually, grains, eggs, and fruits are cooked with sugar and water. For example, Sesame Paste, Simmered Papaya, and egg with Lily Bulb are popular traditional snacks. Cantonese Sweet Water is available throughout the year, with thirst quenching ones sold in summer and lung nurturing, stomach-warming desserts prepared in autumn and winter. Sweet Water also serves as midnight snacks for Cantonese people.

Dog meat is one of the seasonal dishes in Guangzhou, where winter is rather frigid. Dog meat is nurturing and warms up body quickly and therefore becomes popular during the winter months. Cantonese people believe that dog meat has the therapeutic effect of circulating water within the body and nurturing ones kidneys.

Hakka dishes feature large amount of oil, rich flavors, as wells as salty and crispy taste. Salty Chicken and Pork with Salted Vegetables exemplify typical Hakka dishes. Overall, Cantonese customs leave outsiders with the impression that they value eating well as far more important than dressing fancily.

The Offspring of Businessmen

Cantonese people are quick witted and nimble fingered, producing exquisite handcrafts like Cantonese Embroidery, Jade Sculpture, Ivory Sculpture, Stone Sculpture, Brick Sculpture, etc. Since the Qin Dynasty, Cantonese people have represented China to communicate with the rest of the world. This act of courage reached its peak during the Han Dynasty, when merchant ships carrying large quantities of gold and silk set out from Panyu, pursuing trade against high risks. The commercial fleet established an international trading route that bound Asia, Africa, and Europe was also known as the Silk Road at Sea. In addition to cultivating the business element in Cantonese, the oceans promoted their adventurous personality. Being doers rather than thinkers; emphasizing actions, solid work, productivity, practicality and feelings rather than theories are characteristics of Cantonese people. Marriage is another aspect of life that reflects the Cantonese mind where the extent of wealth is valued more than social class. The Cantonese language also demonstrates that Cantonese value fortune. If you wish to get a job in Guangzhou, you will find that speaking Cantonese is a positive quality since recruitment ads often include a statement like "Applicants who speak Cantonese will be prioritized." The direct reason that Cantonese are so stubborn in this regard is that they find it difficult to speak Mandarin. There are 8,000 Cantonese words that are independent of modern Chinese and psychologically, Cantonese people feel they cannot express their emotions properly with the Mandarin language. This stubbornness of using Cantonese dialect has faced countless criticism. Because of geographical and opportune factors, Cantonese have become wealthy and the "value" of Cantonese also soars with this phenomenon. Although speaking Cantonese is somewhat arrogant and discriminating, the spread of Mandarin has not been stifled in Guangdong, where there are slogans saying "Please Speak Mandarin" almost everywhere in Guangdong. TV stations must have programs in Cantonese because of the fact that in Macau, Hong Kong, North America, and in the rest of the world, there are 50,000,000 Cantonese speaking people. In Guangdong, half of the businesses are accomplished in Cantonese.

To earn a living, Cantonese people do their job in earnest and have no time to indulge in empty talk on philosophies. Geographically speaking, Cantonese incorrectly regard the rest of China as the "north country". They think the pollution and disorder in Guangzhou are caused more or less by poor people from the north searching for job opportunities in this city. Some of these job seekers fail to find a job and run out of money, which is what Cantonese regard as "the source of all evil deeds". For some Cantonese businessmen, money is the most significant measure of success; without money, empty talks are in vain.

Serious Superstitions

Superstitions, namely worshipping deity and offering sacrifices to ghosts, has a long history in Guangdong and had become an indispensable part of Cantonese customs. Cantonese superstition is particularly obsessed with the use of words, especially in a deifying way. Cantonese are especially concerned with the meaning and pronunciation of words. The numbers 3, 8 and 9 are preferred because they sound similar to "grow", "wealth" and "lasting long" respectively. In contrast, the number 4 is avoided because it sounds like the word for "death". In daily social interactions, especially when visiting friends and relatives during festivals, clocks are not sent as a gift because "sending a clock" sounds like "attending upon a dying person". Similarly, Cantonese do not use pears as a gift since "pear" sounds exactly like "separation" in Cantonese. Therefore, when dealing with superstitious Cantonese businessmen, pay attention to the words you say and the gifts you send. Use 3, 8 and 9 as frequently as possible. If the price of a gift ends with the number 8, you may buy it if the price is reasonable.

Because of its special geographical location, the culture of Guangdong has been associated with water since ancient times. Guangdong has flat land, a network of waterways and plentiful rainwater, giving the Cantonese a culture involving water. Cantonese often place fish tanks and raise fish in their homes for certain reasons: "fostering fortune" according to Fengshui principles, enjoying the sight of fish, and giving their home a touch of liveliness. Many businessmen also like having water features in their offices, believing that water brings fortune. This is empirically true to some extent, as economic development seems to favor river banks areas and coastal towns. In addition, Cantonese like using the word "water" in daily life. Water is the quintessence of Cantonese customs.

Less Political Talk

Guangdong is far away from the central political power in China. In ancient times, when transport and communications were less convenient, Cantonese were less bound by orthodox ideas. Compared with people in Beijing, Cantonese show less interest in politics, even nowadays, believing that it is merely empty talk, monotonous in nature and far less practical than doing business. In contrast, Hakka people are famous for their respect for teachers, their emphasis on education and their keen focus on studying; they are in some way programmed with the idea that only studying will make them successful.

Lingnan Architecture

Qilou buildings in Haizhu Road South, designed for both residential and commercial uses

The architecture style of Guangzhou can be described as colorful and glorious, is the product of a set of multicultural techniques, including local, traditional architecture and influences from neighboring South Asian zones, some of them imported by overseas returnees from Singapore, Indonesia, etc. Due to its geographical location near the sea, the Pearl River Delta, and ports like Hong Kong, the area has been exposed to over a century of cultural and commercial exchange. For a long time the port of Guangzhou was not only the busiest (silk) port of the Chinese empire; it was also the only one allowed to trade with the West. These interactions have left their traces building styles, as well as in also in overall culture and in the popular mindset.

Stone base pillar

Traditional indigenous architecture of the area responded to the hot and humid subtropical climate in many ways, such as with large porches and archways, stone base of pillar, natural cross ventilation systems with special perforated bricks and roof structures to let air move through the building, and mobile shading systems of bamboo wicker.

Guangzhou Lingnan architecture's development has experienced several stages: The learning academy and ancestral hall (see Huangpu walking tour; page 148) were the cultural representatives of the Ming and Qing Dynasties; The Sai Kwan Grand House (see Li Wan Museum; page 53) and Qilou building (Enning Lu; page 49) reflect the trends and fashions of the late Qing Dynasty and early Republic of China and the western-style architecture (see Changdi walking tour; page 69) of modern times embodies the post-liberation synthesis of Chinese and western architecture.

Lingnan Arts

▶▶▶

Lingnan Garden (岭南花园)

Lingnan Garden is a Guangzhou-centered architectural style of Chinese gardening. Its formation was influenced by the Suzhou Garden style, but also adopted the regional features of Cantonese architecture and the color of Western-style buildings. Apart from that, it adapts to the climate in Guangzhou, utilizing the decent ventilation. These tendencies lend it its distinctive style amongst Chinese gardens. Lingnan Gardens are often smaller than 3,000 square meters, with a hall and an attic. The scenery is arranged along a circuitous and interesting route, where the adornments are made up of plants and fruits common in Southern China, and the windows and handrails have delicate patterns and vivid colors. Rockery is often located in lotus ponds in which goldfish are raised. The windows usually have colorful engraved glass inlayed in them, which is another unique feature of Southern China. According to the chronicles, ancient gardens in Guangzhou existed by the time of the Southern Han Dynasty (917~971 A.D.), while the Lingnan Gardens that survive to this day were mostly built during the middle to late Qing Dynasty.

Where to See

Yuyin Garden (余荫山房)

- Nancun Village, Panyu District (番禺南村余荫山房)
- Take metro Line 3 and get off at Hanxi Changlong Station Exit C, then walk to the main road take and take bus No.30 until the last stop
- 8:00-17:30
- ¥18

Puppet Show (木偶戏)

Puppet shows were first introduced into Guangdong from Western Fujian during the Yuan Dynasty and became a hit in the western part of Guangdong, which is therefore said to be the origin of Cantonese puppet shows. In the late Qing Dynasty and the early Republic of China period, puppet shows could be found on the streets and were especially popular in Chenghuang Temple, Sai Kwan and Huang Sha (the areas of Guangzhou). In 1956, the Puppet Troupe of Guangdong Province was founded, becoming the new core force of puppet art. This group of puppet artists used rod puppets, which prevailed in Western Guangdong, as the basis of their performance and added in marionettes as well as hand puppets, creating a new form of puppet art with a brand new style and a Cantonese touch.

Where to See

Guangdong Puppet Theater (广东省木偶剧团)
No.43 Hongde Lu, Haizhu District (海珠区洪德路43号)
9:00-18:00

Lingnan Painting (岭南画派)

The Lingnan School of Painting is a genre of Chinese painting that originated in Guangdong after the Xinhai Revolution, with its representative painters - Gao Jianfu, Gao Qifeng and Chen Shuren - being called the "three talents of Lingnan". Influenced by the modern trends in Japanese and Western paintings, they became discontented with the conservative and mimicking norms present in traditional Chinese ink paintings and sought to innovate and create a school of their own. On the basis of traditional Chinese painting techniques, they adopted and combined elements from Japanese and Western oil paintings, forming a unique style.

Where to See

Chen Shuren Memorial Hall (陈树人纪念馆)
See Dongshan Walking Tour (page 125)

Guangzhou Bonsai (广州盆栽)

On verandas, in halls, in gardens, and on both sides of roads – wherever you look in Guanzhou, you're likely to spot a Lingnan Bonsai. Guangzhou is a city in love with them. Even the poorest of families has a bonsai tree in their home, and wealthier families often import them from abroad at great cost.

Lingnan Bonsai is regarded as one of the five art genres in China and uses trees, stones, artificial mini pavilions and pets etc as materials. After artful processing and careful cultivation, the

bonsai reproduce natural scenes for people. Lingnan Bonsai typically makes use of subtropical and tropical evergreen trees, while the stone materials in are generally corallites, calcite, and a few others. Bonsai can be seen in many places, such as small alleys, gardens, parks, etc.

Where to See

1. Zuiguan Park (醉观公园)
See Shiweitang Railway Station (page 141)

2. RONGHUA XIJIE (Ronghua Street West)
See Shamian walking tour (page 63)

Cantonese Opera (粤剧)

Cantonese opera, originating in southern China's Cantonese culture, is one of the major categories in Chinese opera. It is popular in Guangdong, Guangxi, Hong Kong, Macau, Singapore and Malaysia. Like all versions of Chinese opera, it is a traditional Chinese art form, involving music, singing, martial arts, acrobatics, and acting.

Till now, the theatre has staged over 400 plays and the classic programs include Searching the Academy, Guan Hanqing (a notable Chinese playwright and poet in the Yuan Dynasty) and Story of a Mountain Village. Besides, the theatre often organizes activities of creation, research, artistic training, artistic exchange and performance to promote the development of Cantonese Opera.

There are two types of Cantonese opera plays: Mou (武 , "martial arts") and Man (文 , "highly educated", esp. in poetry and culture). Mou plays emphasize war, the characters usually being generals or warriors. These works contain action scenes and involve a lot of weaponry and armors. Man plays tend to be gentler and more elegant. Scholars are the main characters in these plays. Water sleeves (long flowing detachable silk sleeves) are used extensively in Man plays to produce movements reflecting the elegance and tenderness of the characters; all female characters wear them. In Man plays, characters put a lot of effort into creating distinctive facial expressions and gestures to express their underlying emotions.

Note: 粤剧 (Yuèjù) should not be confused with 越剧 (Yuèjù), the theatre of Zhejiang.

Where to See

Lychee Bay (荔枝湾)
See Sai Kwan Walking Tour (Page 50)

Bone Carving and Ivory Carving (骨雕和牙雕)

Guangzhou ivory carving is world-famous for its finesse delicacy. During Ming and Qing Dynasties, Guangzhou was the center of the ivory trade, and the scale of Guangzhou ivory carving ranked the first all around China. In the later Qing Dynasty, Guangzhou the ivory carving industry established an international reputation, and most of the ivory sculptors in the imperial city were from Guangdong Province, especially from Guangzhou City. By the end of the 1980s, the ivory trade was banned worldwide. As the successors of the millennium-old tradition of Guangzhou ivory techniques, the ivory-carving artists started to explore new ideas to pursue the true meaning of art from camel and cow bones instead. The main materials for bone carving are now yak bones and buffalo bones. Bone carving and ivory carving are sister techniques, they appear at the same period of the long history, and require the same skills. Ivory carving makes use of fine material, and is of elegant characteristic; in contrast, the material of bone carving is easy to obtain, and the cost is reasonable. Nonetheless, bone carving may also display the exquisite techniques and three-dimensional, exquisite artistic modeling. In recent years, bone carving works which made by the ivory carving artists have grown very popular with collectors both home and abroad.

Where to See

Chen Clan Academy (陈家祠)
- No.34 Eng Long Li, Zhongshan 7th Road, Liwan District
- Metro Line 1 Chen Clan Academy station exit D
- 9:00-17:00
- ¥10

Guangzhou Color Porcelain (广彩)

Guangzhou Color Porcelain, also called Guangzhou Gold-inlay Color Porcelain, has a history of more than 300 years. It originated as Guangzhou Tri-color Porcelain in the Ming Dynasty, developed into five-color in the Qing Dynasty, and gradually evolved into its current unique form forms during the Qian Long period. There are seven procedures for the colored painting of Guangzhou Color Porcelain: line drawing, color filling, gold inlay, green color filling, Doucai (朵 彩), and flower kilning. Guangzhou Color Porcelain has artistic pottery of more than 500 categories inclusive of over 2,000 patterns. It employs the unique brocade patterns of China, is famous for its rich and gaudy colors, resplendence, rigorous composition, and fine drawings, and is of very high artistic value. It applies western enamel paint and liquid bright gold, but imitates Chinese brocade figures to draw flower patterns, and thus creates a distinctive and unique style. This craft represents a successful integration of Eastern and Western cultures. Guangzhou Color Porcelain articles have been collected by royal palaces, museums and collectors in various countries.

Where to See

1. Guangdong Provincial Museum (广东省博物馆)
- No.2 Zhujiang Road East, Tianhe District
- Metro Line APM Guangzhou Opera House exit B
- 9:00-16:00
- Free admission

2. Chen Clan Academy (陈家祠)
- No.34 Eng Long Li, Zhongshan 7th Road, Liwan District
- Metro Line 1 Chen Clan Academy station exit D
- 9:00-17:00
- ¥10

Cantonese Embroidery (广绣)

Cantonese (Guang) Embroidery is a general name for the embroidery products of the regions of the Pearl River Delta, which make use of the techniques of Yue Embroidery. Guang Embroidery, together with Jiangsu (Su) Embroidery, Hunan (Xiang) Embroidery and Sichuan (Shu) Embroidery, are the four major schools of embroidery in China.

By embroidering all kinds of designs on the embroidery cloth (such as silk) with needle and thread, Cantonese Embroidery expresses the author's thought, emotion, spirit, and feeling towards beauty, which makes the piece resonate with its audience. Cantonese Embroidery has the characteristics of full composition, vivid imagery, clear texture, beautiful color and luster, stitch, and flexibility.

Cantonese embroidery articles mainly include fine paintings, scrolls, hanging screens and table screens; ordinary ones include embroidered pictures, golden and silver floss gowns, quilt covers, caps, shawls, scarves, embroidered garments, embroidered shoes, embroidered bags, and dramatic costumes, etc.

Where to See

Chen Clan Academy (陈家祠)
- No.34 Eng Long Li, Zhongshan 7th Road, Liwan District
- Metro Line 1 Chen Clan Academy station exit D
- 9:00-17:00
- ¥10

Annual Events

Lunar Month	Festival	Lunar Days	Western Dates	
			2019	2020
First Moon	Chinese New Year	1	5 Feb.	25 Jan.
	Seoi Zam Se	10~16	14~20 Feb.	3~9 Feb.
	Lantern Festival	15	19 Feb.	8 Feb.
	Lettuce Fair	24	28 Feb.	17 Feb.
Second Moon	'Polo Birth' Temple Fair	11~13	17~19 Mar.	4~6 Mar.
Third Moon	Tomb Sweeping Day	—	5 Apr.	5 Apr.
	Pak Tai Festival	3	7 Apr.	26 Mar.
	Goddess Mazu's Birthday	23	27 Apr.	15 Apr.
Fourth	Kamfa Festival	17	21 May	9 May
Fifth Moon	Dragon Boat Festival	5	7 Jun.	25 Jun.
Seventh Moon	The Daughter's Festival	7	7 Aug.	25 Aug.
	Ghost Festival	14	15 Aug.	2 Sep.
Eighth Moon	Mid-autumn Festival	15	13 Sep.	1 Oct.
Ninth Moon	Double Ninth Festival	9	7 Oct.	25 Oct.
Eleventh Moon	Winter Solstice	—	22 Dec.	21 Dec.

Chinese New Year / Spring Festive (春节)

Chinese New Year occurs on the first day of the first lunar month, usually in January or February. This is a 15 day celebration, during which time some districts can be quite deserted as many migrant workers return to their home provinces. The flower fair is popular in the days before New Year.

Event

Flower Fair is a traditional cultural activity unique to people in Guangzhou during the Spring Festival. It usually starts several days before the Spring Festival and lasts until midnight on New Year's Eve. New Year's Eve is the climax of the flower market, when huge crowds of people surge to the streets. It is customary for most of the families to visit the fair after the reunion dinner on New Year's Eve and buy a potted tree with tangerines hanging on it. The tangerine symbolizes good luck and wealth to the local people and the chrysanthemum symbolizes longevity. There are 9 Flower Fairs in each district. Every district has a flower fair, maps listed below with yellow sections are 5 of the 12 flower fairs with easy access to metro. Every district has a flower fair, maps listed below with yellow sections are 5 of the 12 flower fairs with easy access to metro.

Where to See

Yuexiu District (越秀区)

Haizhu District (海珠区)

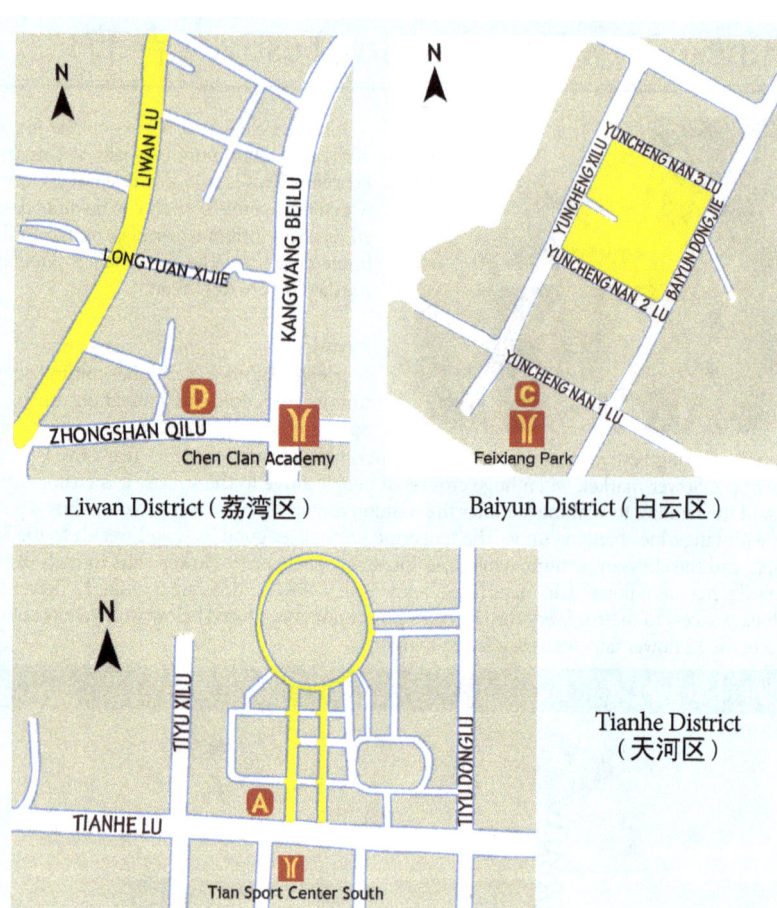

Liwan District (荔湾区)

Baiyun District (白云区)

Tianhe District (天河区)

Seoi Zam Se (水浸社)

Zhu Village is divided into several districts. Wen district is one of them. Established above the water peculiarly, the Altar of Land and Grain is called "Seoi Zam Se". The most conventional surviving custom in Canton, which once enjoyed great popularity, is called "Light a lantern for the birth of a boy".

Event

Any family who gave birth to a baby boy in the past a year has to festoon the altar with lights during 10th~16th of Lunar January, praying to god to bless their sons. The altar, lantern, roof, and memorial tablet are set up in the water, through which people have to wade to reach the pot where they can place and light their lanterns, thus giving tribute. Afterwards, the family should return to the altar daily at around six o'clock every morning and evening to worship with incense; this lasts all the way up until the Lantern Festival. This altar, built in the Hongwu period of the Ming Dynasty (1368-1398), is the only Seoi Zam Se in Canton.

Where to See

Zhu Village (天河珠村)
📖 See the map of the Daughter's Festival (page 37)

Lantern Festival (元宵节)

Throughout China, the Lantern Festival takes place on 15th day of the first lunar month. As early as the Southern Han Dynasty, candles were lit up in the Flower Pagoda of Changshou Temple (the present Six Banyan Temple) to welcome the coming harvest. In modern times, the lantern festival is still held each year around the country. Lanterns of various shapes and sizes are hung in the streets, attracting countless visitors. Children will hold self-made or store-bought lanterns to stroll with on the streets, extremely excited.

Event

The lantern fair in Guangzhou is a civic exhibition of decorated lanterns. They are usually held in Yuexiu Park, Martyrs' Park and Guangzhou Cultural Park.

Where to See

1. Yuexiu Park (越秀公园)
🚇 Metro line 2 Yuexiu Park station exit A
2. Martyrs' Park (烈士陵园)
🚇 Metro line 1 Martyrs' Park station exit C
3. Cultural Park (文化公园)
🚇 Metro line 6 Culture Park station exit A

Lettuce Fair (生菜会)

According to folk legend, at between 11 pm on the 26th day of the first lunar month to 1 am on the next day, the Goddess of Mercy opens the coffer, offering different kinds of treasures to people. For example, people may ask for treasures like money, luck or success in their careers. Workers, farmers and businessmen hope to come across good signs at work, and people also pray for a smooth path and a better life in the coming year. Every year at this time, many believers, in spite of their busy lives, dress up to visit the temple and pray, hoping the Goddess of Mercy will kindly loan them treasures. The Lettuce Fair, which originated in the late Ming and early Qing, has a history of more than 300 years and is popular in Guangzhou, Nanhai (one of the districts in Foshan city) and Shunde (one of the districts in Foshan city). People eat lettuces on the Lettuce Fair hoping to bring in vigor (the pronunciation Chinese word for "lettuce" (生菜 shēng cài) is similar to the pronunciation of the phrase "getting rich." (生财 shēng cái).The Lettuce Fair later became connected to belief in the Goddess. Recently, under the social climate of high value on material goods and commerce in the Pearl River Delta, Lettuce Fair developed more utilitarian purposes, such as the acquisition of wealth and the birth of male heirs.

Event

The Lettuce Fair takes place between 11pm on the 26th of the first lunar month to 1 am on the next day. During the Lettuce Fair, villagers gather around the Kwan-yin temple in Kengkou to celebrate. Villagers perform the lion dance, and you can find people rushing to be the first to burn incenses and make prayers to the goddess. In addition to blessing, villagers touch sea snails and clams. People also eat special lettuce buns stuffed with clams, lettuce and Chinese chives. Almost all of the ingredients for lettuce bun carry some particular folk meaning. For example, silk noodles, because of their appearance, symbolize a long life. Also, due to the similarity in the pronunciations in Chinese, pickles refer to offspring, clams to wealth, and Chinese chives to a long time. With all the meanings above, lettuce bun indicates a hope to be rich and lucky for a long time.

Additionally, people can bring home a head of lettuce bound by red strings which signifies bringing home luck.

At least 6,000 kilograms of lettuces are prepared and given out at the Lettuces Fair every year. In the main square of the temple, which covers an area of 100 square meters, lettuce is wrapped and piled up next to a minimum of eight donation boxes. Lettuces can be taken after any amount of cash donation (generally ¥5 Yuan or ¥10 Yuan) is made into the boxes, with either.

A typical activity during the Lettuce Fair is touching snail shells to pray for the birth of male heirs. There is a large stone trough near the temple, about one meter deep and filled with water and uncountable clams and snail shells. As the folk legend goes, if a pregnant woman puts her hand into the water with her eyes closed touches a clam, she will give birth to a girl, and if she touches the snail shells instead, she will give birth to a boy. Therefore, lots of young women gather here for the prophecy power of the stone trough.

Where to See

Kwan-yin Temple (芳村坑口观音庙)
- No.69 Kengkou Xincun, Liwan District.
- Take metro Guangfo Line to Hedong station exit C, walk along Dongjiao Road South about 1 km.

"Polo Birth" Temple Fair (波罗诞)

Polo Temple also known as the Nanhai God Temple, people used to come here to pray to the Sea God for protection. Having undergone centuries of frequent repair and renovation, it has become a grand temple.

The temple is located by the Pearl River Estuary with raging waves in view. Whether arriving or departing, sailors would have a stopover here to pray to the Sea God for protection and smooth sailing. Even the Emperors sent officials here to worship the South Sea God. The temple, therefore, is also an important part of the legacy of the "Silk Sea Route".

Event

The temple fair, which dates back over 1,000 years, is one of the largest folk fairs in Guangzhou. It falls between February 11th and 13th of the lunar calendar. During these three days, the areas around the temple, both water and land, are crowded by fairgoers. The local saying goes that the biggest event for Guangzhou natives is the temple fair, followed by their own wedding.

Where to See

Nanhai God Temple (南海神庙)
- Nanhai God Temple, Miaotou Village, Huangpu District.
- Take metro Line 13 to Nanhai God Temple station exit A.

Tomb Sweeping Day (清明节)

Tomb Sweeping Day falls around the spring equinox, usually on April 5th. It involves visits to the family tombs for cleaning and making offerings.

Event

Because cremation has recently become more popular than burial, this custom has gone through extreme simplification, particularly in cities. Citizens in Guangzhou formerly went to the gravesites of deceased family members to burn incense and perform ritual offerings while clearing away plant overgrowth from the gravesite. A modern memorial service in a crematorium often consists of burning paper money and accessories (Joss paper include paper currency, credit cards, cheques, as well as paper-made clothes, houses, cars, toiletries, electronics and servants) and fire crackers.

Where to See

Zhonghua Permanent Cemetery (中华永久墓园)
- Daguan Road North, Tianhe District.
- Take metro Line 6 to Huangbei station exit D, follow the traffic direction walk until the traffic light, turn left cross the road and walk along DAGUAN BEILU about 1.4 km.

Pak Tai Festival (北帝诞)

Pak Tai, emperor of the North (the 3rd day of the 3rd lunar month), is popularly considered to have become the god of the North after his death. Because the Cantonese believe that the North is dominated by the water element (among the five elements of gold, wood, water, fire and mud), the water of the South is deemed to come from the North, and the Cantonese worship Pak Tai accordingly. Canton lies in the coastal region, and the Cantonese live by the sea and traditionally made a living by fishing. Pak Tai, being the god of water, controls the water sources. Therefore, Cantonese worship him and pray to him for sufficient water to allow farming, fishing, and trading. The oldest Pak Tai temple, which is located in Foshan city, was named Zǔ Miào , meaning primogenitor of Pak Tai temple.

Event

On the third day of the third lunar month, lion dance performers in Pan Tang region gather at Renwei temple and worship the statue of Pak Tai in the morning, praying for good harvest for the year. Then, the statue of Pak Tai is carried out of the imperial palace by the villagers of Pan Tang and moved around Pan the village for parade, with the lion dancing team leading in the front and villagers playing gongs and drums all the way through. Other traditional activities are also arranged at the square in front of Renwei temple, such as stacking flowers into large mounts, setting off firecrackers, and plays of gratitude for the goddess and lion dance performances. In addition, some modern events like exhibition, Cantonese art performances, children's dance performances, book reading, Chinese writing and drawing lectures, together with the traditional events take place for the celebration of Pak Tai festival.

Where to See

1. Renwei Temple (仁威祖庙)
📖 See Sai Kwan walking tour (page 51)

2. Pak Tai Temple (黄埔村玉虚宫)
📖 See Whampoa walking tour (page 151)

Goddess Mazu's Birthday (娘妈诞)

Mazu, literally "Mother Ancestor", is the indigenous goddess of the sea who is said to protect fishermen and sailors, and is invoked as the patron deity of all Southern Chinese and East Asian persons. Born as lín mò niáng in Fujian around 960 CE, there are many touching stories about her helping people in shipwrecks, so she was thought to be the incarnation of the goddess of the sea and was paid homage by over 100 million believers in more than twenty countries.

Worship of Mazu began around the Ming Dynasty, when many Taoist temples dedicated to her were erected all across Mainland China, later spreading to other countries with Southern Chinese inhabitants.

Mazu is widely worshipped in the south-eastern coastal areas of China and neighboring areas in Southeast Asia, especially Zhejiang, Fujian, Guangdong and Hainan, as well as Vietnam and Taiwan all, of which have strong seafaring traditions, as well as migrant communities elsewhere with sizeable populations from these areas. Mazu also has a significant influence on East Asian sea culture, especially in China and Taiwan.

Mazu's birthday-festival is on the twenty-third day of the third lunar month of the Chinese calendar. It falls in late April or early May according to the Gregorian calendar.

Event

On the 23rd of the 3rd Lunar Month every year, Longtan village enters a state of excitement almost as extraordinary as that of Chinese New Year. The Mazu deity is escorted with utmost respect by the parade crowd from the ancestral hall in the early morning. The parade ceremony begins at about eight in the morning. More than 230 participants dressed in bright-colored ancient costumes join the parade, the Mazu deity sitting serenely in a palanquin carried by eight people, two women scattering flowers in front of the parade. The parade crowd passes through the village and stops in each ancestral hall one after another to pray for good weather for the coming year, as well as for peace and prosperity.

Opera troupes perform Cantonese opera in a makeshift stage at the same time. Long Tan Village is a distinctive and ancient village full of water culture, where rich historical and cultural resources such as ancestral halls, memorial archway, ancient bridges, trees, and more are preserved.

Where to See

1. Longtan Village (龙潭村)

Take metro Line 8 to Lujiang station exit D then transfer bus No.264 and get off at Longtancun Paifang stop (6 bus stops) then walk across the footbridge.

2. Nansha Matsu Temple (天后宫)

No. 88 Tianhou Lu, Nansha district.

Take metro Line 4 to Nansha passenger Port station exit B then walk towards the pagoda direction.

Kamfa Festival (金花诞)

According to legend, during Ming dynasty there was a provincial governor in Guangzhou who loved his wife very deeply. One day his pregnant wife went into particularly extreme labor pains. The provincial governor asked a doctor for help, doctor but the doctor was too tired and fell asleep on the chair, providing little help. He then dreamed of a white-haired elder who told him, "If you can ask Madame Kamfa to come to your house, your wife and baby will both be safe." The Provincial governor woke up and asked his retinues go out in search of a girl whose name was Kamfa. They found over seventy; when one of them entered into the house, his wife completed her labor and gave birth successfully and safely. The news spread out all over Guangzhou and the neighboring area. People respected the girl Kamfa as a god, no one dared to marry with her. The girl eventually grew tired of living without a companion and committed suicide by drowning herself in the lake. In order to express peoples' respect and love of her, people built a temple to consecrate her and her death. April 17th of the Chinese lunar calendar was designated as the Kamfa Festival.

Event

At 9am in the morning, there is a group of people lining up before the gate of Kamfa Ancient Temple. They are mostly villagers from (nearby) Changzhou and other believers coming for worship. They take turns worshiping the goddess of Kamfa by burning the incenses and offering sacrifices. A livelier scene was that both the parents holding children and the elderly with grey hair rush up in a crowd to get the birthday buns (a kind of bread that people usually have on birthday hoping to live longer lives) as soon as the principle announces "Time for birthday buns". Moreover, the villagers struggle to throw cards with red ribbons over the branches of the longan tree in front of the temple. This activity of making wishes in front of the wishing tree is a yearly custom at the birthday of Kamfa goddess for the Changzhou people. Accordingly the temple gained popularity by attracting a large number of pilgrims.

Where to See

Kamfa Ancient Temple (金花古庙)
- No.26 Fujufang Street, Huangpu District
- See Changzhou Island Bike Tour (page 179)

Dragon Boat Festival (端午节)

The Dragon Boat Festival occurs on fifth day of fifth lunar month, usually in May or June. This festival commemorates the sacrifice of Qu Yuan, a famous poet who drowned himself in the river by way of making a statement against government corruption during the Warring States Period. According to legend, local fishermen tried to rescue him, beating drums and throwing dumplings in the water to scare fish away and keep them from eating Qu's body. The highlights are dragon boat racing along the Pearl River, Dragon Boat Water Parade between villages and eating rice dumplings wrapped in bamboo leaves.

Event

In Longtan Village, villagers organize a religious ritual known as The Dragon Boat Water Parade which takes place the day before the Dragon Boat Festival. On the same day, they also organize a traditional dragon boat banquet at which thousands people gather and have dinner outside. The dragon boat banquet was originally offered to boatmen to provide them with enough energy to row. Over time, the Banquet gradually evolved into an event for all villagers, neighbors and visitors. According to tradition, the Dragon Boat Banquet is held at lunchtime at the entrance of the village or ancestral halls. The Dragon Boat Water Parade provides an opportunity to experience Guangzhou's living culture up close, and to squeeze in a visit to an old water village community at the same time.

The Guangzhou International Dragon boat racing is held the First Saturday after the Dragon Boat Festival, normally along the Pearl River between Guangzhou Bridge and Haiying Bridge. It usually starts at afternoon, but spectators should be sure to get to the shore side more early and to pick a good position.

Where to See

Longtan Village (龙潭村)
See Goddess Mazu's Birthday (page 34)

The Daughter's Festival (乞巧节)

In Chinese mythology, the Daughter's Festival, falling on the July 7th of the lunar calendar, is the annual meeting day of the lovers, Cowherd and Weaver Maid, on the magpie bridge. In the legend, as the 7th daughter of the Jade Emperor, Weaver Maid is ingenious and dexterous. During the festival, people, mostly women, perform rituals, praying for wits, dexterity and marital bliss.

Formerly, villagers made use of common materials from daily life, such as plant pith, colored paper, sesame and husks of rice, and then shaped them into various forms such as fruits, flowers,

figures and utensils. Thus began Qī Qiǎo custom (and also known as the Daughter's Festival) gradually grow into a common festival.

According to the records, celebration of this festival dates back to the Han Dynasty (206 B.C.-A.D. 24) and reached its height in southern China regions.

Event

Zhu Village in Tianhe District will also hold Qī Qiǎo Festival is weakening; now the leading role of this festival is played by elder women's associations. Although the Qī Qiǎo Festival falls on the 7th day of the 7th lunar month, people start to prepare for the Qiqiao handicrafts exhibition in March.

Where to See

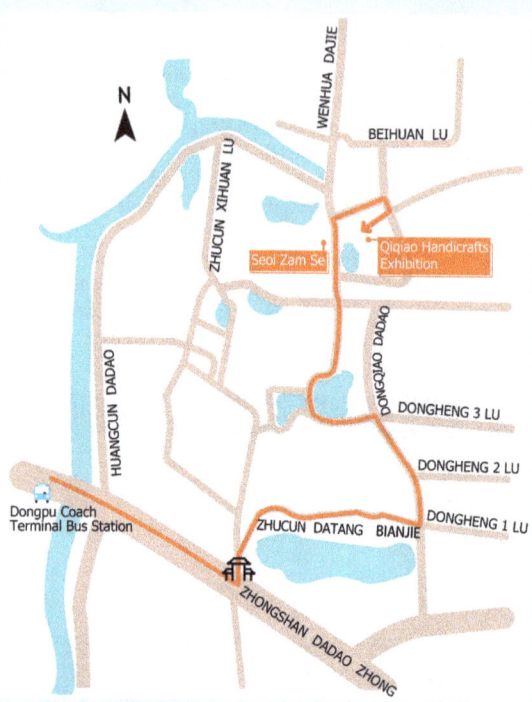

Zhu Village (天河珠村)

🚇•🚌 Take Metro Line 8 to Pazhou Station Exit C, transfer bus No.B7 until terminal station (9 stops), then follow the route.

Ghost Festival (中元节)

Hungry Ghost Festival is a traditional and historical event celebrated on the fifteenth day of the seventh lunar month. It has its roots in the Buddhist festival of Utlambana and Taoist culture during the Tang Dynasty. This festival represents the connection between the living and the dead, earth and heaven, body and soul. It was commonly known as Chinese Old Souls' Day. It is a feast for commemorating the souls of the deceased. It is generally believed that the gates of hell are opened to permit unborn souls and wandering ghosts to  wander on earth and intermingle with the human world for food and other necessities. Because of this, people offer food and joss papers to these hungry ghosts in temples or in front of their residences along the foot way with the hope that the ghosts will not enter their houses and cause trouble. Large amounts of Joss sticks and paper money were heavily burnt to ask for good blessing to the household, family, and business.

In southern China, the Hungry Ghost Festival is usually on 14th of the seventh month of the Chinese lunar calendar. Legend also tells that refugees celebrated the Hungry Ghost Festival one day earlier in order to flee the Mongolian invasion in late Song dynasty.

Although it is a religious festival, the Hungry Ghost Festival has some significance not only among the Buddhist and Taoists, but also among many the pagans who prize filial piety and pay respect to their forefathers.

Event

On 15th of the seventh month of Chinese Lunar Calendar, nearly one thousand delicate handicrafts made by villagers are displayed on a big table within their ancestral hall of Liang clan for people to appreciate, and worship their ancestors according to the ritual ceremony. The activity is called Bǎi Zhōng Yuán, which has a history of more than 500 years, the activity lasts 4 days, during which time people thank the Three Great Emperor-Officials and pray for a good harvest, good fortune, and prosperity in the upcoming year. More than forty tables are laid out and various vegetarian dishes are served out of giant basins. Visitors need only donate ¥5 or ¥10 to enjoy an exotic traditional meal here. According to tradition, during these 3 days villagers have to eat vegetarian food in order to receive blessings, and on the 19th, the final day of the festival, they can have abundant meat. There will be an organized performance of dancing & singing in the evening. This area might be the only one that has been handed down with this custom and culture through the ages in Guangdong province.

Did you know

There are three paper-made clothes handing on the wooden screen above the table, they represent the Three Great Emperor-Officials, which are the Heavenly Official Who Confers Blessings (天官赐福); The Earthly Official Who Absolves Sins (地官赦罪); The Water Official Who Eliminates Misfortunes (水官解厄). In the Southern and Northern dynasties, the Three Officials were combined with the Spirits of the Three Origins (higher, middle and lower). On 15th of the first month, the 15th of the seventh month and the 15th of the tenth month, the birthdays of the Three Officials of Heaven, Earth and Water, respectively, Taoists go to temples to burn incense and offer sacrifices.

Where to See

Chebei Village (车陂梁氏宗祠)
🚇 Take metro line 4 & 5 get of at Chebei station Exit C then follow the route.

Mid-autumn Festival (中秋节)

Mid-autumn Festival is on the 15th day of the 8th lunar month, usually in September or October. Cantonese moon cakes are enjoyed during this holiday. Lian Xiang Lou and Taotao Ju's moon cakes are especially famous. Children play with hand-made paper lanterns. In the evening families enjoy reunion dinners together, and then go out to bask in the moonlight. Each family erects a bamboo pole in front of the door on which colorful lamps and lanterns are hung. Offerings to the moon include moon cakes, shaddocks, taros, water chestnuts and bananas. After the ceremony, families eat porridge and river snails, and chat together until midnight. Guangzhou people consider Mid-Autumn Festival a major family-reunion day, no less important than Spring Festival.

Event

Fire Dragon Dance in Qinghu Village. According to local legend, in the autumn of 1860, a few days before the Mid-Autumn Festival, a large number of locusts spread across Qinghu Village and ate the crops, making the villagers very anxious. An idea came to one of the villagers, the villager made a huge dragon from straw and covered it with incense sticks, which he then lit on fire. They took the dragon out to the fields and danced until midnight, frightening all of the locusts away. From that time on, the Fire Dragon Dance has been carried out according to tradition

The fire dragon is more than 70 meters long with its body divided into 32 segments, all of which are stuffed with straw and twine in colored lights instead of incense sticks, accompanied by drummers and erupting firecrackers, villagers danced for a whole night. On the festival night, the streets and alleyways in the area are packed with fire dragons joyfully dancing to drum music against the backdrop lit by colored lights, creating a fantastic atmosphere for the festival.

Where to See

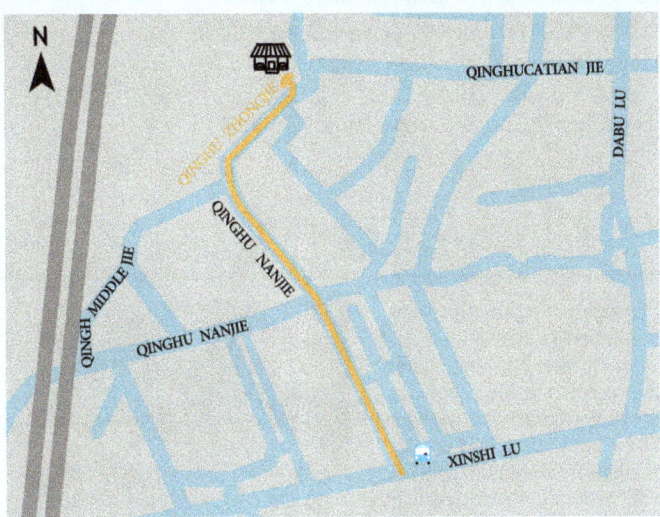

Qinghu Village (清湖村)

 Take Metro Line 2 & 3 to Jiahewanggang Station Exit B, transfer bus No.739 and get off at Qinghucunkou stop (9 bus stops) then follow the route.

Double Ninth Festival (重阳节)

Double Ninth Festival is on the 9th day of 9th lunar month, usually in October. The festival may have begun as early as the Warring States Period (475 - 221 B.C.). According to the Yin/Yang dichotomy that forms a basis to the Chinese worldview, Yin represents the elements of darkness and Yang represents life and brightness. The number nine is regarded as Yang. The ninth day of the ninth month is a double Yang day, hence the name "Chóng Yáng Festival". ("Chóng" means "repeat" in Chinese.) The ninth month also heralds the approach of winter. It is a time when the living need warm clothing, and filial Chinese sons and daughters extended this to make the festival a time for providing winter clothes for their ancestors. The Double Ninth Festival, therefore, also became an occasion to visit the graves of dead family members. Clothes made of paper would then be burnt as offerings. This is also the fall version of the Tomb Sweeping Day in April.

Event

For Chóng Yáng Festival, Cantonese people normally go hiking, have chrysanthemum wine and wear cornel for protection against evil and disaster. This has been a traditional folk custom in China and hiking, so far is still a very popular event in Guangzhou during the Chóng Yáng Festival. From the perspective of the Cantonese, hiking is not for acquiring protection against evil but rather for gaining luck, improving one's destiny and to making wishes come true. Baiyun Mount is a popular spot among climbers especially those young people who go climbing. They set off in the evening, spend the night at the peak, and come back down in the early morning of the next day. They prepare of small paper-made windmills and little flags with wishes written on them and they stick them into the ground when they reach the peak of the mountain. It is said that one can easily figure out what Canton teenagers are passionate about by looking at what is written on the little windmills and flags at the mountain peak.

Where to See

1. Baiyun Mountain (白云山)
🚖 Take taxi from Beijing Road costs around CNY ¥30

2. Longtousan Forest Park (龙头山森林公园)
🚖 Take taxi from Beijing Road costs around CNY ¥90

3. Lotus Mountain (莲花山)
🚖 Take taxi from Beijing Road costs around CNY ¥140

Winter Solstice (冬至)

Winter Solstice, which literally means the Deepest Moment of Winter is on December 22nd. Celebrated on the longest night of the year, Dōng Zhì is the day when sunshine is weakest and daylight shortest. The coming of winter is celebrated by families and is traditionally the time when farmers and fishermen gather food in preparation for the coming cold season. It is also a time for family reunions.

Event
Cantonese people observe the day with a family feast, which often includes preserved duck and sausages. However, the highlight of the day's festive dishes is hot soup served with flour dumplings (汤丸). You can have this dish in many dessert shops.

EXPLORE GUANGZHOU

In each area of the city
we will help you to discover the top sights and
the best ways to experience local life

Many of the walks and biking in this book depart from
the well traveled tourist trails and instead investigate less
well known parts of the city. Guangzhou is a relatively
safe place to wander, but you will want to follow the
usual precautions observed by city dwellers, from taking
care when crossing streets to dressing down and wearing
appropriate footwear to simply being constantly aware of
your surroundings.

Walking Trails

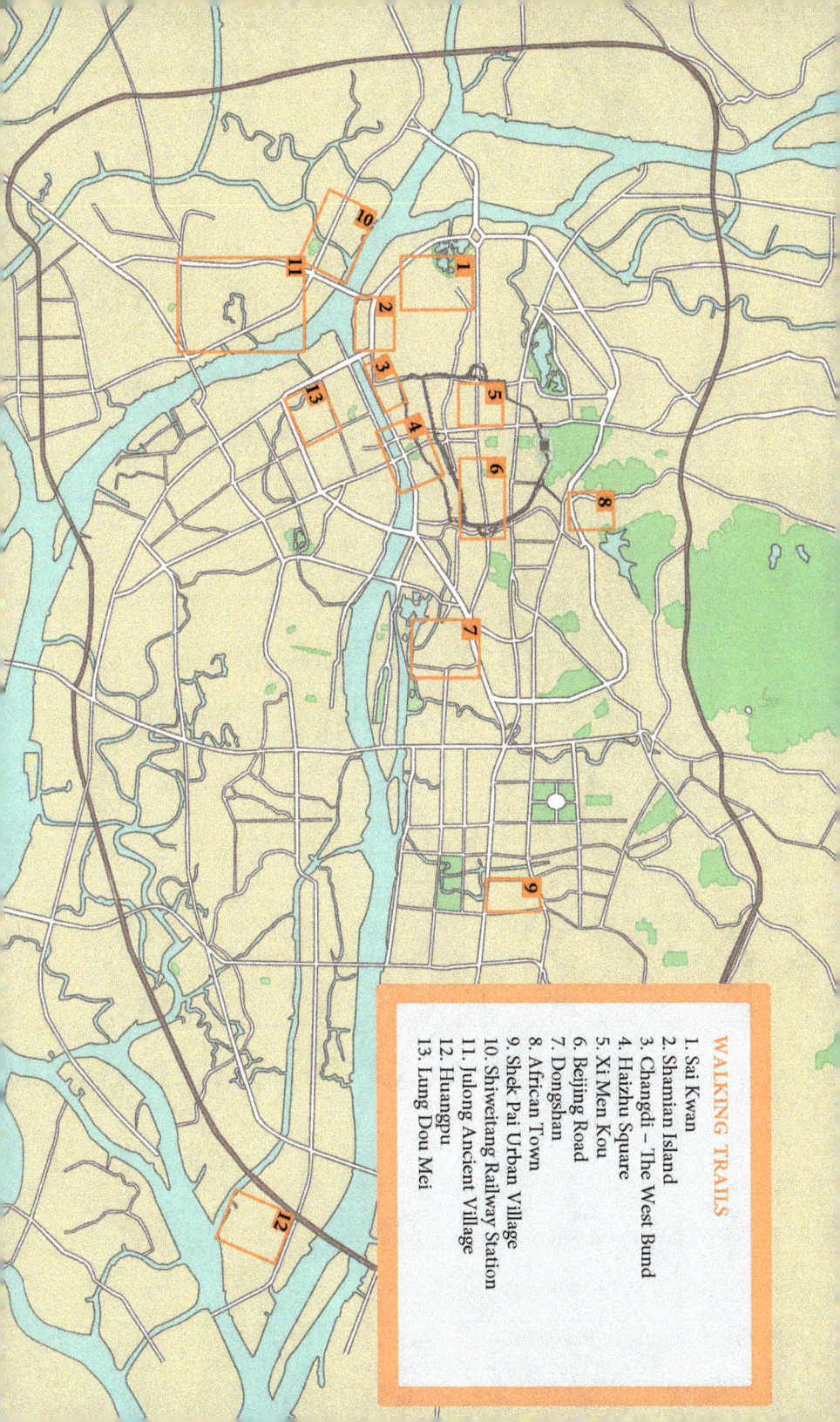

Sai Kwan

HIGHLIGHT: The impression of old Canton
START POINT: Metro line 1 Changshou Lu station Exit E
FINISH POINT: Metro line 5 Zhongshanba station Exit A
LENGTH: Approx. 4 hours (3.7 km)

Historical Background

Sai Kwan, romanized as Xiguan in Mandarin Chinese, which has a history of two thousand years, is endowed with a rich cultural heritage dating back to the Tang Dynasty. This culture is on full display in an area from Liwan Lake and Litchi Bay to the arcade buildings and Sai Kwan Grand House on Enning Road. On Enning Road and Longjin Road, 1100 years of history has been preserved in the Sai Kwan Grand House with towering gatehouses, elaborate decorations, and the brick and pebble doorsteps in the Fengyuan Community. Shopping arcades dating back to the Republic of China period can be seen on Enning and West Longjin Roads. "Lingnan culture is concentrated in Liwan and Sai Kwan where customs are the richest in Guangzhou".

The Litchi Bay Cultural and Leisure Zone covers an area of approximately 580,000 square meters, bounded by Pantang Road and Longjin Road West on the east, Huangsha Avenue on the west, Zhongshan 8th Road on the north, and Duobao Road on the south. People passing by the Litchi Bay Creek would reminisce about "litchi trees with reds fruits lining the emerald creek". The ancient alleys and the reflection of the hills on the surface of the creek give people the feeling of traveling back in time. The areas around the Litchi Bay are typical of Lingnan water towns, enriched by a great culture that spans thousands of years. Places of historical interest around the Litchi Bay include the Litchi Bay Creek, Litchi Lake, Renwei Temple, Literature Pagoda, Liwan Museum, the former residence of Chiang Kuang Nai, the ornate boathouse, Haishan Club, the former residence of Chen Lianbo, Liang's Ancestral Hall, and Sai Kwan Grand House. The Litchi Bay is also the origin of Sai Kwan Grand House, Lady Sai Kwan, the "five treasures" of Sai Kwan, Sai Kwan gourmet food, Cantonese Opera and variety show, and many other enduring Guangzhou cultural icons. Dubbed the "Sai Kwan Cultural Expo Garden", the Litchi Bay is the most culturally endowed place in Guangzhou, displaying elegance and sophistication. The theme of the area is gourmet, Lingnan culture and Sai Kwan characteristics.

Itinerary

Start at Changshou Lu metro station Exit E, turn right and walk south on BAOHUA LU, there are many local food and dessert stores, such as Shun Kee Dessert Store (①, page 57), Chan Tim Kee Fish Skin Store (②; page 57). Sit down and have a bowl of porridge and fish skin (fish skin is featured here), it looks unsightly but tastes very refreshing, a flavor particularly worthy of recommendation. Other snacks available in the small alley of SHILIUFU DAJIE ③, are Ginger Vinegar with Pig Trotters and Eggs and Pork Blood Soup.

The archway leads to Zhan Tianyou Memorial Hall

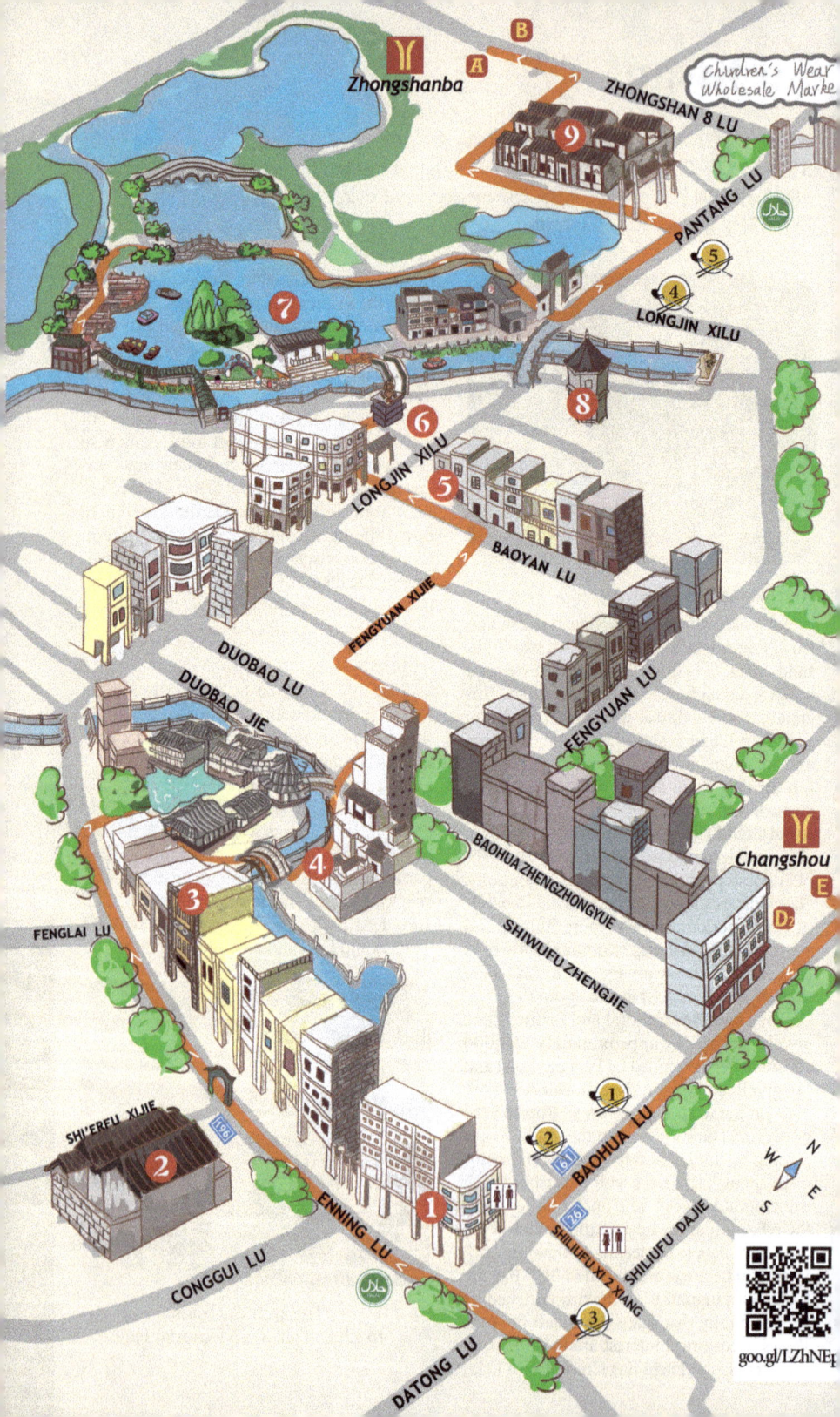

After tasting some local snacks walk to ENNING LU where you will see **Golden Voice Cinema** ❶ , formerly known as 'Golden Voice Theater' , located at No. 265 ENNING LU, built in 1932. It has a long history as an important part of Guangzhou Sai Kwan culture, leaving good memories in thousands of people's hearts, it will be rebuilt to serve as a cinema museum. Keep walking until No.196 ENNING LU, there is a rounded gray archway on your left hand side, walk inside the alley about 50 meters to **Zhan Tianyou Memorial Hall** (❷ ; page 51), located in the SHI'ERFU XIJIE, next to the Zhan Tianyou primary school. The reconstruction of the Zhan Tianyou memorial Hall is also a typical Sai Kwan dwelling house. It still retains the use daily necessities of the old plain furniture that gives it a great sense of history. Return to ENNING LU which is also known as 'Cantonese Opera Street'. **Pat Wo Wui Kun Association** (❸ ; Page 52) is the spiritual ancestral home of Cantonese opera artist, located at No.177 ENNING LU.

There are 7 custom copper shops along ENNING LU. The shops sell copper bowls, pots, spittoons, chopsticks, abacus, copper mahjong, copper fans, etc and other odd copper products. In the past these were daily household utensils used by rich Sai Kwan businessmen. Copper wares were popular in Sai Kwan area before the 1960s. The traditional marriage gift in Guangzhou was 2 copper basins and 2 pairs of shoes. The hand made copper production is a long process where a copper pot will take 2 to 3 days to finish and sell for around RMB ￥ 650, a machine made pot would sell for around RMB ￥ 250. Sai Kwan copper art was listed in a national non-material cultural heritage list in 2009. You are even welcome to keep it as a souvenir.

Copper shops

Then visit the new technology-infused **Cantonese Opera Art Museum** (❹ ; page 53) and learn all the details of Cantonese opera. The museum is organizing a serious of workshops and exhibitions to promote Cantonese opera.

Walk along a small canal to FENGYUANSHI. You will see a meat and vegetable market in a small alley filled with yelling crowds people 4pm~6pm, here you will experience how natives in Guangzhou live. If your stomach gets queasy from watching fish or chickens get butchered before your very eyes don't go inside, if you are interested in what the local people buy for their main evening meal go and have a look. Animals of all variety are on display and being butchered to be taken home for a good fresh home cooked meal! Also watch where you step because there are open drains for the blood to be washed away.

Walk north on the small alley of FENGYUAN XIJIE, turn right at BAOYUAN LU, No.5~23 and No.8~34 BAOYUAN LU there are old residential buildings ❺ , you can feel massive history through storm and anxiety.

Cross LONGJIN XILU to FENGYUAN BEIJIE, and visit **Li Wan Museum** (❻ ; page 53) and walk around **Lychee Bay** (page 50) absorb the atmosphere of the local area. There is a Four-Faced Buddha **Erawan Shrine** (page 52) from Thai people displayed in front of the small bridge. Walk across the bridge and enter the charming Liwan Lake Park. On the right hand side is a pathway along a canal lined with lots of local snack stalls selling traditional local snacks, such as Cantonese pudding, sweetened water chestnut and gingko in soup, and Cantonese-style pickled radish, etc.

In Pantang the five excellent products produced in this district are water caltrop, arrowhead, water bamboo shoot, lotus root, and water chestnut. Pantang is located near Renwei Taoist Temple, Pantang Water Chestnut Cake uses a local product, water chestnut flour, as an ingredient. The method of making the cake is frying granulated sugar until they becomes yellow and dissolves into a syrup, blending in half-cooked water chestnut cake, then cooking it well by a strong fire. The cake is gold yellow and transparent, with elasticity, smooth taste with the delicate fragrance of water chestnut cake. It is pleasant to the palate, with a pure and fresh taste when the water chestnut cake is eaten with tea or having a meal.

Walk down the bridge and turn left and you will see a Cantonese Opera shown on the stage in the park every Tuesday, Thursday, and

Sai Kwan

Saturday afternoon.

Take a walk round the **Liwan Lake Park** (❼ ; page 56), visit the traditional southern Chinese garden with artificial rocks in the pond with goldfish, exit at the east gate of the park. There is a **Literature Pagoda** (❽ ; page 51) on the other side of the Longjin Bridge. A traditional ceremony will be held on the 3rd of March of the Chinese Lunar calendar every year. People who come here will meet the four born stars of wisdom of China on that day.

Just ahead of PANTANG LU, you will find **Renwei Temple** (❾ ; page 51). If you come here during the Pak Tai Festival (page 33), you will see the Lion Dance at the Renwei Temple Bazaar. Finish your trip at metro line 8 Zhongshanba station.

Tips :

1. If you feel energetic take 2 stops to Xicun Metro Station Exit D from Zhongshanba metro station, visit **Dui Shan Yuan Garden** (page 56).
2. Pat Wo Wui Kun only opened during forenoon 9:00~12:00 everyday.
3. Lychee Bay has classic Cantonese Opera performance everyday from 2 pm to 5 pm. It's free of charge, the opera troupe is mainly composed of retired people in Liwan District of Guangzhou. As a amateur opera troupe to promote and support the development of the Cantonese opera in Guangzhou. There's a basket placed in front of the stage for donations, ideal for audiences that wish to donate as well as offer encouragement and support.
4. While walking along BAOHUA LU, be aware of pricing fraud at clothing stores. A lot of shops place a cheap price tag in front of the shop front or above the products to provoke people to buy but the actual prices are higher than the price tags shown, than what you pay. If this situation occurs, you can refuse to pay or dial 12358 to the Guangzhou Price Bureau to complain, however this is always an unsuccessful effort in this unenforceable law-sanction country.

Points of Interest

Lychee Bay (荔枝湾)

Lychee Bay is located in the Pantang region, west of Liwan District of Guangzhou, this is in the vicinity of the time-honored Sai Kwan City, along the banks of the Pearl River. This romantic attraction is home to celebrities of different dynasties and a showcase of Lingnan Culture such as Sai Kwan Resident Community, Miss Sai Kwan, Five Treasures of Sai Kwan, Sai Kwan Delicacies, and Cantonese Opera. More than 2000 years ago, Lu Jia, the notable chancellor in western Han dynasty, embarked on a diplomatic visit to the state of Yue. When he went by and stopped, he ordered his fellows to plant the litchis and dig up the lotus pond. This is the story about how Litchi Bay got its name. Liwan District carried out an overall environmental improvement project in 2009 and 2010 to beautify the area for the Asian Games. After sewage treatment of the Litchi Bay, the stream, neighboring buildings, and streets were restored to their former historic features.

Renwei Temple (仁威祖庙)

This temple is one of the best traditional Southern Chinese temples in Guangzhou. It is beginning establish in four year of Song Dynasty (1052), it is a temple reserved for the worship of deities. The traditional Beidi's (North Emperor) Birth Bazaar has been held here on March 3rd of Chinese Lunar calendar (around the turn of March and April) for centuries. The annual public fair and gala features charity rice distribution, prayer, lion dance, parade, and basin food dinner. Visitors can pay tribute to the Northern Emperor at the temple and pray for blessings. While the three halls on the front side are dedicated to the deities of the Taoist pantheon, in the back, there is a hall with white and red wooden plates commemorating locals' deceased family members. At the square in front of the temple you can watch magic shows, performances of ventriloquism, Cantonese opera, and folk music.

- Miaoqian Street, West Longjin Road;
- Take Bus 66, 2, 8 and 25 to Pantang Stop, and then walk five minutes;
- 8:00-17:00 or 6:30-17:00 (On the 1st day and the 15th day of each month in the Chinese lunar calendar)
- Admission is free.

Literature Pagoda (文塔)

Originally built between the late periods of the Qing Dynasty, this pagoda was constructed to offer sacrifice to writers and poets. As legend goes, the supernatural mortal of the Wenqu Star always holds a pen in his hand, if touched by his pen, one would be able to become famous or successful. Thus, the pagoda was designed in a pen-like shape and is also called 'Pagoda of Fame and Success'.

- No.104 LONGJIN XILU
- 09:00~17:00
- ￥5

Zhan Tianyou Memorial Hall (詹天佑故居)

Zhan Tianyou, also known in the West as Jeme Tien Yow, was a distinguished railroad engineer. He was the chief engineer of the Imperial Peking-Kalgan (Beijing-Zhangjiakou) Railway, the first railway built in China without foreign assistance in 1909, as well as the technical advisor of the Kowloon Canton Railway project in the early 1900s. Zhan has since been revered as the "Father of China's Railroad." Zhan's former residence which was his place of birth and where he spent his childhood, is very typical of a Sai Kwan style house between late Qing Dynasty and early Republic of China. The wooden doors, redwood furniture, stained-glass windows, brick walls, and a musty yet alluring smell takes you back some 150 years in time.

- No.42 YACAI XIANG, SHIERFU XIJIE
- 10:00-17:30 from Tuesday to Sunday
- Free admission

Pat Wo Wui Kun Association (八和会馆)

Pat Wo Wui Kun Association is the umbrella body for Cantonese opera groups and artists. After being restored, it looks like a typical Sai Kwan building during the Qing Dynasty. In 1889, under the reign of Emperor Guangxu (1875-1908), Pat Wo Association was established in Huangsha, Guangzhou to promote and foster the development of Cantonese opera in both Guangdong and Guangxi. In the early 20th Century, the singing language of Cantonese opera had gradually shifted from Guilin Mandarin to Cantonese. With the development of Cantonese Opera, Pat Wo Wui Kun Association established many branches all over the world.

- No.177 ENNING LU;
- Take Bus No. 2, 3 and 82 to Enning Road Stop
- 9:00~12:00
- Free admission

Erawan Shrine (四面佛)

In Buddhism, the Erawan Shrine isn't the Buddha but an angel in a higher heaven or class of celestial beings. In Brahma sense, the Erawan Shrine is the supreme essence of the Hindu universe.

The four faces symbolize the four books of the Vedas, the Hindu scriptures and the source of all knowledge in the creation of the universe. The eight hands, symbolize the omnipresence and power of Lord Brahma. The upper right hand carries a rosary, symbolizing the cycle of life from creation to death. The upper left hand carries the Vedas, symbolizing knowledge and intellect. The lower left hand carries a pot of water representing cosmic energy of creation. The lower right hand bestows grace and protection. The front face represent career, the second face represents romance, the back face unexpected lucky money, and the fourth face represent health.

Erawan Shrine most likely helps you but we cannot say 100% because it depends on your karma. If your karma is bad then no god or Buddha can help you. Give more donations perform good deeds, and help people and the gods and Buddha will help you; you will become lucky and be closer to the gods and Buddha.

Cantonese Opera Art Museum
(粤剧艺术博物馆)

The Cantonese Opera Art Museum is located in the core historic area of Guangzhou. It opened in 2016, and is designed in Chinese garden style, with characteristics of Lingnan culture and a graceful water town. The Cantonese Opera Art Museum is not only a space for exhibition, study, education and display of the Cantonese Opera art. It is also a cultural space with the Lingnan cultural memory, connecting the Lingnan heritage with the current life of successors and ordinary people. This museum is divided into north and south sides. The south side is set as the main exhibition hall, designed in a antique style, basically for exhibition, show, education, research, and public activity. The north side is areas for preservation of cultural relics and Cantonese opera development.

- 📍 No.127 ENNING LU
- 🕘 9:00-16:00 from Tuesday to Sunday
- 💲 Free admission (passport required for entry)

Li Wan Museum
(西关民俗博物馆)

Li Wan Museum, located west of Guangzhou, is representative of architecture from ancient Guangzhou. The museum takes advantage of stairs and corridors to present Sai Kwan cultures and local customs. Displays of wedding and seasonal clothing, give visitors a thorough idea of Sai Kwan culture. Local rich businessmen generally built Sai Kwan Mansions at the "Sai Kwan Corner" of Guangzhou. The ground floor plan was based on a vertical central axis, with a main hall in the center and symmetrically 3 halls and 2 corridors at each side. Along the central axis there are the porch, entrance hall, middle hall, main hall, the first chamber room, the second hall, and the second chamber room. Each hall has an entry and between two halls there is an open lane (tiān jǐng), on which a little attic with a wing or dormer window is constructed for skylight and air circulation. The academy room, side hall, bedroom, stairs, and kitchen are located along the central axis in order. A courtyard decorated with artificial landscapes and ponds is usually located at the right side of entrance hall and connected to the main hall. The academy room is positioned at the back of the courtyard; on each side of a grand mansion, there is a Qingyun lane.

- 📍 No.82 FENGYUAN BEIJIE
- 🚌 Metro line 5 Zhongshanba station Exit B; Bus No. 8, 25, 55, 66, 74, 226 and get off at Lonjinxi Road Stop
- 🕘 9:00-17:30 from Tuesday to Sunday
- 💲 ￥8
- 📞 +86 20 81939917

Room Descriptions

A: Main Hall was the host's living room. Although most of Sai Kwan residences were two-story buildings, without the upper floor, the main hall is fairly tall and spacious. Main halls were well decorated places where families gathered, worshiped their ancestors, made major decisions, and met very important guests.

The men and women guests were separated. Facing the Three-ply Doors, the male host and male guests would sit on the left hand side, the female host and female guests would sit on the right hand side. There are 3 Lucky Gods displayed at the front of the main hall, traditionally they are arranged from right to left, Good Fortune (福), Prosperity (禄) and Longevity (寿).

The main hall is the main part of Sai Kwan residence, the roof of main hall is about 6~8 meters high and is the highest point in the building. The main girder is made of a hard giant wood, which is painted with red oil and must be furnished on a lucky day with a worship ceremony. Its hip rafters are painted with black oil and its lining tiles are painted in white.

B: Side Hall, also known as Partial Hall, located to the west of Main hall, is for meeting general guests. In the display cabinet, some items used in the 1930s and 1940s are exhibited, including electric heating device, dresser mirror, camera, dressing case, lamp, silver ebony chopsticks, black wood ruler, etc.

C: The Study Room, located to the east of main hall, is decorated as it used to be. There are bookshelves, an antique cabinet and a desk with brush pens, ink, paper, and ink stone. The walls decorated with old style painting frames on them look very artistic and an old phonograph on a desk plays beautiful music. A small yard outside with some beautiful green plants looks so peaceful as if it was a freehand brushwork painting. This was also a room where secret talks with guests were held.

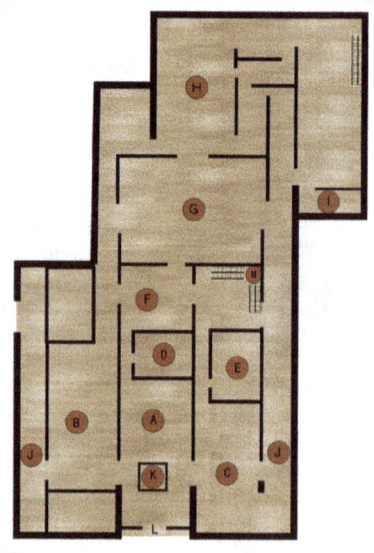

G: Small courtyards with roofs divide halls. Side windows provided courtyards with adequate ventilation and sufficient light. Most of courtyards, especially those that connect the guarding door, Sedan Chair Hall, and Main hall form a square. The floor of courtyard is decorated with granite with floor drain holes that are, usually golden thread shaped, which might have to do with an old saying "water symbolizes fortune".

J: There are two Qingyun lanes on both sides of the residence to represent 'Quick Success'. The lanes lead through to the end of the residence, are about 1.4~2.1 meters wide, were mainly passageways for women and servants to move in and out. These areas functioned as ventilation, lighting, airing, planting, and separating neighborhoods as well.

K: Sedan Hall: Important guests chiefly visited in a sedan chair, and entered from the Three-ply Doors. This room is used to store the guests sedan chair during their visit.

L: Sai Kwan mansion is unique with the Three-ply Door system, A complete Sai Kwan door has: breviped ceiling-fan door (also known as screen door), the sliding rail bars, and hardwood door. The sliding rail bars is a movable fence, horizontal opening and closing, consisting of 13 or 15 hard

A. Main Hall
B. Side Hall
C. Study Room
D. Master Bedroom
E. The Marriage Customs
F. Dinging Room
G. Patio
H. Exhibition Hall
I. Kitchen
J. Qingyun Lane
K. Place for Sedan Chair
L. Three-ply Door
M. Stairs

round batten (typically mahogany or hardwood). The battens must be singular, because dual have the same pronunciation with funeral in Cantonese, they believe it is inauspicious. When someone is at home during the day, they usually only shut the sliding rail bars. The screen door and sliding rail bars are good for air circulation and security purposes, and adapt to the Lingnan hot and rainy climate. The hardwood doors which are 8 cm (0.2625 ft) in thickness have a cross latch buckle door, to prevent thieves from entering. A pair of copper rings function as a door knocker.

M: Sai Kwan Residences usually have an odd number of wood stairs. With Western style wooden railings, the wood stairs look smooth and elegant. Young lady's boudoir was designed lively and brightly. Decorated with smart and graceful furniture, the boudoir fully reflects a young lady's decent life and good taste.

Young lady's boudoir on second floor

Cantonese style stained-glass windows, known as Manzhou windows, inherited the features of traditional ones and sliding windows in a square frame. Combined etching skills with Chinese traditional painting techniques, the windows were designed diversely with a wide range of patterns from flowers, landscapes, and figures.

Usually, there are horizontal tablets, brick carving or decorations shown at the top of the gate. Some are semi-circular colored glass windows with butterfly patterns, commonly known as 'Butterfly windows'. The gray sketch line arched over the window shows the obvious influence of Western Architecture.

Skylight is a special window in a roof that operates with a rope hanging from above. Skylights consists of cedarn lattices, transparent or translucent tile made of mica sheet, on a wooden pulley and track. It has dual the function of ventilation and lighting.

With blue-brick decorated walls, elaborate interior design, well-planned settings, elegant redwood furniture, exquisite wood carvings, stained glass, typical Manzhou windows and barred windows, Li Wan Museum shows you the charms of southern China culture.

Skylight & butterfly window   Three-ply doors system

- No.155 LONGJIN XILU
- Free admission

Liwan Lake Park (荔湾湖公园)

Liwan Lake Park displays the elegant and gentle beauty of southern China with a lake as its central attraction. The park is located in the Pantang area in Liwan District. Liwanhu Park was built in 1958, covering an area of about 400,000 square meters, and the lake covers about two thirds. Part of the park's charm comes from the fact that there are many facilities that allow visitors to enjoy the beauty of the place while exercising in the gymnasium or swimming at the Olympic size pool. For those with children, the park has a children's amusement park with several rides. Visitors coming during the summer months can enjoy the aroma of the blooming lotus flowers that adorn the banks of the lakes.

Dui Shan Yuan Garden (对山园)

Dui Shan Yuan Garden construction began in 1929 and concluded in early 1931, almost at the same time as the construction of the Sun Yat-sen Memorial Hall, located in Zengbu Park. It also known as 'Little Sun Yat-sen Memorial Hall' by locals, as it is very similar with Sun Yat-sen Memorial Hall. The Garden owner was Huang Guanzhang, a munitions director general and Guangdong bank vice President from 1929~1936. He was in charge of the construction of Sun Yat-sen Memorial Hall since 1929 and used his power to demand higher construction funds for his villa Dui Shan Yuan Garden which cost at least 1.5 million yuan at that time. The garden structures combine with China's northern and southern elements and a little bit Western style. You can see the main shrine has northern palatial architectural style, the wing-rooms are Lingnan residential style, the decorations are both Chinese and Western styles. The wing-rooms encircle the main shrine into a rectangular quadrangle courtyard with 4 lane doors in each corner of the quadrangle courtyard to ventilate and lead to all directions. There is a side room in the northwest corner of the main shrine and a European style push-pulled bell-shaped window in the east and west side rooms.

Huang Guanzhang didn't live here for a long time since he and his family went to Hong Kong after the Anti-Japanese War broke out. He died in 1945, according to his last words, Daozheng middle school was set to be in this garden between 1946~1949. After that it became the training center of an acrobatic troupe; later more than thirty families lived here, then it was abandoned

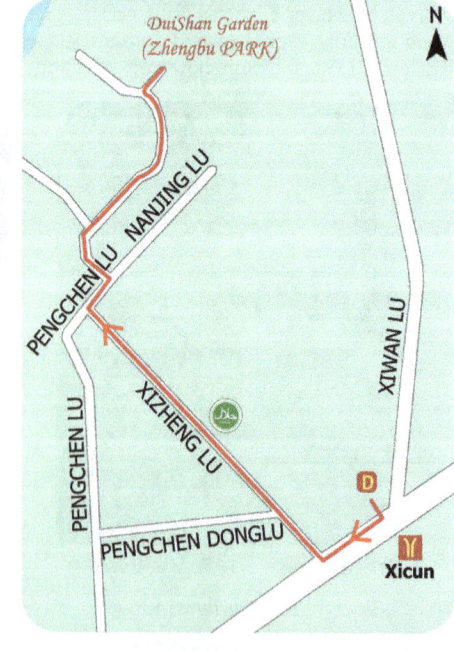

for 60 years after the 1950s, now it has become a nice quiet Zengbu Park in Guangzhou's old industrial area.

There are two 24 meters high circular limekiln towers near the garden, they are the remains of a calcium carbide factory from the 1970s, this area was also the first industrial area in Guangzhou in 1931.

Where to Eat

Shun Kee Dessert Store
(顺记冰室)

Shunji is an old brand name for ice cream in Guangzhou. In Shunji all the ice creams are made the old ancient way by hand mixing a powder to form a slurry to serve people the most delicious ice cream. The most famous ice cream here is the coconut ice cream which is made from the meat of a fresh coconut. This wonderful ice cream has a strong fresh coconut smell and has a distinct flavor. Many honored guests and monarch from abroad have tasted this ice cream and take delight in talking about it.

Menus		
	芒果雪糕	Mango Ice Cream
	椰子雪糕	Cocoanut Ice Cream
	榴莲雪糕	Durian Ice Cream
	红豆冰	Red Bean Ice
	红豆雪糕	Red Bean Ice Cream
	西关蛋糕仔	Egg Puffs
	椰子和芒果雪糕	Coconut and Mango Ice Cream

📍 No.36 Baohua Road, Liwan District (宝华路 36 号)   🕑 7:30-23:30

Chan Tim Kee Fish Skin Store
(陈添记)

This shop has a history of three generations and has been located in a small narrow alley since 1978. They have inside and outside tables, but most of locals enjoy eating at street side tables, to view the old buildings full of Guangzhou tradition. This shop only sell three items: Smooth and Crispy Fish Ski ¥ 25 (Main ingredients: Peanut kernels, green onion, ginger, caraway, soy sauce, sesame, etc.), Sampan Congee ¥ 7 (Main ingredients: pork slices, fried peanuts, sliced fried egg, cut deep-fried dough sticks), and Steamed Rice Rolls ¥ 3.

Menus		
	艇仔粥	Sampan Congee
	猪肠粉	Steamed Rice Rolls
	鱼　皮	Cold and Dressed with Sauce Crispy Fish Skin with Peanuts

📍 At the end of an alley beside No.61 Baohua Road   🕑 9:00-22:30

4 You Xiang Dian Restaurant
（又想点）

Traditional Cantonese tea houses with a trolley revolving at the center of the table have basically died away, today teas are usually cooked immediately after ordered. Lots of locals who live nearby often come here have a cup of tea and Dim Sum. There is a tea set on the table, including a water feeder automatic electric pumping device, this tea ceremony is introduced from Chaozhou-Shantou region (eastern Guangdong Province) kungfu tea style. You have to serve tea by yourself, the Guangzhou Style is pour hot water over the tea leaves in a tea pot and wait for a few minutes. On the first floor, people are eating and smoking while reading the newspaper, the second floor is non-smoking zone. How many servings you should be eating? You can order 3 or 4 items from the lists for 2 or 3 persons. If you are a meat eater, you can mix item with the vegetarian menu.

Menus		
	虾饺	Steamed Shrimp Dumpling
	烧卖	Steamed Pork Dumplings
	蛋挞	Bake Egg Custard Tart
	核桃包	Steamed Walnut Buns with Condensed Milk Filling
	叉烧包	Steamed BBQ Pork Bun
	牛肉肠粉	Steamed Rice Rolls with Beef and Water Chestnut

📍 No.157 Longjin Road West（龙津西路 157 号）　　🕒 7:00-20:30

5 Ling Kee（凌记）

Famous for the most unique Rice Flour Noodle in Guangzhou. They use the highest purity of high quality rice, and sprinkle with black salted turnip instead of the dried radish on surface. You will see long lines of people waiting outside the restaurant which tells you how popular the restaurant is.

Menus
濑粉
Rice-flour Noodle with Dried Radish
炸鱼皮
Fried Fish Skin
萝卜糕
Fried White Radish Patty
椰子冻糕
Coconut Parfait
芒果冻糕
Mango Parfait
三酱猪肠粉
Rice Noodle Roll with Sweet Soybean Paste, Peanut Butter, Chilli Sauce and White Sesames.

📍 Opposite to Renwei Taoist Temple on Pantang Road　　🕒 8:00-21:00

Featured Food

Crispy Fish Skin 👍👍👍
(爽滑鱼皮)

True to its name, this dish provides extra crispiness and is typically made of grass carp, which is frozen after cooking. It is often sprinkled with garlic chives, soy sauce, peanuts, and sesame seeds making it extra fragrant and crispy. The garlic chives inhibit the smell of the fish skin while the peanuts and sesame seeds add to the crispiness of the dish.

Ginger Vinegar with Pig Trotters and Eggs 👍👍
(猪脚姜醋)

Chinese ginger vinegar is very good for your health. It supposedly helps to warm your body and expel "wind" from your body. According to Chinese medicine, excess "wind" inside your body can cause all sorts of ailments including joint pain, arthritis, headaches, etc. This dish is traditionally made for women who have just given birth and the dish is shared with friends and visitors in celebration of the arrival of a new baby. However, it can be enjoyed by anyone, at any time of the year. I love the flavor and the texture of the pig's feet. Everyone makes this dish slightly differently but the steps are simple where most of the time is spent resting the ginger and vinegar.

Double-layer Milk Custard 👍👍👍
(双皮奶)

Cooking ingredients of Shuang Pi Nai are full fat milk, egg white, and white sugar. The making of authentic double-skin milk is very precise. The milk come specifically from water buffalo milk. Pour the fresh milk into a small boiler and boil until it boils over. Remove the milk from the heat and pour it into a rice bowl to cool until the milk surface forms a skin. Using a chop stick, perforate a small hole in the skin and gently pour the milk out through the hole into a bowl which contains egg white. Stir the milk and egg white well. Then pour the mixture back into the rice bowl with precious milk skin, this will cause the milk skin to float to the top of the liquid. Next steam the milk for about ten minutes. The well-done double-skin milk is pure white and coagulated like jelly with two skins. If like you can add the lotus.

Shopping Paradise

Shang Xia Jiu Pedestrian Street
(上下九步行街)

Shang Xia Jiu Pedestrian Street is located in the Liwan District which is a prosperous traditional commercial district. This street is the first commercial pedestrian street in the city is lined with more than 200 stores. Brand name restaurants and teahouses open here from 13:00 to 21:00 on weekends and holidays; and every night, Shang Xia Jiu Lu is restricted to pedestrians only.

Walking along this street, on both sides, you will see the featured arcade houses, next to old style buildings that exists in this city and its neighboring areas that reflect the strong Lingnan Culture. The arcade that is formed by the protruding second floors of the buildings protects the pedestrians from the rain showers. The sculptures located everywhere on the street showcase the old Guangzhou lifestyle. This is an old street of the city and it features a very interesting mix of older Chinese and European architecture.

Fu Li Children's Clothing Wholesale Market
(富力儿童服装批发市场)

Fu Li Children's Clothing Wholesale Market is located at Fu Li Square with more than 500 stores, covering children's clothes, infant supplies, children's goods, etc. More than 80% of the stores are manufacturers from Guangzhou or neighboring cities with clothes covering different ages and different styles for different seasons. For every season more than 700 styles are presented, attracting customers coming from China and other parts of the world.

Shamian Island

HIGHLIGHT: British and French Colonies in Canton, with delicate colonial-era architectures.
START POINT: Metro line 1 & 6 Huangsha station Exit F
FINISH POINT: Huangsha Dock
LENGTH: Approx. 2.5 hours (3.6 km)

Site of foreign district on Shameen Island, Canton, 1883, looking west from the Mainland

Historical Background

The Canton System (1757–1842) served as a means for China to control trade with the west within its own country by focusing all trade on the southern port of Canton. The policy arose in 1757 as a response to a perceived political and commercial threat from abroad on the part of successive Chinese emperors. From the late 17th century onwards, Chinese merchants known as Hongs (háng) managed all trade in the port, operating from Thirteen Factories located on the banks of the Pearl River outside Canton.

After The Treaty of Nanking was signed on the 29th of August 1842, China had to open more treaty ports and allow foreigners access to the interior, ending a long period of Canton being the major commercial center that it once had been. At this time, Macau's commerce was in a steep decline, and Hong Kong had been in existence since 1842 as a result of the treaty ending the First Opium War, and on its way to becoming the commercial center it is today, but the foreign enclave in Canton still attracted a majority of the foreign traders.

Thirteen Factories were burned down in The Battle of Canton during the Second Opium War in 1857, the entire trade area first moved to temporary quarters on Honam Island across the Pearl River. By the middle of 1860, the Anglo-French forces had defeated the Chinese and were occupying Beijing. In the Convention of Peking on 18th October 1860, bringing The Second Opium War to an end, the treaty included the establishment of concessions, then the trade area moved from Honam Island to a man-made Shamian Island which was entirely cut off from the local population, accessible only over two guarded bridges (French Bridge and English Bridge). By 1861 the two concessions were in place on the island, and lasted until June 1945.

French bridge, c. 1939

Itinerary

Begin at Exit F Huangsha metro station, walk north on DATONG LU about a block to reach a small alley called QIAODONGXI. You will see narrow alley where older buildings are being torn down and newer ones being built at very fast pace. You can see glimpses of Chinese architecture, both traditional and modern, as it appears today. The feature you most often see from the traditional local dwelling houses is the typical **Three-ply Doors System** (page 54), the design is an ancient security entry that is well-decorated.

Continue walking east on HEXI LI until you reach QINGPING LU, It is part of **Qing-**

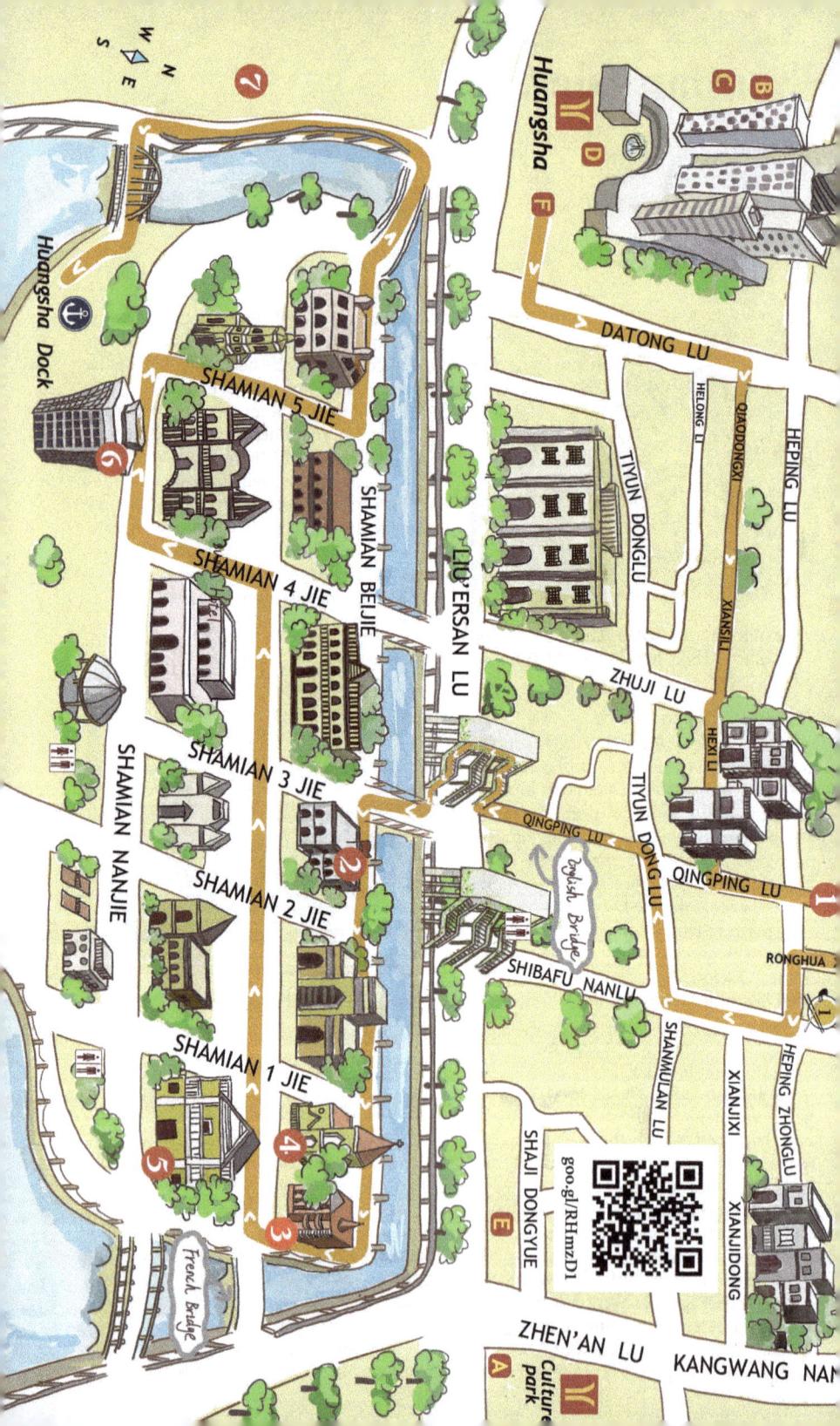

ping Market (❶; page 66), this market is the largest medicine market contains over 1,300 different herbs. If you have been traveling too long and feel tired, you can take some herbs to lift your spirits and boost your energy here, such as Gouji berries, it taste sweet, steeped with tea or hot water and drink, it's good for eyes. Or try some dried figs as a snack, they have small amounts of many other nutrients. Figs have a laxative effect and contain many antioxidants.

Bonsai stores in RONGHUA XIJIE

Continue walking north on QINGPING LU and you can see various pets and pet supplies to be sold here. Goldfish is available at shops on the street near the Holiday Inn, goldfish in the aquarium represent living flow, which makes your living environment more vibrant and your home more pleasant. So it's no surprise that this popular pet trade is even more prominent in Guangzhou.

Turn around and cross RONGHUA XI-JIE, where merchants are selling all kinds of **Guangzhou Bonsais** (page 24). Traditional residents love bonsai, when you walk through the small alleys in the older districts of Guangzhou, you will find that there are many bonsais are placed on both sides of alley. Then have your breakfast or lunch at **Jook Yuen Bamboo-pressed Noodles Restaurant**(❶, page 67), try the traditional handmade bamboo-pressed noodles. These special noodles cannot be mass-produced for you since you need a man to astride the bamboo pole.

Continue walking back to QINGPING LU, you will have a chance to discover more exotic medicinal materials, such as dried deer antler, dried deer penis, live scorpions, live centipedes and dried leeches etc.

Walk over the footbridge, you approach the English Bridge.

Qingping pet market

The Traveler's Handbook of China, 1915, p. 369

With heavy gates shut at night on the bridges, and with guards stationed there during the day to allow no Chinese to pass unless carrying a pass, Shamian was safe. Making light of the risks posed to Europeans by the unruly Chinese, Carl Crow wrote, "Zest rather than danger is added to residence there [on Shamian] by reason of the occasional disturbances in Canton".

British bridge and Shaji massacre martyrs memorial, August 1949

Shamian Island

Demonstration, Canton, 23 June 1925

View at Victoria Hotel, Shameen, Canton, 1900

On June 23rd, 1925, over a hundred thousand Hong Kong workers and Guangzhou people from all walks of life launched a large-scale demonstration here to protest against the May 30th massacre conducted in Shanghai by the Japanese and British imperialists. When the demonstrators were passing at the entrance of English Bridge (where Liu'ersan Road is now) on the opposite side of the Shamian concession, they were mowed down like grass by the guns of the French and the British troops. In the massacre 61 people were killed and more than 170 seriously wounded. This is known as the shocking 'Shaji Massacre'. In memory of this anti-imperialism movement, a monument was built on the eastern side of the West Shamian Bridge (English Bridge). In 1950, the Shaji Massacre Martyrs Memorial was moved to the east of Shamian Island (across from the former site of Canton Customs House, page 80).

Walk off the England Bridge, turn left and walk east on Shamian Beijie. The buildings and streets of the former British and French concession have been beautifully renovated, creating an oasis of tranquility in an otherwise bustling and hectic metropolis. The first building you will see on your right is **Guangdong Victory Hotel** ❷, formerly known as the Victoria Hotel, it was the most comfortable hotels in the far east, where the foreign tourist could meet a competent and reliable guide at that time.

A Pictorial Handbook To Canton, 1905, p. 7~8

On arriving at Canton the tourist should proceed at once to the "Victoria Hotel" and procure a reliable guide. Several of these men come on board the steamer as soon as she is moored alongside the wharf, but it is not advisable to take any of these. Only well known and reliable men are allowed on the British Concession - where the "Victoria Hotel" is situated.- and the Tourist can only there rely upon obtaining a competent guide. Strangers should not endeavour to see the sights of the City without a guide, for by so doing they will derive little pleasure from their visit. Visitors are strongly advised to spend at least two whole days in viewing this wonderfully interesting old City. The Victoria Hotel - on the British Concession of Shameen - is generally acknowledged to be one of the most comfortable Hotels in the Far East, and the Manager is always ready and willing to afford every information to Tourists.

Tourists enjoy coffee, as well as air conditioning to cool down in the summer. Go all the way to the end and turn right pass the Station Restaurant, you will see a Kafelaku coffee shop which is located in the center of Shameen Main Street, it used to be the French police station.

Walk a few block reach the red building on No.2 Shamian Street, built in 1909, it used to be the **Imperial Maritime Customs Building** ③ for the customs senior officials, it is the most western featured building of romantic style. This building is designed by an Australian architect called Purnell, he designed many impressive buildings in Guangzhou, including the Five-Genii Gate Power Station (page 90), Pooi To Academy (page 124) and the South China Cement Factory in Haizhu District. This was later requisitioned by Sun Yat-Sen for his headquarters in 1917, today becomes the Memorial Museum of Generalissimo Sun Yat-sen's Mansion. At least there are more than 10 Purnell's architectures still exist in Guangzhou, including the three mentioned above. In Melbourne, some of Purnell's buildings appear to have been influenced by his years in Guangzhou. In 1914 Purnell designed his own two-storey brick house named "Shameen" at No.17 Munro Street, Armadale in Melbourne, the house is still there and has not changed very much over the years.

Cement factory Canton 1907

Keep walking you will see the **Church of Our Lady of Lourdes** ④, it was built by French in 1892. Trees and buildings are blended in one harmony. Many Chinese visit this central garden for doing exercise, the romantic atmosphere makes this area a popular place for couples taking wedding photos.

Take a visit to the newly opened **Guangdong Foreign Affairs Museum** (⑤ ; page 66). For those who appreciate colonial buildings, this area is an oasis in a crazy city, enjoy the comfortable and romantic European style island.

Return to the central avenue, in the street stands many bronze statues, the statues represents many of Guangzhou's historical changes. Visit the historical **White Swan Hotel** (⑥; page 67), which recently refurbished, everything still looks stunning after those years. The interior is fabulous representing many Chinese culture, arts and antiques, which is worth seeing. Sitting at the bar with a beer in hand overlooking the Pearl River while boats cruise up and down the river. It's a great place to escape the crowds and the heat, prices aren't cheap but a great view.

Then cross a small bridge and take a look at **Huangsha seafood wholesale market** ⑦, where everything is kept alive in tanks, 600 tons seafood are sold here every day. You can see the alligators and turtles are sold here, in a very Cantonese style seafood market, including endangered species. Chinese tradition claims that stewed turtle cures cancer and alligator meat relieves asthma, although the Chinese Government is taking steps to monitor their trade, custom and culture won't change overnight. There is a famous saying, Cantonese eat everything on four legs except the table and anything that flies except an airplane. When people didn't have enough to eat in the past, there was a lot of famine, so people learned to eat everything.

Finish your trip at Huangsha Dock or return back to Huangsha metro station.

Connecting The Walks

There is also a ferry running from Huangsha Dock to Fangcun Dock, which runs every 10 minutes carrying foot-passengers and bicycles. Fares are from ￥1 RMB for a foot passenger and 1.5RMB for a passenger with a bike. If you still have energy, take a ferry to Fangcun and pay a visit to the oldest **Shiweitang Railway Station Walking Tour** (page 138) or **Julong Ancient Village Walking Tour** (page 142).

Points of Interest

Qingping Market (清平市场)

The market is located north from Shamian Island. Cantonese are known to eat just about any animal, and the market is world famous for its wild animal trades. Animals sold here only for pet, not for pot. It is still a great place to visit for exotic goods. The modern front of the market has quite a few stalls selling dried herbs used in Chinese Medicines. The real charm here lies just behind the modern exterior. The modern exterior is built onto a series of old historical narrow alleyways with shops selling herbs.

- Qingping Road
- Metro Line 1 Huangsha Station Exit D

Guangdong Foreign Affairs Museum (广东外事博物馆)

This is the first local museum dedicated to foreign affairs in China and displays over 200 exotic gifts given by governments and individuals from countries around the world over the past 30 years. The exhibits are divided by continent and are displayed in 5 exhibition halls. The museum building was built in 1890. The two-story Baroque building was the French consulate during the Republic of China period, about 100 years ago.

- No.20 SHAMIAN NANJIE
- 9:00am-11:30am every Tuesday, Thursday and Saturday
- Free admission

📍 No.1 SHAMIAN NANJIE

The White Swan Hotel
（白天鹅宾馆）

The White Swan Hotel is opened in 1983, the hotel is China's first five-star hotel, operated with Chinese and foreign cooperation. In 30 years of operation the hotel has hosted 150 heads of State and royalty from more than 40 countries. The Queen of England has eaten roast suckling pig there. Former US President Nixon stayed at the White Swan Hotel twice; once in 1985 and the other time in 1993. There were many foreign families who wanted to bear children, but were infertile. Due to complex adoption laws, it is a long and costly process in many countries, including the United States. For that reason, many people chose to adopt foreign children. The United States is a main source of adopters for Chinese children, and about 90% of Chinese children are adopted by Americans. The cost of adopting a Chinese child is about USD $15,000. Since 1991, American citizens have adopted more than 70,000 children from China. U.S.CIS stipulates that visa applications for adoption of Chinese children are only available in the Guangzhou Consulate. The White Swan Hotel is only a few streets away from the former old U.S. Consulate. Therefore, the White Swan Hotel in Guangzhou became a gathering place for foreign adopters. While walking through the corridor of the white swan hotel, the sound of crying babies could be heard from many rooms. In 2007, China implemented a new Adoption Law. In the meantime, due to the active prevention measures taken by the government to tackle abandonment crimes, fewer and fewer abandoned babies are available for adoption, and global fever of adopting Chinese children gradually recedes.

Where to Eat

① Jook Yuen Bamboo-pressed Noodles Restaurant
（竹园竹升面）

Zhu Yuan Bamboo-pressed Noodles Restaurant originally was located at No.8 HEPING XILU. This noodle restaurant had a televised interview in a documentary called 'A Bite of China' in 2012. This televised documentary attracted a lot of attention from the local people and the landlord took advantage of the occasion by raising the rent immediately, from the original 9,000 RMB per month up to 180,000 RMB per month. The boss Lee of the restaurant was forced to move. The Liwan district government came forward to communicate with the landlord to

resolve the situation, but the restaurant eventually moved to the next block. Bamboo noodles are traditional noodles made the old-fashioned artisanal way where the noodle master will astride a bamboo pole to knead the noodle dough. The novelty of bamboo noodles is not only in the bamboo technique. There are "special" ingredients and it is said that the really good quality bamboo noodles are made using essential ingredients like top-grade flour and duck eggs. This bamboo pole method of producing noodles is supposed to give a more delicate and firmer texture to the noodles while the other distinct feature is in the taste of the noodles which has unique flavors as opposed to 'non bamboo noodles' which usually are bland and can (or need to) soak up foreign flavors.

No.107 Shibafu Road South
（十八甫南路 107 号）

 8:00-20:30

Menus

鲜肉云吞面	Noodle Soup with Pork Wonton
牛腩面	Noodle Soup with Beef Brisket
牛腩捞面	Tender Beef Brisket Lo Mein
猪手捞面	Pig Knuckles Lo Mein
蟹子鲜虾云吞面	Wonton Noodles with Crab Roe and Shrimp
炸酱捞面	Meat Sauce Lo Mein

For Vegetarians:

蚝油捞面	Oyster Sauce Lo Mein
姜葱捞面	Ginger and Onion Paste Lo Mein

Changdi – The West Bund

HIGHLIGHT: The historical central business district of old Canton
START POINT: Metro line 6 Yide Lu station Exit A
FINISH POINT: Metro line 6 Culture Park station Exit D
LENGTH: Approx. 2 hours (2.3 km)

Historical Background

During the period of Republic of China, there is a saying that, "Shanghai has the Bund, Guangzhou has Changdi."

The Bund (present-day CHANGDI DAMALU) with the crowded quayside. Looking north east, c. 1920.

A century ago, on the north shore of Pearl River, Eastwards from Shamian Island, there was a road which was built up to form a wide concourse known as the CHANGDI DAMALU, commonly known as the "The Bund" by Guangzhou people. The Bund stretches from West of Shamian Island, to the East of Dashatou, with the total length of about 4.5 km. It can be divided into the West, the South, and the East Bund sections. The Changdi, as it is known today, usually refers to the West Bund that stretched from West of Renmin Bridge, east to Haizhu Bridge.

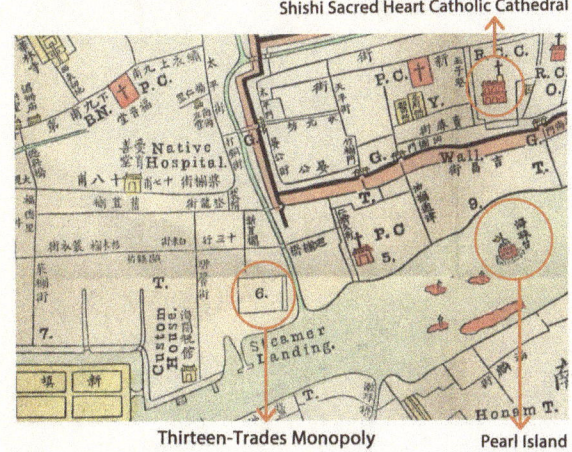

A few kilometers eastward from Shamian Island and past the Steamer Landing lies which was later built up to form the Bund.

In the early Qing Dynasty, the East Bund area was still part of the Pearl River outside Guangzhou city. After Qianlong implemented "single port commerce system" policy, there appeared Thirteen Hongs of Canton (present-day Guangzhou Cultural Park) on the north shore of the river in Guangzhou. By observing the paintings that went abroad at that time, one could find that the buildings were mostly commercial buildings with Western-style, double-slope roof, with two to three floors. The first floor was for offices, warehouse, sales office, and so on, while the second floor was used for housing. The first and second floors were constructed with verandas composed of a continuous arch. The architectural style was the Colonial Veranda style which combines the Western architectural features adapted to the local hot climate and colonial needs. In 1856 after the British and French launched the second Opium War, Thirteen Hongs of Canton were destroyed by the fire.

After sedimentation increased during the late Qing Dynasty the Bund area turned tidal flats. In 1889, Zhang Zhidong the governor-general of Guangdong and Guangxi provinces ordered the establishment of the bund at the north shore of Pearl River to prevent flooding and promote commercial activities. Since then the appointed successors continued to build up the bund. Filling and construction projects took place in several phases until the year of 1931 which is what people see today.

From the end of the Qing Dynasty to 1930s, Changdi gradually had been built up several landmarks, which created new records of the highest architecture in Guangzhou and form dominant city skylines at that time. There were many government offices, commercial banks, foreign banks set up institutions, enabling the Bund to be the most centralized place of wealth in the contemporary Guangzhou. Changdi witnessed ancient Guangzhou giving way to modernization in recent decades, and the architectural evolution, which is an important symbol of the contemporary construction development in Guangzhou.

The busy Bund fronted by commercial buildings, c. 1937

Itinerary

Tour start from the metro line 6 Yide Lu station Exit A, head off south along Haizhu Nanlu, this is a narrowed road lined up by thousands of traditional dried seafood stores, dried food plays an important role in Cantonese culinary culture.

Take the first turning on the right, there is a school called **Changdi True Light Middle School** (❶; page 74) with a long cultural history, which was established in Guangzhou in 1872, it's the pioneer of Chinese women's education.

Head to the opposite direction on CHANGDI DAMALU, a large number of houses and buildings surrounding this geo-depression region suffered in the hundred-year inundation occurred in 1915.

Dried seafood stores at HAIZHU NANLU

The Great Flood of 1915, the East Asia Hotel on the upper right.

Journal of The American Asiatic Association, 1916, Page 308

The year 1915 will not stand in the annals as a prosperous one for trade-this is the opinion of most merchants apart from the showing of Customs returns. Politically, although closing in the gloom of a menacing revolution already rife in Yunnan, the year was free from disturbance in this province under the strong government of General Lung Chi-kuang; but prevalence of brigandage and piracy in the interior and the strained Sino-Japanese relations-happily of short duration-adversely affected business. Moreover, the unprecedented flood in the summer, by destroying rice and silk crops, considerably reduced the trading power of the country. Further, a short age of tonnage, coupled with a diminution of supplies brought on by the prolonged war in Europe, abnormally increased the prices of many commodities, thus greatly hampering trade. The year 1915 has gained beyond question, in the Canton region, the title of the Year of the Great Flood; and it is to be hoped that this distinction will never be disputed in after years. Inundations, local and partial, there are every year; but never before, so far as authentic records show, has there been so widespread and destructive a flood as occurred this year from the 1oth to the 20th July. The old city of Canton, being higher than the adjoining sections, was for the most part free from the flood; but the new city, the southern and western suburbs, and the Island of Shameen were submerged for 10 days to a depth of 6 to 10 feet; and the surrounding country for many miles in every direction was for the most part under water, villages being laid low, crops entirely destroyed, property of all kinds swept away, and an untold number of lives lost. In previous years, while the country adjoining the banks of the West River has suffered seriously from the overflowing of that river, Canton and its immediate vicinity have escaped serious damage. The disastrous flood of 1915, so far as it affected Canton, was due principally to the bursting of the dikes of the North River, whereby the waters of that river-which would otherwise have been carried between its banks to Samshui and thence into the West River, the Fatshan branch, and the network of streams which flow through the delta country to the sea-escaped, through immense breaches in the east bank, about 30 miles northwest from Canton, and overflowed the whole country to Canton and beyond. In Canton and Shameen the lower floors of houses were inundated to a depth of several feet, and locomotion was possible only by boats. At the height of the flood on the 13th July a fire broke out in the western suburb and, it being impossible to use the ordinary means of extinguishing it, spread rapidly until about 450 houses were destroyed, with great loss of life from burning and drowning. After the subsidence of the waters no time was lost in planting new crops of rice and other food products; and while great deprivations and misery persisted for some weeks, during which food was dispensed to many thousands of people by charitable organizations, recovery from the great calamity seemed to come more quickly than would have been believed possible; and with the maturing of the new crops, which, however, were sadly cut down in amount by the long drought which followed the floods, the dire distress began to abate and life in the flooded regions to resume its normal course; but the ruins of hundreds of villages remained, mute witnesses of the calamity that had befallen the country, where, from the fragments of their houses, the people have made themselves tiny hovels of rudely heaped-up bricks, loosely covered over with sticks and straw, to serve as their only shelter from heat, cold and wet, until savings can be accumulated for rebuilding on the old sites. The devastation wrought by this flood, though greater and farther reaching than that of any previous flood in recent times, is exceptional only in degree; for almost every year some parts of the delta are flooded, and more or less loss of life and destruction of crops and of property occur.

You come to the **East Asia Hotel** (❷ ; page 75) and the **Civil Finance Building** (❸ ; page 75), there was a time where Sincere Department Store was located, the company name 'Sincere' was known far and wide by Chinese in the early period of the Republic of China.

Red pillar monument

Take the first turn on the right, walk until you reach the end of Xindi 2 Henglu, on the left you come to a red pillar monument, the location was the site of **Pearl Island** (❹ ; page 76) on the Pearl River (Canton river). It was used as the Dutch Folly Fort which the Europeans used during the Second Opium War and later became the Haizhu Park in the early Republic of China. Today two skyscrapers stand in the same place, which is at the water's edge and no longer an island due to land reclamation.

Turn right walk along the riverside about 300 meters, on the right you come to the **Oi Kwan Hotel** (❺ ; page 76), now the building is classified as historical site, and protected by the city government. The rooftop revolving restaurant was the highlight of the hotel, but it temporarily closes in May 2018 for hotel refurbishment.

A view taken from Oi Kwan Hotel looking over the old city

Continue walking to the traffic light you can see the **Sun Yat-Sen Memorial Hospital** (❻; page 78), which is one of the most prestigious ophthalmic institutes in the world, and the **Former Mission Building** (❼; page 77), where American Southern Baptist pioneer in missionary Robert E. Chambers once worked.

Walk to the **XIHAO 2 MALU** (❽; page 78), along this short street are buildings that once housed department stores, restaurants, cinemas, hotels, discotheques and much more, in the past was a haven for the older generation.

Walk to the end of XIHAO 2 MALU you reach RENMIN NANLU, here was the location of the west ancient city wall, the city walls were demolished to build roads and facilitate transportation in

Renmin Nanlu, c. 1920s

1918. All of the older buildings on Renmin Nanlu were built or significantly modified during the 1920s and 1930s. Historians generally called it the Wall Street of Canton, it is also the birthplace of Chinese commercial banks. They feature many of the architectural styles of their era.

Cross the road and continue west on YANJIANG XILU, many of the more notable buildings along the shore, such as the **Former Xidi Da Sun Department Store** (**9**; page 79), **Guangzhou Postal Exhibition Hall** (**12**; page 79), the **Former River Affairs Office** (**11**; page 80) and the **Former Chinese Imperial Maritime Customs** (**10**; page 80) etc. They are associated with the district's early 20th-century development.

Return to the post office then cross the road and visit the **Culture Park** (**13**; page 81), which was the original location of Canton's Thirteen Factories. Soak up more Canton trading history at the Guangzhou Thirteen Hongs Museum inside the park. The annual Lantern Fair Exhibition and the Late-autumn Chrysanthemum Show are held respectively in February and November in the culture park, it provides an opportunity to view thousands of varieties of beautiful chrysanthemums. Finish your trip at metro line 6 Culture Park station.

View of Thirteen Factories, c. 1800

Connecting The Walks

One metro stop away from Culture Park station you reach Huangsha station, which is the starting point of **Shamian Island Walking Tour** (page 61), or one block walk on Liu'ersan Lu to the west.

Points of Interest

Changdi True Light Middle School (长堤真光中学)

Formerly know as the True Light Seminary, it was used to be a primary school. The United States missionary Ms Harriet Newell Noyes founded the first school for women in Guangdong Province on June 16th, 1872 and provided an access to education to women who could not enter the traditional academy in Guangzhou. She had sufficient resources to supply free education, food and accommodation to women. When the school first opened, there were only six students. The school was ordinary a residential bungalow located in Shakee, on the opposite side of Shamian Island. It was moved to current location after having an early disastrous fire in 1875 and the number of students increased to 40, the school enrollment increased to over 100 students in 1887 and in 1894 had 200 students. The Women's School and the Bible Women's School were merged and renamed as "True Light Middle School". Ms Harriet Newell Noyes was the school principal from 1872 to 1919. In 1919, the first graduation ceremony was held. After she returned to the United States in May 1923, she received a letter from Eugene Chen, the secretary to Sun Yat-sen, thanking her for her contributions in helping with Chinese women's education.

📍 No.348 CHANGDI DAMALU

East Asian Hotel (东亚大酒店)

The East Asian Hotel is formerly known as the Oriental Hotel. It was originally one of the four major corporations in the period of the Republic of China, the Sincere Company was founded by Ma Yingbiao while he was living in Australia. It opened in 1914, and was one of the leading luxury hotels in Guangzhou before the liberation. It was renowned in Southeast Asia, Hong Kong and Macao. Many wealthy merchants, military dignitaries, celebrities, foreign tourists, overseas Chinese visiting relatives, stayed in the East Asia Hotel. At that time the hotel owned shipping terminals for passengers and cargo. In 1925, the hotel opened its branches in Hong Kong and Shanghai. During the night of 14th October, 1949, the East Asia Hotel raised the first five-star red flag in Guangzhou.

📍 No.320 CHANGDI DAMALU

Civil Finance Building
(民间金融大厦)

This is the origins of Sincere Company. In 1913, Australian Chinese Ma Yingbiao founded the Sincere Company in the new prosperous business districts of Guangzhou. Sincere company

mainly traded upscale and mid-range imported foreign goods. It also ran hotels, restaurants, entertainment enterprises, insurance, banking and other affiliated enterprises, to provide customers around the world the latest production goods and products. At that time, overseas Chinese operating department stores usually first set up headquarters in Hong Kong, then had its affiliates in Canton, enabling the direct importation from Hong Kong. It changed the custom of bargaining, setting a precedent for the practice of fixed pricing. Sincere Company also hired a saleswoman for the first time. The Changdi Sincere Company was destroyed by fire in 1976. In the eighties, it was reconstructed at the old site and named "Huaxia Department Store", which is now the "Guangzhou Civil Financial Building".

📍 No.316 CHANGDI DAMALU

The Dutch Folly Fort, c. 1857

The Ruins of Ancient Pearl Island (海珠石遗址)

There were three little sandbars in Guangzhou Pearl River during the ancient times, of which the largest was Pearl Island. Since the Song Dynasty, it has become an island, on which was built a Ci Dao Temple. During year of Emperor Shunzhi's reign, the construction of Pearl Fort took place, which the West called "Dutch Folly Fort". In 1925, the city government opened it up as Haizhu Park. In 1932, the appointed city mayor Chen Jitang dredged the river, blew up the reef, constructed a causeway, and rebuilt the road. Haizhu Park and part of the Changdi were connected into one, now the CHANGDI DAMALU. Part of it sunk to the river bottom, Haizhu Park and the Pearl Island no longer exist.

📍 At the end of XINDI 2 HENGLU

Haizhu Park c. 1925

Oi Kwan Hotel (爱群酒店)

Oi Kwan Hotel (now known as Aiqun building) was previously one of Guangzhou's best known landmarks. Built in 1937, the hotel was a 70-year history dating back to 1937. Once the highest building in South China, it had the first rotating restaurant in Guangzhou. It hosted opening and closing receptions for the Canton Fair 10 times running since its inception in 1957. For more than half a century, Aiqun Mansion is a big part of Guangzhou's history. Designed by architects Li Bingyuan and Chen Rongzhi, the 64 meter, 15-floor Aiqun has a floor space of 800 $^{m^2}$ and a shape imitating U.S. Woolworth Building, retaining an air of elegance, simplicity and harmony. At the time, Aiqun was a place of conspicuous consumption where guests were expected to pay at least $5 HK dollars as tips, the value of a month's food for the poor. During the 1950s and 1960s, Aiqun Mansion was Guangzhou's most important location for activities involving foreigners and one of Guangzhou's best-known landmarks.

Oi Kwan Hotel

U.S. Woolworth Building

📍 No.113 YANJIANG XILU

Former Site of Mission Building (光楼)

In 1899, Robert E. Chambers opened the China-America Baptist Publication Society in the Baptist church in Guangzhou, and began to concentrate entirely upon literature ministry. At the same time, he started the "True Light Magazine", the earliest Chinese language Christian periodical in China. In 1915, as a product of Chambers' planning, the Baptist Publication Society erected

a building in the center of Guangzhou, with the name "Light House". In 1925, reeling from the workers strike in Guangzhou, they decided to move the publishing house to the flourishing commercial center of Shanghai. The property is owned by The Canton Municipal Bank in 1932.

📍 No.107 YANJIANG XILU

Former Site of the Canton Hospital (广州博济医院)

The Canton Hospital was founded by Protestant medical missionary Peter Parker in November 1835 which was the first Western-style hospital in China. In beginning, it was only intended for the treatment of eye illnesses. Parker didn't charge for his services, he relied on support from missionary colleagues and local business firms and merchants to stay open. In addition, this

Boji Building, built in 1935

Front gate of Canton Hospital

hospital also led to Western-style medical education in China, when Parker and Dr. EC Bridgman trained three young Chinese men to help out in the hospital. In 1866, the Boji Medical School was established in the hospital, it was the first western-style medical school. Sun Yat-sen began to study medicine at Boji Medical School in Guangzhou in 1886. A year after, he studied medicine at the Academy of Western Medicine in Hong Kong from September 1887 to July 1892. Until 1930, it became part of Lingnan University. During the Japanese invasion, Boji hospital was used as a Japanese hospital. Today it is the Second Affiliated Hospital of Sun Yat-sen University.

📍 No.107 YANJIANG XILU   💲 Free admission
🕗 8:00-17:30

XIHAO 2 MALU (西濠二马路)

The road was built in 1921, located at the commercial center of Renmin Road South, and wholly dedicated to commercial, business, and entertainment. Some shops were open all night. Before the 1990s, this road was getting more and more prosperous and bustling. Although it wasn't officially named as a commercial walking street, it was not unusual to see the Xi Hao Second Street as the earliest walking street in Guangzhou. Xi Hao Second Road was once the bustling place for reformation movement in Guangzhou, also the center for Guangzhou nightlife. As time passed, all these had become history. Most of the original shops have disappeared. Those which stayed were mostly the food stalls, which changed their business practices.

Former Xidi Da Sun Department Store (城外大新公司旧址)

The former Xidi Da Sun Department Store was the first concrete building in Guangzhou which was founded by Mr. Cai Xing and Mr. Cai Chang in 1918. On the eve of Japanese invaders' occupation, Xidi Da Sun Department Store burned for three days and four nights, all the products as well as the facilities were destroyed by the fire, leaving only a framework until 1949. Later on, through the reinforcement and restoration by the government on the basis of the original structure, Xidi Da Sun Co. Ltd. started business on the eve of the National Day in 1954 and renamed itself Nanfang Mansion. In 2004, it was transformed into an electronic products wholesale market.

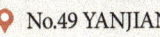

📍 No.49 YANJIANG XILU
🕙 10:00-18:00   💲 Free admission

Guangzhou Postal Exhibition Hall (邮政博览馆)

Guangzhou Postal Exhibition Hall is the former site of the Qing Post Office, founded in 1897, used to be the Guangdong Post Office during the era of the Republic of China. It was destroyed by fire in 1916. However, it was designed and rebuilt in the same year by the British citizen Danby. In 1938, Guangzhou fell to the Japanese, who burned most properties in the West Bund. The buildings were looted again, and all doors, windows, flooring, and decorative furniture were burned. But, fortunately, the buildings structure had not been destroyed. The following year, they were restored to their original appearance by the Chinese national Yang Yongtang. For centuries, it has been the Guangzhou Post Office for National Government and the People's Government. In the year of 2002, it was designated to be the Postal Exhibition Hall. The first floor was to be the Philatelic Exhibition Center, while the doors in exhibition halls of second and third floor have eight mailboxes. Put the corresponding postmark into different boxes.

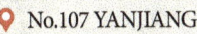

📍 No.107 YANJIANG XILU
🕙 8:00-17:30   💲 Free admission

Former Chinese Imperial Maritime Customs Canton (粤海关旧址)

Administrator of the Canton Customs was set up in 1685, also known as Hoppo, it is one of the earliest established customs in China. The original site was the location of Guangzhou Hotel today, before it was moved to the current location in 1865. The current building was completed and opened for use in May 1916. It was designed by British architect David Dick. Before the first opium war, Canton Customs was completely autonomous. After the two opium wars, Guangzhou was occupied by the British and French forces, largely staffed at senior levels by foreigners. At that time, Shameen Island belong to the concessions, where Canton Customs base camp was set up on the island. To facilitate foreigners dealing with trade affairs, the Chinese Imperial Maritime Customs Canton was established at the current location in 1865, the primary focus of the activities of the Customs was the servicing of Chinese government debt. In 1926, the Nationalist Party Kuo Min Tang began the process of military reunification of China by the leader Chiang Kai-shek. Canton Customs' tax department thus returned to the the Guangzhou National Government in 1931. Now it is known as the China Customs Museum.

📍 No.29 YANJIANG XILU   💲 Free admission (passport required for entry)
🕘 9:30-16:00 every Wednesday

The Former River Affairs Office (塔影楼)

After the Revolution of 1911, Chen Shaobai resigned from the post of Director of Foreign Affairs to Guangzhou to set up an industry. He proposed China set up Guangdong Airlines, with routes flying between Hong Kong and Guangzhou. Subsequently, he served as general manager of the Guangdong Airline, operating the Guangzhou-Hong Kong route.

At the end of 1918, the British merchant ships suffered from enormous losses in the first world war. To revive the shipping industry, the British purchased the old ships in Hong Kong at high prices. Chen Shaobai took advantage of this circumstance. In 1919, the company's ships were all sold to the United Kingdom. He terminated the operation of The Guangdong Airlines, purchased Lianxing terminal, and built the four-and-a-half story building next to it.

📍 No.36 YANJIANG XILU

Cultural Park (文化公园)

Guangzhou Cultural Park was the former Qing Dynasty's concession to the European and American trade zone. In 1951 the Guangzhou municipal government organized "South China Local Specialties Exhibition and Interchange Conference", to solve the shortage of resources, and promote the sales of goods. After the conference, under the instructions of Guangzhou mayor Ye Jianying, the decision was made that the exhibition site was to be retained. It's name was then changed to the Guangzhou Cultural Park in 1956. Since 1959, the Cultural Park has held a free chrysanthemum exhibition every November. In 2016 the Guangzhou Thirteen Hongs Museum was launched within the park, with a large amount of precious historical literature to show the illustrious history of Thirteen-Trades Monopoly.

Guangzhou Thirteen Hongs Museum

- No.2 XIDI 2 MALU
- Free admission
- The Culture Park 6:50-21:30;
  Guangzhou Thirteen Hongs Museum (passport required for entry) 9:00-16:00 from Tuesday to Sunday

Haizhu Square

HIGHLIGHT: Guangzhou's historical old axis – linking up a number of historical sites and modern structures
START POINT: Metro Line 2 & 6 Haizhu Square station Exit B3
FINISH POINT: Shishi Sacred Heart Cathedral
LENGTH: Approx. 4 hours (3.5 km)

Historical Background

Haizhu Square is the first city riverside square. It is also one of the centers of Guangzhou's foreign trade, exhibitions, foreign guest meeting spots, and cultural activity centers after the 1949 communist revolution in China. During the Qing Dynasty, areas around Haizhu Square were lively and prosperous for trading. It had two large fruit markets and one subsidiary agricultural produce trading market. In the late Qing Dynasty, lots of residences had been built, with many people gathering in this area.

In 1938, Guangzhou was bombed by the Japanese army, and most of the areas in downtown Guangzhou were heavily damaged. The Five-Genii Gate Power Station and Haizhu Bridge in the Haizhu Square area were the main targets. Although these two spots were not being bombed directly, people who lived around here suffered greatly. Many residential buildings were bombed out and the whole area was destroyed. There were three war disaster areas in Guangzhou: Haizhu Square, Huangsha, and Culture Park. The Haizhu Square area was the most heavily damaged.

The north bank of Haizhu bridge (right) after suffered from Japanese military attack, the Haizhu Square was built here later on.

After the Anti-Japanese War, the government of Kuomintang focused on the Chinese civil war instead of cleaning and rebuilding the areas in Guangzhou that were damaged during the war. Haizhu Square became filled with trash and weeds. After Kuomintang was defeated in the Chinese civil war, on October 14th, 1949, the Kuomintang army blew up Haizhu Bridge before they withdrew from Guangzhou. When the People's Liberation Army went into Guangzhou the first mayor, Mr. Jianying Ye, gave the order to repair the Haizhu Bridge to restore travel between the north and south banks of the Pearl River. At the end of 1951, the first traffic square was built and named "Haizhu Square", as the square was located at the north end of Haizhu Bridge near the site of the old Haizhu Stone. It is adjacent to Guangzhou's famous old commercial districts such as Changdi Road, Xidi, Beijing Road, and so on.

In April 1958, the Standing Committee of the National People's Congress of Guangzhou renovated Haizhu Square. Construction started right after planning was confirmed. In 1958, the Chinese Export Commodities Exhibition Hall (Qiaoguang Road) was built on number two Qiaoguang Road. It was five floors high, and used as the exhibition hall for the 3rd and the 5th Canton Fair. In 1959, the new Chinese Export Commodities Exhibition Hall (Qiyi Road) was established on the south side of Haizhu Square. The 6th Canton Fair was held in this exhibition hall. A total of 29 Canton Fairs were held until 1973. After 1959, the Chinese Export Commodities Exhi-

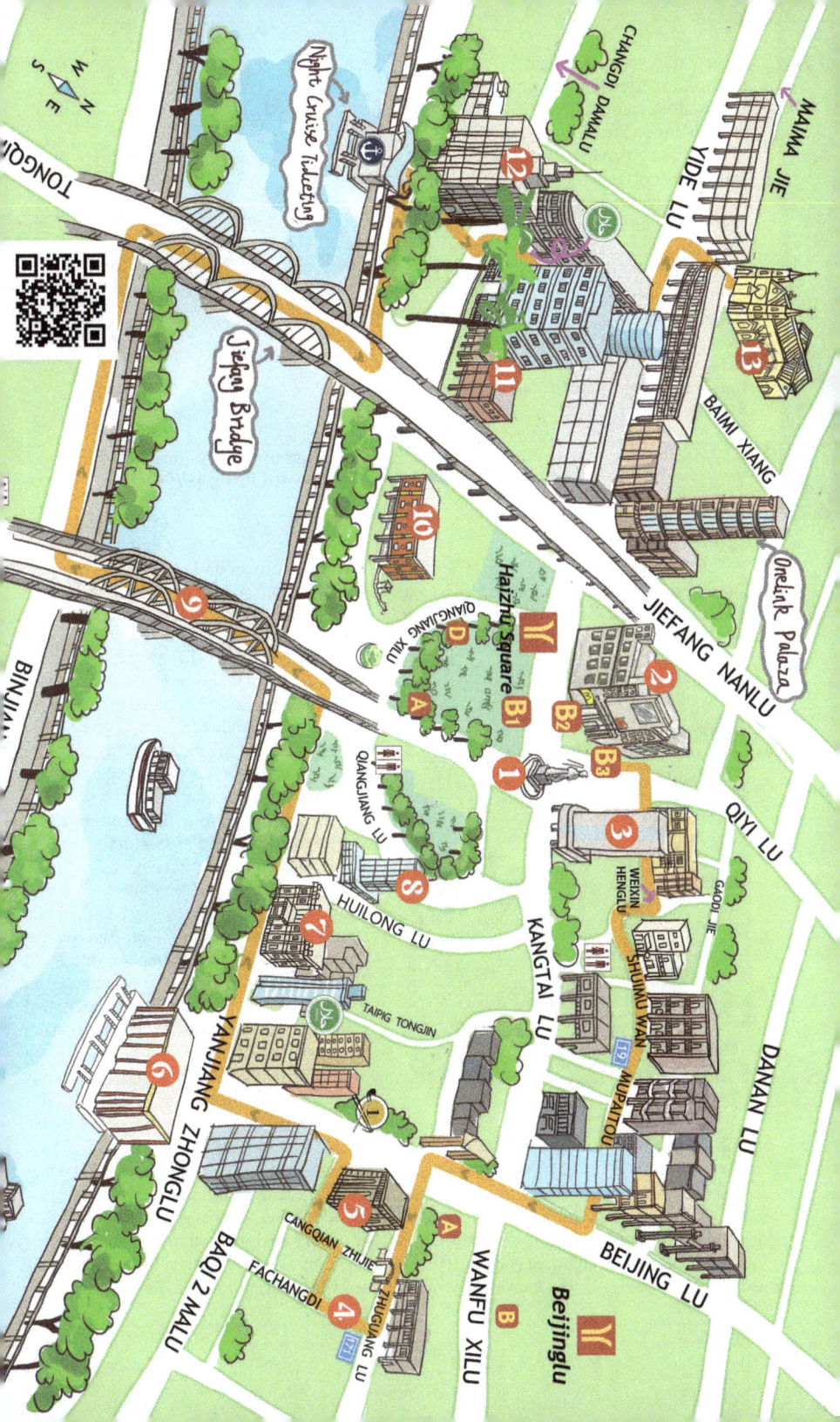

bition Hall (Qiaoguang Road) had became the Guangdong Industrial Museum, and now it is a lively seafood restaurant.

For a long time, Haizhu Square was not only the most famous foreign trade center in Guangzhou, but also in China. The combined view of Haizhu Square and the Guangzhou Liberation Monument was selected as "the Loyalty of Pearl River" in the Eight Sights of Guangzhou, and it became a famous signature in landscape of Guangzhou.

Haizhu Square captured from the south bank of the Pearl River, 1970s.

Itinerary

The tour begins at Exit B3 Haizhu Square metro station. Turn around and look up, there is a **Guangzhou Liberation Monument (❶** ; page 88) behind you. You will also see **the former site of Chinese Export Commodities Exhibition Hall (❷** ; page 87) and **Guangzhou hotel (❸** ; page 88) around you.

MUPAITOU Street

Walk north to WEIXIN HENGLU towards MUPAITOU where lots of elderly locals gather, this is the site of the original Pearl River shores, originally used for the timber rafts moored during the Song Dynasty (960-1276). Most of the residential buildings are two-story masonry and wood structure built in 1950's. There are over 300 stalls on either side of the street piled high with fruits, vegetables, cooked food, groceries, general merchandise, private slaughtered meat, fresh fish, seafood, newspapers, books, etc. You can buy some Cantonese take away Dim Sums on this street, such as Steamed Dumpling with Pork, Mushrooms and bamboo Shoots in addition a cup of Soya-bean Milk, normally traditional Cantonese take these as breakfast or snack when people get hungry.

At BEIJING LU, turn right and walk across a traffic light, walk east on ZHU-GUANG LU and turn right near the house numbering of No.171, there's a small alley called FACHANGDI, which in Chinese means **"Execution Ground"** ❹. FACHANGDI was an ancient execution ground in Guangzhou during Qing Dynasty. During 1854~1855, the Taiping rebelled against the ruling Manchu-led Qing Dynasty, after a failed rebellion, the viceroy butchered and decapitated over 70,000 people at the execution ground at one summer time. It surrounded by similar pottery workshops, they took the opportunity to use the blood-drenched soil to make even durable and stronger earthen brazier. When no execution was going on, it's a narrow alleyway crammed with pottery drying in the sun.

Glimpses of China and Chinese Homes, 1902, p. 172, EDWARD S. MORSE

Nearby was a simple enclosure surrounded by high walls, known as the execution-grounds. At the time of my visit, the ground was covered with pottery in the form of little kitchen braziers; apparently some one had hired the place for the temporary storage of his pottery stock. Near the walls were larger jars, in which the heads of the executed were placed. Judging from the description of the Spanish prisons in Cuba, Porto Rico, and the Philippines, Spain is the only European country which must be placed on a level with China in this respect.

Travels From The Grandeurs of The West to Mysteries of The East, 1909, p. 284, CHARLTON B. PERKINGS

The principal execution ground is in the heart of the city and is about 200 feet long and 100 feet wide, and surrounded on three sides by brick buildings. In this small space hundreds of thousands of people have been executed. In a small room adjoining this fatal spot there lives an old man, the official executioner, a veteran in the service. He was appointed by Li Hung Chang when the latter was Viceroy at Canton. As a compensation he is allowed twenty cents, Mexican, by the Government for each decapitation, provided he beheads with one stroke. Often the head is not completely severed from the body, and to make certain of his twenty cents he saws the head off without lifting the axe after the first stroke. This old man, like "Johnny-on-the-spot," is always at hand, for he never knows when an execution may take place.

Walk across CANGQIAN ZHIJIE then return to BEIJING LU, you will see the **Former Nan Guan Cinema** ❺ near the corner. Founded in 1908, Nan Guan Cinema is one of the oldest movie theaters. It closed in 1998 but had reopened in 2010 after undergoing a 1 million Yuan renovation. The interior decoration was quite nostalgic with an early 20th century feel. The cinema also stored over 300 films, mostly old movies such as 'Tunnel Warfare', the movie was an important part of local life and relates to many of the elderly's personal memories, but it was closed again in May 2013. Today, this former Nan Guan Cinema has been converted into a night club.

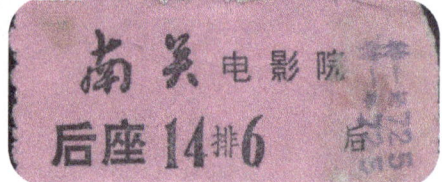

The former Nan Guan cinema

Tickets of Nan Guan cinema in 1970s

Continue walking south on BEIJING LU for a few minutes to reach **Tianzi Dock** ❻ , which was built during Qing Dynasty Yongzheng Period more than 270 years ago. It used to receive officers of the feudalistic government, other boats were prohibited to moor alongside the wharf, so the people call it Tianzi (the Son of Heaven) Dock.

Continue walking to west on YANJIANG ZHONGLU, you will see the **Former Central Bank** (❼ ; page 89), which was built in 1924. Now it is used as Industrial and Commercial Bank of China. Dozens of meters ahead, you will see the **Former Overseas Chinese Tower** (❽ ; page 88). On your right there is a trendy seafood restaurant and next door is a popular restaurant known for breakfast and crowded for dinner too. This five story building was once used as the Chinese Export Commodities Exhibition Hall (Qiaoguang Road) in 1958.

The front is the **Haizhu Bridge** (❾ ; page 89) which is the oldest bridge crossing the Pearl River in Guangzhou. Walk over the bridge, and you will see some sculptures that reflect the history of the Haizhu Bridge. At night YANJIANG ZHONGLU is one of the three main bar streets in Guangzhou.

Once there was a Dawn Market on the bank of the Pearl River between Haizhu Bridge and Jiefang Bridge open from 5am to 8am. The market opened early in the morning in order to hide from the authorities. Both the sellers and buyers are from the lowest level of the society and the goods sold here are cheaper than other places. The booths are mainly run by the elderly who sell abandoned products which they collect from bins or donated goods, to make a living. When the sun rises and the traffic becomes busy, these markets disappear and these poor people hide in the dark side of the prosperous city. These unlicensed vendors were unsightly in public places and posed a danger to the people in the area. This dawn market was banned in 2015.

You can see the abandoned Guangzhou **Five-Genii Gate Power Station** (❿ ; page 90) across the river. At present, no decisions have been made about its future.

Part of a site of the Hospital Franco-Chinois Paul Doumer

After crossing Jiefang Bridge, walk west about 100 meters, across the road on the north side, it was the **Former Site of the Hospital Franco-Chinois Paul Doumer** (⓫ ; page 91) , you still can see an old two story building engraved with the architectural year '1903' on the top.

Continue to **The former Eng Aun Tong Pharmaceutical Factory** (⓬ ; page 91), this building used to be a factory and office of Tiger Balm in 1930s. Cross JINGHAI LU and walk toward north to YIDE LU, which is a traditional dried seafood road. Finish your trip at **Shishi Sacred Heart Catholic Cathedral** (⓭ ; page 92).

Tips:

1. If you would like to go shopping for stationery, dried seafood, decors, clocks, soft toys, key chains, purses, gifts, or souvenirs, you will see many shops along Yide Road and OneLink Plaza. Scan QR codes for detailed location on Google Map.
2. There is another You Xiang Dian Dim Sum chain restaurant just off Beijing Road , see page 58 for Recommended food.

You Xiang Dian restaurant

Connecting The Walks

From **The West Bund Walking Tour** (page 69) is 330 meters due west, once finish visiting the catholic cathedral, return to Yide Lu heading west and you will soon be at the starting point of The West Bund Walking Tour, as well as the metro Line 6 Yide Lu station.

Points of Interest

The Site of Former Chinese Export Commodities Exhibition Hall (广交会旧址)

This is one of the most famous structures of the "Three Form" architecture. It consists of a main building at the center and two side buildings on the north and south. The main building is 10 floors high, and the side buildings are 8 floors high. It was built in August 1959 and designed by Mr. Lin Keming with the help of other architects. It took only 10 months to complete, starting from the design process. 29 Canton Fairs were held in this exhibition hall. The 8th to 10th floors of the main building were for receiving guests. The top floor of the side building at the north was where the grand symposium was held in every Canton Fair. And the top floor of the south building was the office. The rooftop was designed to be an open-air garden based on the climatic features in Guangzhou. It could be used to hold symposiums. Now the building is used for a clothing market.

No.1 QIYI LU   9:30-20:00

Guangzhou Hotel (广州宾馆)

Guangzhou Hotel was built in 1968. It specialized in receiving guests who came to Guangzhou for the Canton Fair. Since the beginning of Canton Fair, accommodating all of the visitors had been a problem. In 1965, Premier Zhou Enlai decided to build a large, upscale hotel funded by the government to solve this problem. Guangzhou Hotel is 86 meters high with 27 floors. It was the tallest building in China between 1968-1976. The Guangzhou citizens used to call it "27 Floor" back at that time.

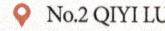 No.2 QIYI LU

The Former Overseas Chinese Tower (华侨大厦旧址)

This building was built in 1957 and was the earliest skyscraper around Hiazhu Square. The purpose of building it was to solve the housing problem for the overseas Chinese in Guangzhou. It was a hotel that specialized in receiving overseas Chinese, as well as their relatives. In the 90s, the Overseas Chinese Tower was expanded. A new 39-floor building was built on the south side and renamed the "Hotel Landmark Canton". The Chinese Export Commodities Exhibition Hall (Qiaoguang Road) was located on the south side of Overseas Chinese Tower.

 No.8 QIAOGUANG LU

Guangzhou Liberation Monument (广州解放纪念碑)

The Guangzhou liberation monument was built to memorialize the victory of the CPC army in Guangzhou. The monument is 11.5 meters high, was carved from granite by Pan He and Liang Mingcheng and sits on a base that is 3.6 meters high. The length of each side is 4.3 meters. At the front and sides of the base, there is carved Ye Jianying's inscription, "All Power Belongs To The People". On top of the base stands a soldier with a rifle in his right hand and a bundle of flowers in his left hand. In 1959, the 10th anniversary of the liberation day, Guangzhou government erected the monument in Haizhu Square. It was listed in Guangzhou Eight Scenic Spots in 1962 and declared a major site to be protected. Dismantled during the Cultural Revolution, and planned to erected statues of Chairman Mao. It was rebuilt in July, 1980.

The Former Guangzhou liberation monument

Former Central Bank
(中央银行)

August 15th, 1924 personally founded by Sun Yat-sen's central bank, it had the right to issue currency notes. 1927, Nanjing, the Nationalist government set up after the new central bank in Shanghai, Guangzhou, the central bank in March 1929 renamed the Central Bank of Guangdong, in January 1932 and renamed the bank of Guangdong. With the new type of banking industry growing in Guangzhou, Guangzhou's pawn industry started declining since 1928.

📍 No.193 YANJIANG ZHONGLU

Haizhu Bridge (海珠桥)

Haizhu Bridge was the first draw bridge in Guangzhou. After several ups and downs over more than 80 years, survived damage and reconstruction, the bridge has witnessed Guangzhou's many changes. On the 15th February 1933, excited people in Guangzhou rushed toward the Pearl River banks to have a look at the first bridge across the Pearl River in the pass two thousand years. In November 1929, the Guangzhou municipal government official and American Cautious Prosperous Business Firm, Mark Sincere Company signed and started the construction of the Pearl River Iron Bridge. After more than 3 years of relentless efforts, the first bridge was finally completed on the Pearl River. The bridge length is 356.69 meters, main span 182.90 meters. According to experts, the entire bridge construction used more than 1,700 tons steel and iron which was imported from the U.S. Surprisingly, the bridge floor could open and close rapidly. The bridge floor like two large arms could open in the middle automatically to allow the steam vessels to pass under the bridge and close slowly automatically after vessel pass. Only several centimeters separate the two arms and the open and close procedure only took 5 minutes. As the first and only one over the river and movable bridge in Guangzhou at that time, Haizhu Bridge become the symbol of the city of glory in people heart. On October 1938, the Haizhu Bridge floor was bombed by Japanese aggressors and the movable parts were badly damaged.

The equipment was disassembled and transported to Japan, so the Haizhu Bridge could no longer open and close. Large vessels no longer pass along the Pearl River. The Republic of China government carried on repairs to the Haizhu Bridge after the Anti-Japanese War. It still bears the load of transportation between both sides of the river. On 14th October 1949, China's People's Liberation Army attacked and liberated Guangzhou and the Haizhu Bridge was bombed by Kuomintang when they retreated from Guangzhou. In 1950 Mayor Ye Jianying commanded that the Haizhu Bridge be repaired as soon as possible to regain the north-south transportation. On 7th November 1950, Haizhu Bridge the main body was repaired in the middle and the bridge was back in use. In 1974 and 1995, the bridge experienced two extensions and reinforcement, both sides had bicycle ways and sidewalks added and it is one of Guangzhou busiest bridges. There is a picture called 'Work hours Transportation' about the Haizhu Bridge in 1988. It is highly recognized domestically and internationally and it was selected in the 14th session of international news picture exhibition and yearbook. The Haizhu Bridge is known as 'The world's ninth big marvelous sight'. From bicycles, motorcycles, and automobiles on the bridge, it has become the Guangzhou city develop with the Chinese economical vicissitude is best to witness, Although the Guangzhou Pearl River has constructed more than ten bridges, greater, more imposing, and with more ingenuity than the Haizhu Bridge, but this bridge is the most glorious and celebrated and considered the soul part of the City.

Haizhu Bridge and the crowded Pearl River crammed with sampans in 1933, the Five-Genii Gate Power Station in lower left-hand corner.

Haizhu Bridge and Pearl River, 2016

Site of the Five-Genii Gate Power Station (五仙门发电厂)

This was the first power station in Guangzhou. In 1900, a British firm set up a company of electric light and built power station called Five-Genii Gate Power Station. Later, the power station was taken over and expanded by the Canton government. When Canton government realized the benefit of electric power, they

1910

started to paved roads and put up power poles. In 1918, street lamp that supplied with electricity appeared in Canton. The Five-Genii Gate Power Station was the first power station of Canton but the power station was closed down in 1975.

The Former Site of the Hospital Franco-Chinois Paul Doumer
(中法韬美医院旧址)

This was formerly the Hospital Franco-Chinois Paul Doumer founded by French in 1903. As plenty of remaining building materials sit unused in the dock soon after the Sacred Heart Cathedral was built, the French consulate proposed to the Qing government that French provided money and China contribute property to build the Sino-French hospital. The name of the hospital was in memory of Paul Doumer (1857–1932), as Governor-General of French Indochina in the early 1900s, he was France 13th President of the third Republic either. In the period of the Republic of China, many military and political officials received treatments and the very best health care possible at this hospital. The hospital took on the task of helping wounded soldiers and refugees before Guangzhou was occupied by Japanese imperialists, part of several buildings had been destroyed by Japanese air strikes during the World War II.

The hospital was then renamed several times afterwards, and now it's the First Affiliated Hospital of Guangzhou Medical University and the First Clinical Medical Institute of Guangzhou Medical University.

Hospital Franco-Chinois Paul Doumer

The Former Eng Aun Tong Pharmaceutical Factory (永安堂制药厂旧址)

Eng Aun Tong is located in Yanjiang Road West, built by Burmese Chinese Aw Boon-Haw in 1937. It was a private property engaged in production and sales of the Tiger Balm in Mainland China. Aw inherited the formula from their herbalist father who left China. Tiger Balm is made from a secret herbal formula and a household name in many East and South Eastern Asian countries. It was the second tallest building before 1949.

Eng Aun Tong in 1935

The famous-brand product "Tiger Balm" from Eng Aun Tong

After the Chinese people's liberation army captured Guangzhou, Eng Aun Tong was taken over by Provincial Federation of Trade Unions, the building was used as a temporary center of operations and office building until in the early 1990s. In 1967, there was a fierce warfare in Eng Aun Tong between the conservatives and insurrectionists during Cultural Revolution. After the third plenary session of the 11th central committee of the Chinese communist party, the Chinese Government ended the political struggle and concentrated on economic development. They wanted to attract overseas Chinese to come back and invest and they realize they had to mend their relationship with the overseas Chinese, thus return property back to overseas Chinese. The firstborn daughter of Aw Boon-Haw donated the building to the Guangzhou municipal government as children's library in 1995.

With the development of Zhujiang New Town, the Children's Library was moved to the former Guangzhou Library, this building is left empty again since 2014.

No.149 YANJIANG XILU

Shishi Sacred Heart Catholic Cathedral (石室圣心大教堂)

It is one of the oldest church structures in the city, the largest of its kind in Southern China, and currently in use for worship. Shishi Sacred Heart Cathedral was the residence in the Viceroy of Guangdong and Guangxi Provinces inside the Qing Empire. Following the Second Opium War, good Sino-French Treaties of Tientsin was launched by Emperor Daoguang in February 1846. The treaties guaranteed compensation for chapels destroyed and items acquired in the mission. The French Government asked for compensation for chapels destroyed and characteristics within the mission. While using support of Emperor Napoleon III as well as the Catholics of

France, the early priest apostolic of Guangdong, was accountable for the appearance and oversaw the expansion process. After 25 years of construction, it was completed 1888. The whole project was more costly than 400,000 gold francs. The cathedral, similar to the truly amazing medieval cathedrals of Europe, consists of solid masonry. It is probably one of only a handful of chapels in the world being entirely built of granite, including all the walls, support beams as well as the twin towers. The granite stone pieces were moved from Kowloon, Hong Kong by sailing ships henceforth, it is nicknamed "Stone House" by citizens.

- Metro Line 2 Haizhu Square Station Exit B1
- No.56 Yide Road
- Free admission
- weekdays 8:30-11:30 and 14:30-17:30; weekends 8:30-17:00

Xi Men Kou

HIGHLIGHT: Experience the local daily activities and exotic cuisines
START POINT: Metro line 1 Ximenkou station Exit C
FINISH POINT: Relic of Large West Gate Barbican
LENGTH: Approx. 4 hours (3.1 km)

Historical Background

View of Large West Gate of Canton, c. 1893~1919

Xi Men Kou, which literally means "Large West Gate" in Chinese, was the main entry and exit of Guangzhou for people in Ming and Qing Dynasties. It was a plain, outside gate through which there is a road leading to Zengbu, Xicun, Bantang, etc. Farmers would enter through the large west gate carrying fruits, vegetables, and other fresh produce to sell in the town. People often pawned something when entering or leaving the city. Therefore, there were many pawn shops near the city gates. Baosheng Pawnshop, founded in the Qing Dynasty, was situated outside the large west gate. It was the third biggest pawnshop in Guangzhou at that time. The battlement of Large West Gate was demolished in the 1920s due to road construction, and nowadays the site sits near the intersection of Zhongshan Sixth Road and Zhongshan Seventh Road.

During the reign of Emperor Qianlong of the Qing Dynasty, the government banned maritime trade. The only open port was in Guangzhou. Businessmen were despised in the Qing Dynasty, so they were banished of the city and only allowed to do trading outside of the Large West Gate. The relocated businessmen built up the foreign trading commercial firm (also called Foreign Firm) outside of the city. This made the adjacent markets become more and more prosperous, and the place had slowly formed into the wholesale market it is today.

In the Qing Dynasty, the neighboring areas of the Large West Gate were a thriving industrial park. It had a coffin, funeral and interment service markets from the Republican period. Nowadays, except for the spectacular view of historic sites, different kinds of markets, and shops, Ximenkou has also become a good place to enjoy daily life for Guangzhou citizens.

Baosheng Pawnshop

Itinerary

The tour starts at Ximenkou metro station Exit C, Walking out of the subway station, you will face Guangxiao Road, which used to be one of eleven archery ranges in Guangzhou old town in Qing Dynasty. Historical records indicate that sons of "Eight Banners" of the Qing Dynasty learned shooting and riding from their childhood. (In the past, there was a horse ranch close to the Archery Lane next to the Guang Xiao Road.) The horse ranch was situated in the area from today's Guang Xiao

Road to the south of Renmin North Road. There were no residents near the archery range, which was only open for the armies of the Yellow Banner and Red Banner to practice horseback shooting. After Guangzhou government demolished the city gate to build roads in 1921, residents gradually gathered in the areas of eleven archery ranges so the place was getting busy.

In 1921, China Discipline and Self-care Evangelization Society bought lands in Guangxiao Road and entrusted Priest Tan Woxin to build a new church. Beginning in December of 1921, the construction project was completed in October of 1924. It took three years and cost 70 thousand silver dollars to build the new church and it was named **Guangxiao Church of Christ in China** ❶

Guangxiao Church of Christ in China

If you're interested in Cantonese flavors and herbal soup then try the Cantonese stew soup in **Shun Homg Fung Stewed Soup Store** (; page 102).

Continue walking north on GUANGXIAO LU until you reach **Guangxiao Temple** (❷; page 100). Continue walking east on JINHUI LU toward HUIJI XILU, along quiet and romantic alleys, in great contrast of the noise Zhongshan Rd. These buildings were built in 1920s~1930s by overseas Chinese and the architecture combines Chinese and Western elements, as well as strong Lingnan architectural features. You will see the **Former Site of Ta Kung Pao Newspaper Office** (❸, Closed to visitors) located in HUIJI XI 2ⁿᵈ lane where at the front of the building there is a child statue holding a roll of newspaper in its right hand. Ta Kung Pao is the oldest active Chinese language newspaper in China is located at the Wen Wei Po newspaper office

Former Site of Ta Kung Pao Newspaper Office

former site. They established the office here during 1951~1970. Opposite of No.33 HUIJI DONGLU is one of the filming locations of 'A Road and a Will', which is a 1997 Hong Kong modern serial drama produced by TVB and the series was broadcasted on TVB Jade.

General's Mansion c.1878

Continue walking north on HUIJI XILU, then along winding alleys and you will arrive at the entrance of **Liurong Temple** (❹; page 100). The temple enshrines three large Buddhist statues, the biggest copper Buddhist statues in Guangdong province.

Guangdong Guest House hotel

Opposite the temple you will see the red gate of **General's Mansion** 5, which is now the back door of the Guangdong Guest House. According to historical records it was the General's Mansion in the Qing Dynasty, until Emperor Xianfeng, 11 years of Qing Dynasty (1861). Part of the buildings seized by the British to be used for their consulate. In 1928, the Republic of China took it back from the British and rebuilt it as Jing Hui Park. In 1931 it was reconstructed as a villa and renamed to Orchid Garden Guest House. In May 1962, government changed its name to Guangdong Guest House hotel . The four-star Guangdong Guest House has received heads-of-state from over 120 countries since 1952 and is the only garden style four-star hotel in the city center.

Continue walking south on LIURONG LU until you reach the crossroad. The place on your left was used to be a weekend flea market and Jiangjundong appliances shopping mall, a popular place for secondhand computer, cell phone and electrical accessory sales. Guangzhou metro corporation took back the land in 2015 for further development projects, it serves as a parking lot temporarily.

Cross the road and approach the next sight **Tao Street** (6 ; page 101). This area is the local man's paradise for electrical appliances and second hand items, most of buyers are middle aged men. Experience and see what are these men are interested in.

After visiting the man's paradise, walk toward the historic streets of GUANGTA LU and MANAO XIANG. Dating back to the Tang Dynasty more than one thousand years ago, Guangzhou had become the national center of foreign trade. Therefore, many foreign businessmen came to Guangzhou. At that time, Guangzhou had three main foreign trade partners: Srivijaya Empire in Southeast Asia (present-day Sumatra), India in South Asia and Tazi Empire in the Arab region. Among them, businessmen who lived in Guangzhou were mostly from Tazi Empire because their homeland was furthest away from Guangzhou, and they had to depend on the monsoon season to sail. It might take two years for them to sail to Guangzhou and back. Therefore, lots of Tazi businessmen chose to live in Guangzhou for convenience, and some of them opened shops and even purchased properties and lands, settled down and got married to local women in Guangzhou. The rapid increase in the number of foreigners caused social problems due to the of lack of management. Therefore, Guangzhou government in Tang Dynasty established a "Fan district", namely foreigner district, west of the city to gather foreign businessmen together for the purpose of management. This "Fan district" is near present-day Guang Ta Road. At that time, Arabic businessmen sold Arabic specialties and jewelry made of Carnelian, which were the most popular product amongst rich Cantonese. These pieces of jewelry were so popular that a number of jewelry shops sprung up and concentrated in the market. Besides, local people opened stores here as well to sell necessities to foreigners. Gradually, a new and large commercial district emerged in the west of the city.

If you are a Muslim, pay a visit to the **Huaisheng Mosque** (7 ; page 185), it is one of the oldest Muslim mosques in China. The Mosque is open to Muslims only and serves the Hui ethnic

A view looking north west over Canton city. The Minaret (Huaisheng Mosque) on the left and Flower Pagoda (Liurong Temple) on the right stands out markedly on the city skyline.

group not the general public, but the building is worth admiring from outside. There are also many halal restaurants near the mosque.

Continue walking west to **Lun Wenxu Memorial Square** ❽, an area about 500 square meters. Built with the Ming Dynasty architectural style as the main design element. At the Ming style memorial arch there is a platform for storytelling and a granite stone statue memorializing the number one scholar Lun Wenxu of Guangzhou in Ming Dynasty. Finish your trip at the **Relic of Large West Gate Barbican** (❾ ; page100).

Lun Wenxu Memorial Square

Tips:

There is a dawn market on RENMIN BEILU early in the morning from 2:00 am~7:00 am. The dawn market in Xi Men Kou was formed at the beginning of the 20th century and made its first appearance on Zhongshan 7th Lu, which is located in the western part of Guangzhou. The fact that the relic of Large West Gate Barbarian used to be an ancient time slum in the suburban area, the convention of selling low end commodity goods or stolen goods to the low class people is still practiced today. Cheap foods and low commodity goods include clay pots, potteries, secondhand books and newspaper, clothing, socks, and shoes are the main selling commodities. These days the dawn market serves as a low price supermarket for the homeless without pension, who often sleeps under the Renmin Bridge and make a living by returning recycle materials for money to buy food with. Although large crowds of locals are attracted to this area, many of the items are stolen goods as well as overdue products. Some people remark ironically, "If a burglar breaks into your house and steals things at night, you can retrieve the stolen things at the dawn market the following morning." It seems that the dawn market has never gone out of business in the past century because it meets the demand of the minority in the city, creating a livelihood for manual labor and providing the impoverished with low price commodities.

Other dawn markets in Guangzhou:

Dawn market of RENMIN BEILU and HAIZHU ZHONGLU (yellow sections)

Haizhu Middle Road (HAIZHU ZHONGLU):

It is still a street market for trading stamps as well as ancient coins and notes on a large and professional scale. Since there are shops selling paper antiques, this area is also called the Antique Book Market. In the past quite a few precious treasures, now displayed in museums, were found here. For example, the receipts from fund raising for building the Chen Clan Academy are now displayed at the academy. The swords and trumpets used by the Chinese revolutionaries who tried to overthrow the Qing in 1911, are now exhibited in the Revolution of 1911 Museum, were found at this dawn market, which seems to be selling old second hand goods.

Time: Every Saturday from 5:30am~9:00am.
Categories: books, stamps, ancient notes and coins.

Wenchang North Rod (WENCHANG BEILU)

The dawn market on WENGCHANG BEILU, also known as the Ghost Market, is the oldest one in Guangzhou and dates back to over a century. For several hundred meters along the road, antique shops stand in a row. In the 1980s, antiques stolen from ancient tombs were transported here by antique smugglers from all over China. In the beginning, the market opened daily but since 2003 the market began to open only on Tuesdays. In the Ghost Market, 90% of the "antiques" are counterfeit, only specialists are likely to distinguish the authentic items (only 10%) from the fake pieces. Because this dawn market only opens on Tuesdays, the majority of the visitors are merely curious, therefore only a few serious sellers promote their pricey goods. At dawn, professional buyers of antiques, toys, and secondhand goods are already gathering in the market along with a large number of people attracted by its reputation. When you visit this market, a flashlight, the ability to bargain, and a treasure hunting attitude are all you need.

Time: Every Tuesday from 6:00 am~8:30am.

Liwan Road (LIWAN LU)

Liwan electronic gadget comprehensive market and the secondhand electronic gadget market nearby have been well known for years both in the local area and by IT geeks. In the 1980s and 1990s, imported secondhand air conditioners, printers, and even fine electronic devices were all well liked by locals. These imported solid waste items were mainly from countries in western Europe, the United States, and Japan. The cost of waste disposal was as high as several hundred dollars per ton in developed countries, while transporting their waste to China only cost $10 U.S. dollars per ton.

Time: Every Friday from 10:00am~5:00pm.
Categories: electronic components, secondhand appliances

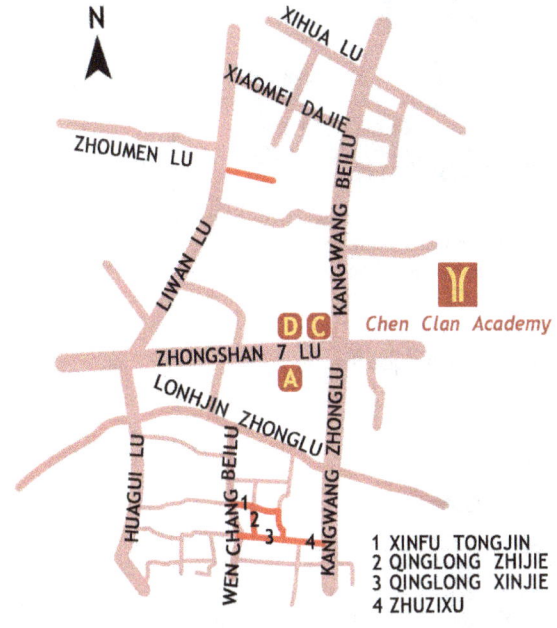

Dawn market of WENCHANG BEILU and LIWAN LU (red sections)

Points of Interest

Guangxiao Temple (光孝寺)

One of the oldest temples in Guangzhou. The Bright Filial Piety Temple (Guangxiao Temple) located on Guangxiao Road was the mansion of Prince Zhao Jiande of the Nanyue Kingdom during the Western Han Dynasty (206 B.C.- 24 A.D.). As the sixth patriarch of Zen Buddhism, Hui Neng, trained at this temple in the 7th Century and it is a popular pilgrimage site for Zen Buddhists. There is also a pagoda where Huineng's hair is buried. Other ancient structures in the temple include Sakyamuni Hall, Samgharama Hall, the King of Heaven Hall, and two iron towers. The temple has been destroyed several times by fire and the current buildings dates back to the mid-19th century.

- Metro Line 1 Ximenkou Station Exit C
- No.109 GUANGXIAO LU
- 6:00-17:00
- ¥5

Liurong Temple (六榕寺)

The temple is known as Liu Rong Temple in Chinese, is situated inside the city and first built during the Five Dynasties period (907-960), it was originally called Bǎo Zhuāng Yán Temple. It was renamed in the Ming Dynasty (1368-1644) as Six Banyan Temple after Su Shi, a great writer of the Northern Song Dynasty (960-1127), who is known to have written the two characters of Liurong when he saw the six ancient banyan trees on a visit to the temple. The thousand Buddha copper pillar cast in the Yuan Dynasty (1271-1368) is kept on the top story of the pagoda. The 184-foot pagoda appears to have nine stories; however, inside there are 17 levels. Because of the colorful exterior carvings, it is popularly known as the Flower Pagoda and is one of the most popular attractions in Guangzhou. The temple dates back to the 6th century, while the pagoda predates it by about 300 years.

- Metro Line 1 Gongyuanqian Station Exit I
- 87 LIURONG LU
- 6:00-17:00
- Admission is ¥5; Flower Pagoda ¥10

Relic of Large West Gate Barbican (西门瓮城遗址)

It was built in Ming Dynasty. Barbican is a fortified outpost or gateway such as an outer defense to a city or castle, or any tower situated over a gate or bridge which was used for defensive purposes. Usually barbicans were situated outside the main line of defenses and connected to the city walls with a walled road called the neck. According to archived records, Zhu ZuLiang was sent by Founding Emperor of Ming Dynasty to set up the city wall after being ousted from the Yuan Dynasty. The walls had been used by Qing Dynasty after Ming Dynasty. During the Republic of China, Sun Ko as mayor of Guangzhou city, destroyed defensive walls and gates in the old city in order to build roads.

ZHONGSHAN 7 LU

Tao Street (陶街)

It could be one of the most crowded electronic flea markets in Guangzhou. Here is the public's technology paradise, outdated computers, cheap speakers, interphone, Nintendo Game Boys, Toto tap, toys and Aviation Aerial Models etc. All sorts of strange things related to mechanical or electronics it can be found here, even the Chinese tea, tea sets, bicycles, military supplies, and astronomical telescopes. It is known as the Man's paradise, they don't have much money in their pocket but it is more about horse trading.

JIEFANG ZHONGLU

Where to Eat

Shun Homg Fung Stewed Soup Store (信行丰炖品皇店)

It is an old Cantonese restaurant which opened in April 1981. Time honored brands relying on word of mouth, legendary ancient means of communication. It follows ancient Chinese medicine diets and theories from the Chinese Nation, using a unique recipe, traditional processing techniques, adhering to Cantonese food culture, to finally create the Cantonese stewed soup and lotus leaf rice. The cashier desk is at the front of the shop and there is a menu board with yellow bottom red characters. A wide range of stewed soups are priced from 10 yuan to 28 yuan. They will remove items from the menu if they sell out. How many servings you should be eating? Order one of the items from the list for each person.

No.65 Guangxiao Road (光孝路 65 号)
11:00-21:00

Menus

原只椰子炖竹丝鸡
Braised Chicken with Whole Coconut
淮杞炖竹丝鸡
Braised Chicken with Dry Yam and Medlar
花旗参炖竹丝鸡
Braised Chicken with Ginseng
炖蝎子
Braised Scorpion
淮杞炖鹌鹑
Braised Quail with Dry Yam and Medlar
天麻炖猪脑
Braised Pig Brain with Rhizoma Gastrodiae
冬瓜炖水鸭
Braised Teal with Winter Melon
咸蛋肉饼饭
The Salty Egg Meat Pie Rice
原只椰子炖鹌鹑
Braised Quail with Whole Coconut
牛奶木瓜炖雪蛤
Papaya Stew Wood Frog with Milk
红萝卜瘦肉炖蝎子
Braised Scorpion with Carrots and Lean Meat
花旗参石斛炖瘦肉
Braised Lean Meat with Ginseng and Caulis Dendrobii
土茯苓瘦肉炖龟
Braised Tortoise with Smilax Glabra Roxb and Lean Meat
土茯苓瘦肉炖水蛇
Braised Water Snake with Smilax Glabra Roxb and Lean Meat

> **For Vegetarian:**
> 牛奶炖木瓜　　Braised Papaya with milk
> 冰糖炖木瓜　　Braised Papaya with crystal sugar

② Wing Sang Zap Pak Water Snake Congee Restaurant (荣生集北水蛇粥)

Guangzhou has a long history of eating snake, Cantonese can be considered as the expert in eating snake in all of China. Dishes made from snakes can be divided into dry and wet dishes. Eating snake may scare some people but the water snake with its amino acid has helped people in curing diseases and improving health.

> **Menus**
> 水蛇粥
> Water Snake Rice Porridge in Pot
> 椒盐蛇碌
> Deep Fried Snake with Salt and Pepper
> 九制陈皮骨
> Deep-Fried Spare Ribs with Mandarin Peel

📍 No.62 Guangxiao Road (光孝路62号)
🕒 11:30-14:00 & 17:30-01:00

③ Ching Choi Hin Restaurant (晶彩轩了能菜)

Dare to try exotic insect delicacies in Guangzhou? There is no need for you to go to Southeast Asia when they could be found here. Eating insects is generally received with grimaces and gag reflexes by Westerners. From centipedes to scorpions, creepy crawly things are consumed for their high protein content, appealing crunchiness, and straight-up taste. The Restaurant is a three story building with fashion decoration and the wild insects are imported from Yunnan and Guizhou provinces. The owner believes that Guangzhou people dare to eat the strange insects because people in Guangzhou have enough courage to try something new.

> **Menus**
> 炸蜈蚣王
> Deep-fried Centipede
> 炸蝎子王
> Deep-fried Scorpion
> 七味盐局竹虫
> Baked Bamboo Maggots in Salt
> 蜜蜂蛹炒桂花蛋
> Stir Frying Honey Bee Pupa with Egg
> 黑蚂蚁煎蛋
> Fried Egg with Ants
> 蒜香桂花蝉
> Fried Lethocerus Indicus with Garlic

📍 No.225 Haizhu Road North (海珠北路225号)　🕒 11:00-14:30 & 17:00-21:30

Beijing Road

HIGHLIGHT: A business center and the ancient city of cultural tourism.
START POINT: Metro line 1 Peasant Movement Institute station Exit C
FINISH POINT: Buddha Ancient Temple
LENGTH: Approx. 5 hours (3.5 km)

Historical Background

During the Ming and Qing Dynasties, today's Zhongshan Road used to be the main East-West street of the old area of Guangzhou. There were mostly government offices along the street, which made it the political center of Guangzhou. Beijing Road was the main street from the south of the city to the Tianzi Wharf, which was used for mandarins' landing. Therefore, the local mandarins, their entourages, and families gathered in this T-shaped area at that time, which is today's Zhongshan 4th Road and the northern part of the Beijing Road. To meet their demands, this area gradually became a business center of the city.

Shops and signboards on Sheung-mun-tai street (present day Beijing Road), c. 1870

John Chinaman at Home, 1905, p. 46~47, E.J. HARDY

Nothing impresses one who visits a Chinese city for the first time so much as the signboards that hang perpendicularly from shops and hongs. A good one is a valuable piece of property. In bright colours and gold are inscribed the sign of the firm and some such words as "Never-ending success"; "By Heaven made prosperous"; "Trade revolves like a wheel"; "Virtuous and Abundant"; "Health and happiness rest on all who enter here"—this last over an opium smoking den! Hints like the following may be read: "Gossiping and long sitting injure business"; "No credit given: former customers have taught caution." The shape of the signboard and its colour, as also the colour of the letters upon it, indicate different trades. The brightly painted large paper lamps that hang over the shops also add to the cheerful picturesqueness of the streets of Canton and of other Chinese cities.

In 1920, Guangzhou Municipal Government demolished the city wall to broaden roads. This road was renamed Wing Hon Road from Wing Ching Road, which meant the Qing Dynasty was overthrown and the Han nationality would prosper forever.

Wing Hon Road crowed with people coming and going circa 1920s

In 1936, the Governor of Guangzhou Hu Hanmin died. He was the first president of the legislature of the Nanjing National Government, and was Cantonese, so people renamed the road Hanmin Road to commemorate him. However, in October of 1949, the name

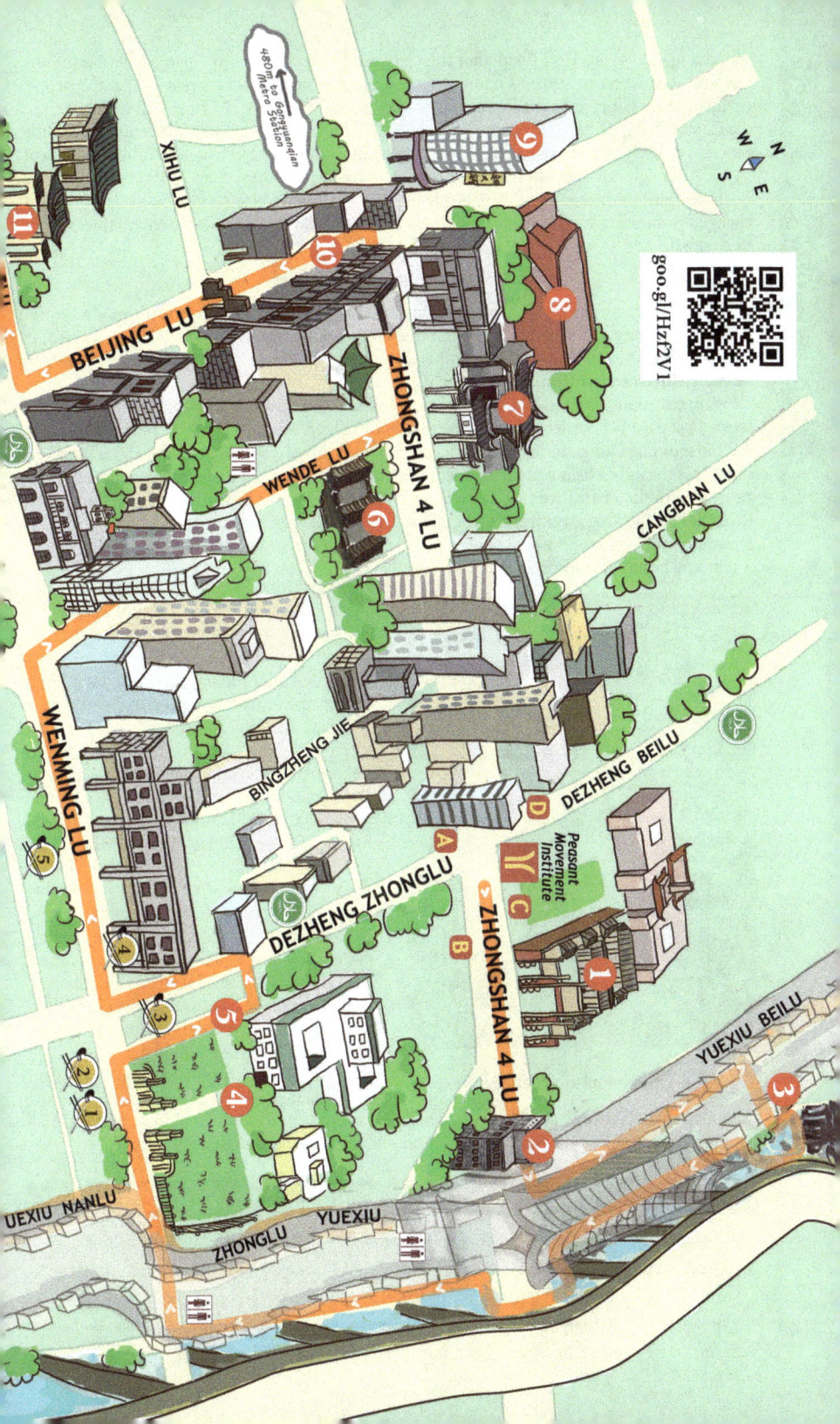

was changed to Wing Hon Road after the Communist Party liberated Guangzhou. During the Cultural Revolution in 1966, its name was changed to Beijing Road, expressing that the people of Guangzhou adhered to the leadership of the Communist Party of China and recognition of the Capital being Beijing. This name metaphorically shows that this road is the central axis in the process of developing the old area of Guangzhou city, so the name "Beijing Road" has been kept so far. Although this area has witnessed tens of Dynasties and more than 2,000 years of history, it still remains as the center of the city. Guangzhou is among the few metropolises that has not changed its location for more than 2,000 years, and it is said that only Rome shares this distinction with it.

Itinerary

Tour start at Exit C Peasant Movement Institute metro station, if you come on Sunday morning, you will see people gather under the tree on Sunday morning to practice their English in Guangzhou Children's Library. Next to the Guangzhou Children's Library is the **Former Site of Peasant Movement Institute** (❶ ; page 110).

Walk east along ZHONGSHAN 4 LU for a block until you reach **Dongping Pawnshop Museum** (❷ ; page 111). After that cross the road and walk on east side YUEXIU BEILU until reach the **Museum of Donghao Moat** (❸ ; page 112), walk toward south along the Donghaochong canal, it is the only existing canal passing through the urban center. The canal had linked the six streams with the Pearl River since the Song Dynasty. Connecting Baiyun Mountain and Pearl River, Donghaochong greenway has a total length of 4.51 kilometers. It is one of the Asian Games renovation projects and now becomes a new destination for tourists in Guangzhou for its green waters and beautiful landscape.

Donghaochong canal

Then cross the road by foot bridge. Walking south along the canal to reach DONGHUA XILU and then turn right cross the traffic light to WENMING LU, there are many local food shops along this road, take a rest and try the Cantonese dessert and stew soup.

There are a few lawns kept inside the fences on your right hand side, this place used to be former examination halls in Qing Dynasty. Examination Hall was used for the triennial provincial examination of male candidates for the "Second Literary Degree". The exams were time-consuming and expensive, a family usually would save all their resources so that one lucky boy can prepare for exams and rise to high office. The old imperial examinations system was abolished in 1905. It successor, the Gaokao was introduced as a meritocratic route to academic and social advancement in 1952, three years after the Communist People's Republic of China came into existence. It is still a gateway to university entrance exam in China today and the most pressure-packed examination in the world, and has even been linked to student suicide. The old Examination Hall has been converted into the **Sun Yat-sen Library of Guangdong Province** ❹ in 1986.

Glimpses of China and Chinese Homes, 1902, p. 172, EDWARD S. MORSE

Another of the many interesting features in Canton was the examination-hall, as it is called, though there was no trace of a hall on the grounds according to our meaning of the word. This famous place consisted of rows of long, narrow sheds running at right angles to a broad area which might be called a yard or avenue. These low sheds were divided by partitions open in front; if they had been furnished with doors they would have resembled the bathing-houses along our seaside resorts. These structures were built of brick, with brick partitions, and the individual. Cells were not over four feet wide.

The number of them has been variously stated to be seven thousand five hundred and ten thousand. The candidates who compete for examination come from all parts of the Empire. These include young men and old men, some of whom have reached the age of eighty or ninety years, who have been competing since they were boys, and appear again and again to win the coveted prize of recognition and, if successful, to get some office under Government with a modest stipend, the balance of their salary being squeezed out of the inhabitants by fraud and persecution. Early in the morning a single text from Confucius or some other ancient classical writer is issued to all, each one receiving the same text. On this they are all to write an essay and deliver it the next morning. An ignoramus on everything but Chinese classics may beat other numskulls in writing the best composition on the text given, and attain some office dealing with matters" pertaining to the nineteenth century.

The imperial examination hall with 7500 cubicles, circa 1873

Near the bus stop turn right and this leads you to a small alley, go through the iron gate about 100 meters you can see an old brick walls, it's called '**Longhu Walls**' (⑤ ; page 112).

Calligraphy and painting stores on Wende Lu

Turn left and continue walking along the alley for a few steps to reach DEZHENG ZHONGLU, and walk back to WENMING LU. Continue walking west on WENMING LU for a block until you reach a crossroad, turn right at WENDE LU, this road is famous for decorative pictures. During the Qing Dynasty, WENDE LU was considered a "Calligraphy and painting street" where shops sold pictures, calligraphies and four treasures of Chinese study (writing brush, ink stick, ink slab, and paper), famous book stores and antique stores aligned this street at that time. WENDE LU is now a major street where shops sell calligraphies and paintings and some stores carry Chinese antique curios and porcelains.

The Temple of Horrors

The next destination is **Wanmu School** (❻ ; page 113) which is at the northwest corner of WENDE LU and ZHONGSHAN 4 LU. Diagonally opposite of it is **Chenghuang Temple** (❼ ; page 113), the temple dedicated to the tutelary god of Canton city, popularly known to foreigners as the temple of horrors' in the old day from its representations of the Buddhist Hells.

John Chinaman at Home, **1905, p. 46~47, E.J. HARDY**

This was the temple of the god of the city, or, as foreigners call it, "The Temple of Horrors." This Chinese Madame Tussaud's was not as gruesome as others of the kind which I have seen elsewhere. On either side of the entrance court are life-sized wooden figures representing people undergoing the tortures inflicted in the ten kingdoms of the Buddhistic hell. They are being bored through the middle, sawn between two boards, precipitated upon turned-up swords, boiled in oil, extinguished by the descent of a red-hot bell. People are having their eyes and tongues pulled out. Others are being transmigrated into lower animals. One figure is being ground, as if he were rice, by a hammer worked by the treading of a coolie. This is the braying a fool in a mortar spoken of in Scripture. A dog waits to lick up the blood. There is a mirror in which the man sees the deeds for which he is being punished. In this temple there is a curious votive offering. One merchant accused another of fraud. The accused hastened to the shrine and declared his innocence. Shortly afterwards he died, and to the wrath of the god before whom he made a false statement his death was attributed. The accuser put up an offering in the form of an abacus, which is an instrument for performing arithmetical calculations by balls sliding on wire. Upon it is inscribed: "Man with man has many reckonings, with God he has but one. That great being sooth in secret."

Canton Shinto Shrine

Wing Hon Park

Next to the temple is the **Archaeological Site of the Nanyue Kingdom Palace Museum** (❽ ; page 114), the museum is built on top of the ancient palace but all the ruins are covered by transparent glass offering an amazing view of the 2,000-year old royal garden structure. This site used to be the former Guangzhou Children's Park before 2,000 and Wing Hon Park in 1933. During

Japanese invasion of China, Wing Hon Park became Canton Shinto Shrine, it was a place for Japanese invaders to commemorate war dead who served the Emperor of Japan during wars.

As you approach the **Former Site of the In-town Da Sun Co. Ltd** (❾ ; page 114). It use to be one of the "Four Great Department Store" in Republic of China. Turn right and walk down the major commercial center Beijing Road. See the **Beijing Road Ancient Path** (❿ ; page 115). You also can try delicious Guangzhou snacks from stalls along Beijing road.

There is a model of a water-dropping clock at the junction of BEIJING LU and HUIFU XILU. As formerly, for time-telling purposes, but it keeps its count of the minutes and hours are accurately as ever. It is the biggest and best preserved water-dropping clock in ancient China, mounded by the blacksmith studio of Xian Yun-xing in 1316 A.D. Originally there was a Double Gateway and the clock was housed on the top of this tower clocking daily for the people. The real water clock is displayed at the National Museum in Beijing since 1959. Then turn right on HUIFU DONGLU, finish your trip at **Buddha Ancient Temple** (⓫ ; page 116).

Clepsydra model, a sign of Beijing Road

Travels From The Grandeurs of The West to Mysteries of The East, 1909, p. 282~283, CHARLTON B. PERKINGS

Among other interesting specimens of antiquity to be seen is the famous Water Clock or Clepsydra, known to the Chinese as Tung Wu Ti Low, or copper jar water dropper. This stands on an arched tower and is approachable by a flight of granite steps. The building was erected during the Tang Dynasty A.D. 626, by a rebel chieftain, and it was restored A.D. 947 by Low Chang, who captured the city. It was destroyed by fire A.D. 1333 and rebuilt in 1366; and again partly destroyed in the bombardment of Canton in 1857 by the British. The Clepsydra is placed in a separate room under the supervision of a man who, besides earning a small salary, sells time-sticks for a livelihood. These sticks are really incense sticks on which the hours are marked off, so that when they burn to a certain point the correct time is known. The clock itself consists of four jars covered with copper plates standing on a brickwork stairway, the top of each jar being level with the one above. The largest of the three measures twenty-three inches high and is of like diameter, containing seventy catties or ninety-seven and one-half pints of water. The second is twenty-three inches high and twenty-one inches in diameter; the third is twenty-one inches high and twenty inches in diameter, while the fourth is twenty-one by nineteen inches.

The Water Clock of the Gongbei Tower, c. 1900

Connection is made between these jars by a trough, along which the water trickles at the base of each jar, and a floating index to regulate the time is set at 5 o'clock both morning and evening, the water being dipped back to the upper jar when the index records the half day, and so on, the water being renewed every three months. Near the jars stand two large drums which record the different watches of the night. Clocks of this description date from 1324. Today, as in the days of old, the attendants place upon the wall at every hour a board upon which is recorded the time of the day or night, and on an other board the periods of the moon are set forth.

Points of Interest

Former Site of Peasant Movement Institute (农民讲习运动所)

It is the original site of Communist training center founded by Mao Zedong in the 1920s. Now it is a museum with displays covering the China revolutionary history. The Guangzhou Peasant Movement Institute was set up in a 14th century Confucian temple and now the site on Zhongshan Road commemorates Guangzhou's revolutionary past. The national revolutionary movement experienced a vigorous growth after the first cooperation between the Chinese Communist Party and carried out by Kuomintang. In an effort to facilitate the imminent Northern Expedition and stimulate the nationwide peasant movement, in May 1926, the Sixth Session of the Peasant Movement Institute, headed by Mao Zedong, was held here. 327 trainees from 20 provinces and regions received education in the theory and methodology of peasant movements. The trainees underwent vigorous military training and took part in important social activities. Upon graduation, they traveled throughout the country to spearhead peasant campaigns against imperialism and feudalism, making significant contributions to the Chinese

Lecture hall

revolution. The Peasant Movement Training Institute was opened as a commemorative site in the 1950's and the lecture rooms and dormitories of the young revolutionaries have been recreated.

Peasant Movement Institute was the original Panyu official school, it was the local official school in the feudal times of China, also a temple of Confucius with Confucianism Buildings, such as Hemicycle Pond (泮池), Arch Bridge (拱桥), the Star of Wisdom Gate (棂星门), Dacheng Palace (大成殿) and Lecture Hall (明伦堂) etc. It had the functions of ceremonies of Confucius and nurturing talents. Panyu official school was built in 1370 of Ming Dynasty. The existing structure was formed from 1747, during the Qing Dynasty it was the highest official school in Guangzhou area.

In the middle of the Lecture Hall (堂倫明), you can see a Confucius statue and a plaque on at the hall-top: Model Teacher for Ten Thousand Ages (表師世萬). This used to be the classroom of the Panyu official school in ancient times. There are eight Chinese characters on the round pillar, the verse means: read and understand Four Books, read Five Classics of Sages, then do the right thing with responsibilities. This is the concept of Confucianism. The two sets of chimes were used for ceremonies of Confucius.

- 📍 No.42 ZHONGSHAN 4 LU
- 🕒 9:30-16:30 from Tuesday to Sunday
- Ⓢ Free admission

Dongping Pawnshop Museum
（东平大押）

This is one of the oldest pawnshops in Guangzhou and the only one in Chinese mainland to have been turned into a museum. This "pawnshop museum" is located in a "Diaolou", a 400 square-meter old traditional watch tower made from bricks and timber. Three stories are opened to visitors with the first floor exhibiting a replica of a pawnshop from the early Qing Dynasty; the second floor displaying historical pictures and documents; the third floor displaying the development and reform of the pawn business in modern times.

Description of items shown in display cabinets:

A: Deng Scale was used for weighing gold, jewelry and other valuable goods. The scale was made from ivory or precious timber – ebony. The trays and scale box are made of intricately carved ivory.

On the 2nd floor of Dongping Pawnshop Museum

B: Touchstone was a stone used to identify gold. In ancient times, the authenticity and fineness of gold are identified by scoring on the Touchstone. When someone took the gold to pawnshop, shopkeeper would score the touchstone with the gold piece then look carefully at the scratch to determine the quality and fineness with magnifying glass. If there was any suspicion, the shopkeeper would put some nitric acid onto the touchstone scratches, which made the impurities corrode. Then, the remnant must be pure gold. This test will be the reference for the price of the gold.

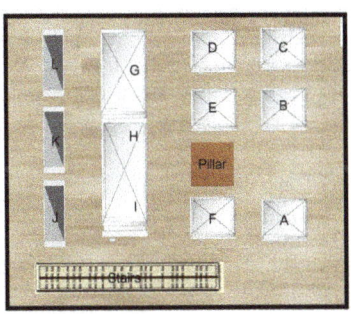

On the 2nd floor of Dongping Pawnshop Museum

C: Pawn character was used for writing pawn-tickets. It was created by a man from Shanxi Province during the Ming Dynasty, the purpose was to avoid people from fake and altering pawn-tickets. In the old pawnshops, the person who was responsible for writing tickets should be only one. It's said that a person must work for 10 years as an apprentice to become a master through study.

D: Business License issued by The Qing Dynasty Government.
According to the rule set in 1728, all civilian pawns need to remit application to chief secretary by local government and pay taxes annually. The license was signed by the province chief secretary and handed over to the county for checking and sending. Generally, the license indicated the expiration date of lawful operation and was updated regularly. It was to be illegal for setting up pawnshops without notifying the government.

E: Account book of Pawnshop in old time
F: Postcard with pawnshop in old time
G: Pawn ticket in The Republic of China
H: Pawn ticket in Qing Dynasty
I: Hong Kong and Macau's pawn ticket
J: Cabinet Zhao Gongming statue which is a god of pawn industry, also named 'God of Wealth', every pawn company enshrines him in order to avoid misfortune for wealth.
K: Mechanical Balance which was used by a pawn weighing gold and other precious items.
L: Republican period telephone; also shown is a pawn ticket for the telephone in 1944. The pawn ticket indicates one telephone at that time could pledge 30 Yin Yuan (Sliver dollar), about 7,000~10,000 RMB now, equal to one high-tech cell phone.

📍 No.1 ZHONGSHAN 4 LU
🕘 9:30-16:30 except for Monday

💲 Free admission
🚌 Yuexiu Zhong Road Station

Museum of Donghao Moat (东濠涌博物馆)

The museum is located along the Donghao Moat. Though not spacious, has two stories and five exhibition halls, A, B, C, D, and E. There are authentic objects, photographs, projections, audio-visual materials, etc, The museum records and exhibits collectively the history and cultures of Guangzhou's rivers and the achievements Donghao Moat. Reconstruction of the Moat has made the area a hydrophilic gallery integrating leisure, ecology, and culture in the recent years. The exhibition also displays life of the townsfolk living by the river in the old days, such as the scene of beautiful fisher maidens rowing the wooden boat to sell the fruits, or the fishermen catching fish; the merchants and shops crowded on both sides of the streets, the Zhan's Garden of great fame, the Guangdong Mint, etc. The past scene of the "old drains" show where dirty water flowed everywhere.

📍 South end of YUEXIU BEILU
🕘 9:00-17:00 close on Monday

💲 Free admission
🚌 Take the bus No. 11, 54, 80, 184, or 236, get off at Dadongmen Stop and walk for about 50 meters

Longhu Walls (龙虎墙)

Longhu Walls is 30 meters long, the place where announcement of the imperial examination results were displayed. Over the walls is Sun Yat-sen library, originally this was one of the four major The Imperial Examination Houses in Qing Dynasty.

Wanmu School (万木草堂)

In 1891, Kang Yongwei, a Chinese modern bourgeois reformer, rented parts of Qiu's family school in the town, where Qiu's descendants would live when taking imperial examinations. He made it a lecture cottage in order to teach his thoughts of reform and to cultivate students for the reform. Gathering students and giving lectures here, Kang teach reformism and this place became the source of the Hundred Day's Reform. In 1893, this place was renamed Wan Mu Thatched Cottage. Kang himself taught here for seven years, cultivating not only hundreds of scholars but an army of assistants for the Hundred Day's Reform. However, with the Reform failing, Kang escaped to Japan and this place was closed down in 1898 by the Qing government.

After liberation in 1949, Qiu's family transferred the Qiu's family school to the Guangzhou government. It later became one of the workshops for the Dong Feng Lock Factory, and then gradually became an area for more than 40 families. In 2004, the Guangzhou government had the Wan Mu Thatched Cottage renovated entirely and planned to build a Yuexiu District Museum here to exhibit historical relics or materials about Kang Youwei and other figures at that time.

- No.3 CHANGXING LI, ZHONGSHAN 4 LU
- 8:15-11:30 & 14:00-17:00 (Monday, Wednesday and Friday)
- Free admission

Chenghuang Temple (城隍庙)

This temple was built in 1370, the 3rd year of the Hongwu Period of the Ming Dynasty and was the largest Chenghuang Temple of its time in the Lingnan Region. "The design of them were about gods torturing devils," said Che Zhirong, the head Taoist priest of the temple. The function of Cheng Huang is to reward good deeds and to punish wrong doings. There is an arc sitting meters from the temple's main hall, inscribed with "Zhong You," (忠佑) meaning "loyalty and blessing." A walk beneath the arc leads to the gate of the main hall. The gold-coated nameplate and sculptures are dazzling and breath taking. Don't forget to take a look at the dragon-boat-like rooftop and the paintings depicting Pearl River scenes, all made by traditional Guangdong artisans. Worship of Cheng Huang is more or less of Taoist origin, so there are some elements of the ancient philosophy within the temple.

There are three gods receiving prayers here. The main god is Liu Yan (刘龑), an emperor governing Guangdong in the early 10th Century. He is worshipped because he built Guangdong into unprecedented prosperity. On his left is Hai Rui (海瑞), a government official in the Ming Dynasty being famous for fighting against corruption, but he himself was very poor. Yang Jiaoshan (杨椒山) sits on the right. Also being a high-ranking official in the Ming Dynasty, he had lifelong combats with corruption and abuse of power, and finally died miserably by a plot of his enemies. Note the big wall on both sides, the 246 square meters golden painting may be the first thing to attract you in the main hall, it is made of real gold. The painting consists of 150,000 genuine gold leaves, that took some 30 teachers and students of Guangzhou Academy of Fine Art half a year to complete. There are 132 immortals from Chinese mythology in the painting, from the Jade Emperor to the God of Wealth.

- Crossing of WENDE LU and ZHONGSHAN 4 LU
- 8:00-17:00
- Free admission

Archaeological Site of the Nanyue Kingdom Palace Museum
（南越国宫署遗址）

The Palace of the Nanyue Kingdom represents the best of Guangzhou's cultural heritage. It is a large archaeological site museum based on the Palace of the Nanyue Kingdom. The Palace of the Nanyue Kingdom is located in the center of the inner city of Guangzhou. Relics from thirteen dynasties, it was not only the seat of the Palace of the Nanyue Kingdom of the Western Han Era and the Palace of the Nanhan Kingdom of the Five - Dynasties Era, but also the seat of various government offices following the annexation of the Lingnan region by the Qing Empire. It testifies to the fact that Guangzhou has all along been the political, economic and cultural center of the Lingnan region.

During excavation of the area, discovered among other things, was the remains of the Palaces of the Nanyue Kingdom and Nanhan Kingdom as well as the royal gardens. The royal garden consists of a large stone pond and a crooked stone brook which meanders around sharp bends, past a crescent-shaped pond, down slopes and through a water gate. It is relatively well preserved and is the oldest Qin-Han royal garden discovered so far in China.

- No.316 ZHONGSHAN 4 LU
- 9:00-17:30 from Tuesday to Sunday
- Free admission

The Former Site of the In-town Da Sun Co. Ltd (城内大新公司)

In-town Da Sun department store

In 1912, Da Sun Co. Ltd. was founded in Hong Kong by Australia overseas Chinese Mr. Cai Xing and Mr. Cai Chang. They gain remarkable achievements through their unremitting efforts. In 1916, the Da Sun company set up a branch store in the middle of the Avenue of Benevolence and Love (the site of the present Xin Da Xin department store on Zhongshan 5th Road). The branch was called In-town Da Sun Co. Ltd., distinct from the parent company Xidi Da Sun (page 79) situated in the West Bund which was founded in 1918. At the time, the In-town Da Sun department store concurrently engaged in items with in rooftop amusement park, western-style restaurant, liquor store, bathhouse and Bing Sutt (a type of traditional coffee house in Guangzhou, which was very popular during 1950s and 1960s. Providing light meals and drinks, it is a unique place where Chinese food meets Western food); The Xidi Da Sun department store concurrently includes businesses such as hotel business, rooftop amusement park, western-style restaurant , barber shop, photographic business, optical shop, etc. The In-town Da Sun department store was remodeled into a new sixteen-storey building and renamed New Da Sun department store in 1989. After the completion of Da Sun Co. Ltd. of Hui Ai Road, two overseas Chinese brothers Cai Chang and Cai Xing from Australia bought the property in the street aside.

The buildings along the street are mainly three-storey, with the combination of commercial and residential mode where the street level is for small shops and the upper level is housing, for the Shang Xiadian, each shop was about 5 to 6 meters width of room.

In order to commemorate the contribution of the brothers Cai Xing and Cai Chang had towards Guangzhou, the Guangzhou government in the Republic of China period named the Changxing Street with the names of Cai Chang and Cai Xing in 1918. In the 1930s, custom made suits became a fashion among Guangzhou's magnates and Changxing Street specialized in high-end suits. In the 1960s, with the domestic economic downturn and political instability, the market of handmade western suits declined, many western suit stores had licenses revoked or closed down on their own. By the early 1980s, the business form gradually changed and there were mainly dentists and watch industry. Nowadays, some clock stores, dentist offices, and snack shops are spread throughout on Changxing Street, compared to the past, more like a atmosphere of ordinary life.

New Da Sun department store

Changxing Street

Beijing Road Ancient Path
（北京路千年古道）

The Ancient Beijing Roads Relic was unearthed in July 2002, under the Beijing Road Pedestrian Mall. When this site was excavated workers found ancient roads and vestiges of five dynasties in eleven different layers. In order to protect the site, the local municipal government covered it with glass fiber reinforced plastic which provides viewing area to visitors. Beijing Road is central axis of ancient

Guangzhou city and the most prosperous commercial distributing center throughout history. It is once downtown of Guangzhou from Nanyue Kingdom period of the Western Han Dynasty to the Qing Dynasty. Beijing Road is the main street in Guangzhou in Tang, Song, Yuan and Qing Dynasties and has become the most prosperous cultural pedestrian mall of Guangzhou since the Ming Dynasty.

Dafo Buddhist Temple (大佛古寺)

It is one of the most famous Buddhist temples in southern China. Aged more than a thousand years this temple was built during the Southern Han Dynasty it reached prosperity during the Qing Dynasty. Buddha Ancient Temple houses the first Buddhist public library in Guangdong province. 664 square meters with more than 40,000 books and 8,000 volumes, the library is a modern facility. It is a professional Buddhist library, occasionally offering Buddhist courses or discussion classes for young people and Zen courses.

- No.509 HUIFU DONGLU
- 8:00-18:00
- Free admission

Where to Eat

1. Rose Desserts and Snacks
（玫瑰甜品店）

This shop has been opened for more than 10 years. In the tiny shop, you will see lots of people waiting in line for the next available table, especially at night time. The owner is quite hospitable, always chats with customers as friends. There are also some images of the menu on the walls around the shop. There are 3 dessert shops opened along this road, only this one will personally serve you by the owner, the other two are managed by staff employees.

Menus

杏仁豆腐
Chilled Almond Jelly

芒果西米露
Sweet Sago Soup with Fresh Mango

芒果杏仁豆腐
Chilled Almond Jelly with Fresh Mango

双皮奶
Double-layer Milk Custard

芝麻糊
Sesame Paste

凤凰奶糊
Scrambled Egg White with Milk and Egg Yolk

姜撞奶
Ginger Buffalo Milk Custard

椰汁西米露
Sweet Sago Syrup with Coconut Juice

杏仁糊
Almond Paste

香芋西米露
Sweet Sago Syrup with Coconut Juice and Taro

杨枝甘露
Sweet Sago Syrup with Coconut Juice and Pomelo, Mango & Pineapple

红豆冰	Red bean ice water
糖不甩	Glutinous Rice Balls with Peanuts & Sesame Seeds
杏仁奶糊	Scrambled Egg white with milk and almond

📍 No.218 Wenming Road（文明路 218 号）   🕒 12:00-23:30

② Lao Sai Kwan Rice Noodles Store
（老西关濑粉）

This shop has two floors, basically everyone will order the Wedding Rice Noodles here with texture is sticky and the soup flavor is strong. If you like a crispy taste you can put a little bit dried radish or spicy dried radish with green onion, then mix them, but don't put too much, or it will be salty, half a spoon is all right. There are a lot of pictures showing the old Guangzhou on the walls of the second floor.

Menus

濑粉	Wedding Rice Noodles with Dried Radish
水菱角	Rice Flour Water Caltrop
炸鱼皮	Fried Fish Skin

📍 No.216 Wenming Road（文明路 216 号）   🕒 7:00-22:00

③ Choi Fook Noodle Store
（才福面家）

Another good place to try for their Wonton Noodles that are economical and practical. The shop front appears in Sai Kwan style decoration. There is an air draft machine in front of the storefront to diffuse the fish soup smell into the air stimulating your smell senses when you walk pass the store.

📍 No.238 Dezheng Road Middle
（德政中路 238 号）   🕒 7am-2am

Menus

鲜肉云吞面	Noodle Soup with Pork Wonton
鲜虾云吞	Soup with Shrimp Wonton
鲜虾云吞面	Noodle Soup with Shrimp Wonton
鲜肉云吞	Soup with Pork Wonton
鲜肉云吞伊面	Crispy Egg Noodle with Pork Wonton in Soup

For Vegetarian:

蚝油捞面	Guangdong-style Noodle with Oyster Sauce
炸酱捞面	Fried Bean Sauce with Boiled Noodles

Beijing Road

④ Ngan Kee Rice Rolls Store
（银记肠粉）

This store was founded in the 1950s. There are 22 branches in Guangzhou, but the most delicious and authentic one is located in Shang Jiu Road. If you get here at lunch or dinner time you will have a hard time to find a seat. Locals usually order a bowl of congee combined with a dish of steamed rice rolls.

📍 No.199 Wenming Road
（文明路 199 号）

🕐 6:30am-1am

Menus

及第粥	Rice Porridge with Pig's Liver and Kidneys
滑鸡粥	Chicken Congee
艇仔粥	Sampan Congee
猪肉肠粉	Steamed Rice Rolls with Pork
牛肉肠粉	Steamed Rice Rolls with Beef and Soy Sauce
鲜虾肠粉	Steamed Rice Rolls with Fresh Shrimps

For Vegetarian:

白粥	Plain Rice Porridge
生菜粥	Lettuce Congee
茶树菇肠粉	Steamed Rice Rolls with Agrocybe Cylindracea
玉米肠粉	Steamed Rice Rolls with Corns
炸面肠粉	Steamed Rice Rolls with Deep-fried Dough Sticks

⑤ Da Yeang Stew Soup Store
（达杨原味炖品）

This is a famous and popular shop selling stew soup in Guangzhou. Various stew soups are available to choose from according to the season and the customer's body condition. Nourishing soup is important for the skin in the dry autumn season.

📍 No.202 Wenming Road
（文明路 202 号）

🕐 11:00-23:00

Menus

原只椰子炖竹丝鸡	Braised Chicken Soup With Whole Coconut
原只椰子炖鹌鹑	Braised Quail Soup with Whole Coconut
花旗参炖竹丝鸡	Braised Chicken Soup with Ginseng
天麻炖猪脑	Braised Pig Brain with Rhizoma Gastrodiae
淮杞炖牛展	Braised Beef Shank with Dry Yam and Medlar
天麻炖鱼头	Braised Fish Head with Rhizoma Gastrodiae

淮杞炖竹丝鸡	Braised Chicken with Dry Yam and Medlar
淮杞炖鹌鹑	Braised Quail Soup with Dry Yam and Medlar
香菇炖鸡	Braised Chicken Soup with Mushroom
淮杞炖乳鸽	Braised Squab Soup with Dry Yam and Medlar
炖羊肉	Braised Mutton Soup
炖龟	Braised Tortoise Soup

Yat Chui Cantonese Restaurant
(壹厨饭店)

This traditional Cantonese restaurant particularly popular with local neighborhood. In most cases people need to wait 30 minutes or more for a table by dinner time. If you want real Cantonese cuisine with huge menu to chose from, this is the place. Staffs don't speak English but Chinese menu with picture is clear. Key point is remember to bring enough cash. They only accept Chinese credit cards and debit cards, and only accept RMB. Luckily there is Industrial and Commercial Bank of China ATM next to the restaurant.

Menus		
	深井烧鹅	Roast Goose
	烤乳鸽	Roast Pigeon
	白切鸡	Sliced Cold Chicken with Ginger Dipping Sauces
	香葱淋鲈鱼	Steamed Weever with Green Onion

📍 No.171 Dezheng Road Middle (德政中路 171 号)
🕒 11am-2pm & 5pm-2am

=== **Featured Food** ===

Roast Goose
(深井烧鹅)

    Roast Goose is one of the traditional roasted dishes of Guangzhou. The best birds are medium and small sized black geese. The roast goose has a brown color the meat is very tasty. There are many famous roast goose shops in Guangzhou but the most famous one is Shenjing roast goose on Changzhou Island of Huangpu District.

Roasted Squab
（红烧乳鸽）

Roasted Squab has been a renowned dish in Guangzhou, being sold in hotels and restaurants city wide. Pigeon meat is nutritious and easy to digest; every 100 grams of pigeon meat contains 22.14 grams of protein and only 1 gram of fat. In addition, the microelements and vitamins found in pigeon meat, the availability is very plentiful. Traditional Chinese Medicine (TCM) practitioners believe that squab is salty and mild in nature, having therapeutic effects for nurturing the kidneys, dissolving toxin, and circulating energy within the body. Furthermore, they say it is recuperative, alleviating thirst, long-time malaria, intestinal bleeding, dizziness, fatigue, and memory loss.

Steamed Fish
（清蒸鱼）

Steamed fish is one of the most common home cooked fish dishes in most Cantonese kitchens. People usually steam their fish with ginger, bird-eye chili, and soy sauce.

Since less oil is added, Cantonese style steamed fish is less fattening, relatively easy to cook, and good for your health. This traditional method of preparing fish preserves its natural flavor while also adding other flavors that complement it wonderfully. The key point for all steam fish dishes is that the fish must be fresh. This method of preparation is simple, yet elegant. When you experience this dish, it is wonderful, moist, has a flaky texture with great flavor and you will want to make it again.

Steamed Vermicelli Roll
（肠粉）

Steamed Vermicelli Roll is a type of rice made food. It is now a popular snack in Tea Houses and hotels throughout Guangzhou. There are some famous brand names for Steamed Vermicelli Rolls such as Yinji, Dakeyi, and Huahui. The traditional method is to put the rice slurry on cloth and steam. Steamed Vermicelli Roll is usually eaten at breakfast or as a late night snack food. This food is prepared by taking a filmy skin and spreading on a stuffing such as ground beef, pork, fillet, shrimp, or deep fried bread sticks, etc. Before it is cooked, they can be rolled into strips.

Rice Porridge with Pig's Liver and Kidneys （及第粥）

It is a rice congee stewed with pork balls, sliced pig liver, and chitling. This rice congee is white and bright colored, intermixed with some red color. There are many stories about the source of this snack. Congee with Pig Liver and Kidneys is called "Ji Di Zhou" in Chinese, which means the Number One Scholar in ancient times. Here is one of the stories: It is said that during the Ming Dynasty there was a poor wise man Lun Wen-xu who lived by selling vegetables. The boss of a congee restaurant respected his knowledge, so he sent the wise man a bowl of porridge every day. At last this wise man got the Number One Scholar and became an officer. He could not forget the favor of the boss, so he went back to his hometown to have a bowl of congee again. The boss asked the chef to cook a bowl of congee with pork balls, sliced pig liver, and chitling. After that the congee at this restaurant was named "Ji Di Zhou".

Sliced Cold Chicken with Ginger Dipping Sauces
（白切鸡）

Baiqie Chicken dish is a simple Cantonese chicken prepared without adding any other flavor except boiled water. It tastes fresh and light, and has the best original taste of chicken. When you eat it add ginger and green onion with a sprinkle of cooked peanut oil. Baiqie chicken skin is tasty and refreshing and the chicken meat is not greasy or strongly flavored. Qingping Chicken is also one version of Baiqie chicken. People prefer live poultry bought in the wet markets, frozen chicken doesn't taste good and does not have the texture of sliced boiled chicken.

Dongshan

HIGHLIGHT: Western style buildings were built by oversea Chinese in 1920s.
START POINT: Metro line 1 & 6 Dongshankou station Exit E or Exit F
FINISH POINT: Yuyuan Villa
LENGTH: Approx. 2.5 hours (3.2 km)

Historical Background

The area of Gui Gang Road in Dongshan district and its neighborhood was not only the earliest commercial district developed in Dongshan, but also contain the earliest business's in which overseas Chinese invested in Guangzhou. Speaking of the development of Gui Gang, we might begin with the introduction of western schools to Dongshan.

Canton Baptist Academy, c. 1899-1909

At the beginning of 20th century, westernization became an inevitable trend in China. In 1889, Chinese Christians and some enlightened people established Canton Private School in Binzheng Street, attracting many young students to study there. In 1907, this school was renamed Canton Baptist Academy and relocated to No.2, Peizheng Road. In the same year, Pooi To Academy, founded in the Five Genii City Gate (the number 18, page 46) in 1888 by the Southern Baptist Convention, was moved to the nearby area. These western schools seemed more attractive for students whose relatives were overseas Chinese and subsequently they built houses and lived near the schools. Before the 20th century, Dongshang was merely a wilderness outside the Large East Gate of Guangzhou city, belonging to Siyou County and Shanhe County. There were many hills which were surrounded by paddy fields, vegetable fields, fish ponds and bamboo forests and there were many groves on the hillsides.

Since the Canton Baptist Academy relocated near Yandun hill, some open-minded overseas Chinese started building houses there. In 1909, Zhong Shurong used money provided by his father, an American Chinese, together with people from his hometown and some other American Chinese, to buy the entire land of today's Yandun Road from villagers of Siyou County. Then, in 1911, they divided it into six sections for sale after clearing the land. At the beginning, Zhong built houses in the west and later his nieces, returning from America, built two houses in the east. Following Zhong and his nieces, the Jiang brothers from Honolulu built two houses in the middle area. But these houses were merely built as dwellings, so a busy downtown had not taken shape here yet.

In 1915, Huang Xieshi, an America Chinese originally from Kaiping of Guangdong province, founded a development company named "Da Yip Tong" and bought 12 thousand square kilometers (4,633 square miles) of wasteland from the government. In this place was a hill shaped like a turtle shell, so it was called "Gui Gang" ("Turtle Hill" in English). The company leveled the land first and then divided it into four sections with four roads as boundaries to sell to people from Kaiping. Considering there were prestigious schools around this area, some Kaiping resident expected it would appreciate in the future. Therefore, a clan with the surname Huang purchased all lands and built houses.

Gui Gang Road and its neighborhood began to boom at that time. Some overseas Chinese and their relatives began to open shops here, such as restaurants, cake shops, tea houses, stationery shops, candy stores, and etc. These shops contributed to the prosperity in Dongshan, thus a commercial district appeared in the area of Gui Gang Road. Besides, the development of businesses here also promoted the development of the real estate industry, in which overseas Chinese in Guangzhou invested.

In 1919, some Chinese who returned from overseas founded the Ka Naam Tong Property Company, whose main business was accepting deposits and investing in properties. The company invested and started the realty business in Miao Qian West Road and Gui Gang 5th Road, boosting development in this area. In 1922, Ka Naam Tong and Nanhuo Property Company co-founded Jiahua Savings Bank and then built the New Asia Hotel and the New China Hotel. After that, some returned overseas Chinese also establish a small private bank in Dongshan, thus starting the financial industry in Dongshan. During the financial crisis in western countries from 1929 to 1933, many of overseas Chinese brought capital back to Guangzhou. Because Dongshan was known for its beautiful environment, cheap lands and western-style schools, many of them chose to build houses here. Gradually, a number of houses in a combination of Chinese and Western styles were built on Orphanage Road, Yandun Road, Peizheng Road, Xin He Pu, Qiming Road and etc., forming a special building complex of overseas Chinese houses in Dongshan.

Itinerary

The tour starts at exit E or F of Dongshankou metro station. Walk south on SHUQIAN LU and if you are interested in Southern Chinese fine arts, you can make a stop at **Chen Shuren Memorial Hall** (❶ ; page 125), it is one of the Linnan art masterpieces.

Continue on until the end of SHUQIAN LU. There is a Dongshan department store on your right hand side, which was opened in 1983, it sold all kinds of daily needs.

Dongshan Department Store

Continue on GUIGANG DAMA LU until you reach the canal, turn left and walk east on XINHEPU LU until you reach **Chunyuan Villa** (❷ ; page 125). This is only one of the five villas open to the public. The Communist Party of China once used it as its revolution base. Unfortunately there is no English description inside. Another point of interest is a gramophone on the 3rd floor which was made in 1956.

Continue walking east on XINHEPU LU and you will see many Chinese and Western architectural styles Mansions. Go around the back of PEIZHENG XINHENGLU and you will arrive at **The Museum of the 3rd Communist Party National Congress of China** ❸ which was held on 12th June 1923. Again there is no English description. Across from the museum is **Kuiyuan Villa** (❹ ; page 126), which now is leased for an art gallery. Walking east on PEIZHENG LU you will find two villas that you can only view from outside, **Jianyuan Villa** (❺ ; page 126) and **Mingyuan Villa** (❻ ; page 127). There is a **Pei Zheng Middle School** (❼ ; page 127) located at Peizheng Road. This school has the look of classical Chinese architecture, it was founded in 1889 and has a long history of nearly 129 years.

Continuing on to the T-junction, you will see a red brick building with green glazed roof located in the front left, it's part of the **Guangzhou No.7 Middle School** ❽. This school formerly known as Pooi To Academy, it was founded by Southern Baptist Convention Missionary Emma Young who set up classes for children and women in 1888 and moved to its present location in 1907. It's officially renamed as Guangzhou No.7 Middle School in 1962.

New premises of Pooi To academy in Dongshan, c.1907

Copper sculpture of Dongshan young Master and Sai Kwan Miss

Walk along YANDUN LU and get into TONGBEI JINSHI and you will see **Dongshan Christian Church** (❾ ; page 128) on your left hand side, it is only open on Sunday. Finish your tour at **Yuyuan Villa** (❿ ; page 127).

This part of the Mansions was the place of residence of dignitaries and rich overseas Chinese business people in the last century. They built a group of western style buildings followed by dignitaries and military officials who also came here to build their houses. At that time almost all of the dignitaries and the rich businessmen lived in large houses in Sai Kwan. For a time the growth of 'Dongshan Mansions' changed the landscape from that of the Sai Kwan traditional mansions and the saying became 'Dongshan young Master and Sai Kwan Miss' or 'dignitaries in Dongshan and rich men in Sai Kwan'.

Points of Interest

- No.10 SHUQIAN LU
- 9:00-17:00
- Free admission

Chen Shuren Memorial Hall
(陈树人纪念馆)

Chen Shuren memorial hall was built on the original residence in 1988. Lingnan style painting was founded in late Qing Dynasty. It inherited the art of traditional Chinese painting and combined with western impressionist painting, the background color of the rendering, foil and ink make it appear very attractive. Chen Shuren is one of the three founders. There are two floors of exhibition, the first is used for display of Lingnan paintings and art exhibitions are held occasionally. His painting, calligraphy works and historical materials are displayed on the second floor.

Chunyuan Villa (春园)

Chunyuan Villa is a three tiered red brick building. The offices of the 3rd central authority of the communist party are located in here, including the international representative Marin and the attending representative Chen Duxiu. Li Dazhao, Mao Zedong, and others used to live in Chunyuan Villa where they discussed and modified the communist party of China's party platform, drafting the declaration and the various resolutions, etc.

- No.24 XINHEPU LU
- 09:00-17:30, closed on Monday
- Free admission

Kuiyuan Villa (逵园)

Kuiyuan Villa was built in 1922 by Ma Zhuowen who was Chinese born in America. It has been built for 80 years. This is a three story reinforced concrete house with the red brick walls still intact. The first and second stories have Greek style columns that have been white washed. A prominent painting is built above the arch and the numbers '1922' on the gate, which could be the year the Kuiyuan was built. Today Kuiyuan is a private courtyard and leased for an art gallery on the first floor. The second floor is a coffee shop where Latte is sold at about ¥40, but comfortable surroundings.

There are two straight betel nut trees reaching into the sky in the front of the house. Kuiyuan courtyard are full of flowers and trees, especially Livistona, a wild profusion of vegetation, thus people gradually call 'Kui Yuan'. The story of Kuiyuan is not much but it played a unique and glorious role. The communist party 3rd National Conference site was here because it is located in the suburbs, a remote and sparsely populated area, ideal for secrecy work. People coming from outside to Guangzhou to attend meetings with representatives said it was a difficult area to find. Fortunately opposite to it is Kuiyuan, in a humble old building which was very outstanding. The '1922' on the gate became coordinates the representatives used to accurately identify the position of the 3rd national conference site. The 3rd national conference site was destroyed by bombs during the Anti-Japanese War; the site was relocated again by Kuiyuan Villa.

- No.9 XUNGUYUAN LU
- 10:00-17:00
- Free admission

Jianyuan Villa (简园)

Jianyuan Villa was built by The Nanyang Tobacco Company Jane brothers. It is known for the 3 story architectural layout symmetry and both have a garden. Exterior besmear is brushed with a rice color, Greek style pillars, and geometric figures decorate the eaves. It was the German consulate before.

- No.13 PEIZHENG LU

Mingyuan Villa (明园)

Mingyuan Villa was built in 1920s or 1930s. It consists of two level red house with, Roman style columns, porches, and iron windows. Bamboo forests encircled Mingyuan at that time, people dug out bomb shelters in the bamboo forests which lead to Peizheng Lu during Anti-Japanese War.

📍 No.8~14 PEIZHENG LU

Yuyuan Villa (隅园)

Yuyuan Villa was built in 1932. It consists of two story brick and timberwork structures with red brick and green glazed tiled buildings. The owner and designer is Wu JingYing (1890~1993). He was one of the oversea students sent by the Qing government to learn manufacturing ship technology in United States. He came back to China in 1920 and was appointed to Shanghai Jiangnan shipyard to work by admiralty. Wu JingYing was called back to Guangzhou as a naval ship construction director in 1925 during Kuomintang-Communist cooperation. He participated in distribution of naval mines around Humen (Dongguan City) waters to prevent Japanese troops from landing in Humen during Anti-Japanese War. On the eve of liberation he took direct orders from the communist party to build war ships to liberate Hainan province. He died in 1993 in a Sydney apartment at the age of 103.

📍 No.42 SIBEI TONGJIN

Pei Zheng Middle School (培正中学)

Canton Baptist Academy, renamed Peizheng School in 1912, had a primary school and middle school. Since the school moved to the current location, Principal Huang Qiming went to southeast Asia and America to raise more than 100 thousand yuan for building new buildings and purchasing new education equipment. Since 1918, Cuba Hall, Australia Hall, America Hall, the library, and other new buildings in school were built. Many overseas Chinese enrolled their children to study here. During the Anti-Japanese War, Peizheng School set up a subsidiary school in Macau and joint schools in the Northern area of Guangdong province and Guangxi province. After China won the Anti-Japanese War, Peizheng School moved back to the current address. The new principal Feng Tang raised 100 thousand dollars from overseas Chinese in the United States and invested the money in improving the equipment and building an auditorium in the school. After so many years, the layout of the campus still seems simple but elegant. During the Cultural Revolution, the school changed its name several times but regained its original name in 1984. Peizheng School witnesses a continuous emergence of many distinguished talents. There are 13 academicians among its alumni including American nuclear expert Luo Zhunian, Nobel Prize winner Cui Qi and Xiu Chengtong who won a Fields Medal and a Nobel Prize in Mathematics.

Dongshan Christian Church
(东山基督教堂)

In 1908, the American Southern Baptist Convention purchased a land and built a church at No. 9, present-day Si Bei Tong Jin. In the same year, a Dongshan Baptist church was established. The church was named Dongshan Baptist Church. It was originally built as a temporary shed-structure. Due to the increasing number of followers at that time, it was expanded and converted into an American-style building with concrete structure in 1923. On each side of the church, there was one God School established by the Southern Baptist Church School. The eastern side was a school for women to receive education and to learn about Christianity, later renamed to Pooi To Academy.

In 1938 October, the Japanese invaded Guangzhou. The church was blocked by the Japanese, the church was requisitioned as hospital for injured armies. After the victory of the Anti-Japanese War, Dongshan Church gradually restored its religious activities. In 1946, the Southern Baptist Church handed over the teaching affair to the Dongshan Baptist Church. Since then, church property has been controlled by the governance of Chinese Catholics. In 1960 there was church alliance implemented nationwide, the Dongshan Baptist Church and several other churches merged, and the name was changed to the Christian Dongshan Church. During the Cultural Revolution, the policy of freedom of religious belief was halted, Dongshan Church stopped the gathering activities. On September 30th, 1979, Dongshan Church was restored and became one of the six earliest chapels which resumed worship.

Where to Eat

① Fan Fong Desserts and Snacks Store (芬芳甜品店)

It has been open for more than 20 years. The must taste dessert is sesame paste and glutinous rice balls in syrup.

📍 No.696 Donghua Road East
（东华东路 696 号）

🕒 09:00-21:00

Menus

糖不甩
Glutinous Rice Balls Boiled in Hot Syrup
芒果西米露
Sweet Sago Soup with Mango
杨枝甘露
Chilled Mango Sago Cream with Pomelo
香草绿豆沙
Sweetened Mung Bean Paste with Vanilla
煎饺
Fried Dumpling
粽子
Glutinous Rice Dumpling
芝麻糊
Sesame Paste
双皮奶
Double-layer Milk Custard

Featured Food

Tong Bat Lat (糖不甩)

Tong Bat Lat (Glutinous rice balls coated with crushed peanuts), whose main ingredient is glutinous rice dough, is a dessert from Guangdong and Hong Kong areas. Tong Bat Lat literally means sugar which does not separate from the sticky ball once it is on the ball. The recipe goes like this: Roll the glutinous rice flour into a dough, cut it into pieces, roll them into balls, soak the balls into boiled water and remove them. Dip the balls in syrup then coat with crushed peanuts or sesame. The dessert tastes soft, smooth, sweet, and savory; therefore it is good for all ages.

It is said there is a local custom concerning Tong Bat Lat and marriage in the villages such as Dongkeng, Chashan, and Hengli of Guangzhou. Accompanied by a matchmaker, a man goes to a young lady's home and asks her parents to marry their daughter to him. If the parents agree, they will cook Tong Bat Lat for him. Seeing the rice balls on the table, the man would be very happy to understand that his promise in marriage with the lady will "stick to" him; to show his wish that happiness should double, he would ask for another bowl of Tong Bat Lat. However, if the parents refuse him, they will cook a bowl of syrup with shattered eggs and dried bean curd sticks for him. In this case, the man would know there is no desire for him to marry the lady. Since they are "shattered", the man should stop bothering them and leave immediately. Although the syrup is sweet the man feels bitter, so he would drink a little syrup and hurry to leave her house. Today Tong Bat Lat has become a famous dessert in Guangdong Province and Hong Kong.

Sweetened Mung Bean Paste (绿豆沙)

Guangzhou located in the south area of China where it is very hot. Cantonese have food paying attention to function as heat-clearing and fire-toxin releasing. Mung Bean Paste is an ideal snack having this function, prepared by slow cooking. Herbs are added to the paste and great pains are taken to remove the mung bean peel to create a softer mung bean paste.

Black Sesame Paste (芝麻糊)

Black sesame paste is typically sold hot in winter and cold in summer, containing crushed black sesame seeds in the form of flour. This dish sometimes also contains glutinous rice balls and can also be found in supermarkets as an instant powder where you just have to add hot water. In traditional Chinese medicine, sesame is used to warm the body, replenish blood, relax the bowels, and nourish hair. Although it is said to help with anemia, constipation, dizziness, and tinnitus, some people find that the black color is disagreeable.

African Town

HIGHLIGHT: Home to largest African community
START POINT: Metro line 5 Xiaobei station Exit D
FINISH POINT: Metro line 5 Xiaobei station Exit D
LENGTH: Approx. 30 minutes ~ 60 minutes (0.7 km)

Historical Background

The tunnel leads to the African Community in Guangzhou

Xiaobei is commonly known as "Little Africa" or "African Town". Thousands of Africans do business here every day. A large number of them are from West African countries like Nigeria, Mali, Guinea, Cameroon, Liberia and the Democratic Republic of the Congo. Most have been in Guangzhou for several years. Thousands of Africans purchase goods like clothes or electronics in bulk, put them in containers and ship them to Africa. Many of them live permanently here both legally and illegally. The Chinese call the place "Chocolate City". Some Africans say that staying in China illegally is inevitable because it is impossible to finish the business they came for within a 30-day time frame and they cannot afford a plane ticket home.

In the 1980s and 1990s, people told stories about Chinese heading abroad to make a living overseas, but now, 30 years later, immigrants are flocking into China as well. To many Chinese people the emergence of the African street is a mirror image of the Chinatowns found in other countries. For these African merchants, Guangzhou is seen as a land full of hopeful business prospects.

Baohan Street, located at the center of Guangzhou. Because of its convenient location it is the most popular street for black people in the city. For Africans who have just arrived in Guangzhou, the advantages are the shopping malls, wholesale markets, subway stations and hotels surrounding the area.

Most shops and restaurants have their names displayed in at least two or three languages: Arabic, English and Chinese. This is now a major feature of the locality. The existing African community helps new immigrants settle in and adapt to doing business in this new environment.

The street is calm during the day and not much different from any other street in Guangzhou. It comes alive at 4 pm and the action doesn't end till around 3 am. It serves as a place for a temporary stay for many new immigrants. It's difficult for Africans to get a business visa in China and many run out of time before finding a business opportunity.

As ties between China and Africa grow closer, more Africans are coming to China in search of opportunities. African merchants are drawn to Guangzhou due to its close proximity to factories and other manufacturing facilities. More and more have come into the city, with most working in international trade shipping Chinese-made products to Africa. Languages can be heard from the Middle East, South Asia, South America and Africa. There are even Australian aboriginals. According to different sources, in 2006 there were approximately 20,000 legal residents and 100,000 to 200,000 illegal residents. That number is set to swell in the coming years. However, for China, neither the government nor the general public had yet adjusted themselves to welcome such an influx of the Africans. In order to arrest black people who stay illegally in Guangzhou, the local

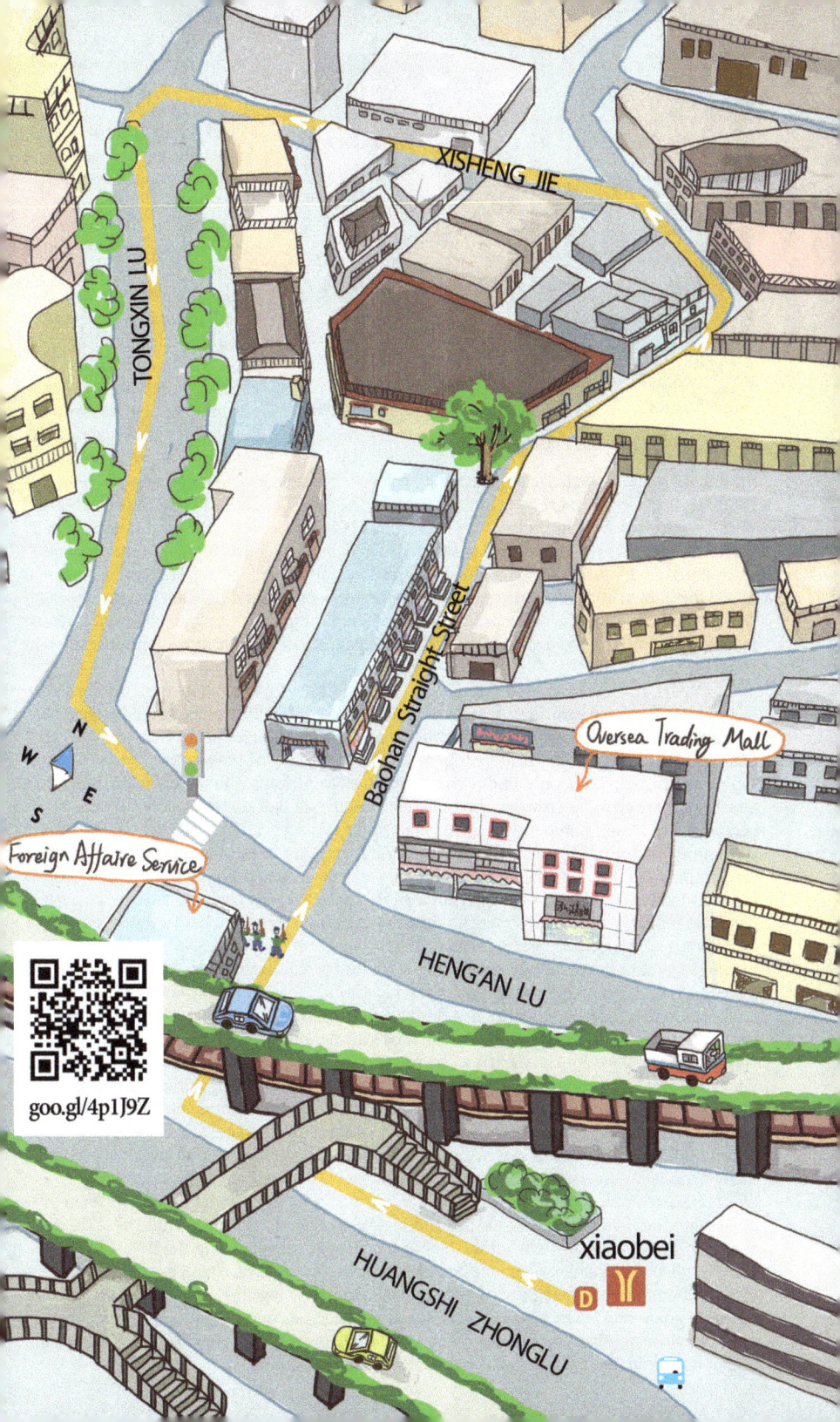

View of Baohan Street in 2014

law enforcement agencies loaded special registration software at more than 2,000 hotels to collect information about Africans. The entire Guangzhou was in the state of emergency on the black Africans.

On July 15, 2009, two Nigerian textile retailers attempted to escape from the visa examination. One of them accidently fell from an 18-meter (60 feet) high-rise building. The two visas were verified to have expired. More than 100 Nigerians protested on the streets of Guangzhou. Subsequently, the government put forward the statement, "regardless of language, nationality, color, we build a harmonious homeland."

In 2010, before Guangzhou held the Asian Games, the visa policy was once again tightened. That year, 40% of African traders left Guangzhou's "Chocolate City," and most of the Africans moved to Huangqi town of Foshan city, which had a slightly looser immigration control policy.

In 2013, China promulgated a new Immigration Control Act. Many African businessmen hoped the infinite cycle of short-term visas applications would be simplified. However, the truth was, the new law made the process of visa renewal more complicated, and foreigners must return to their home countries to apply for renewal. In the past, Africans could also apply for renewal in Hong Kong or Macau.

Most African businessmen in Guangzhou came to China through short-term business visas of 4 to 6 weeks. In the early days, foreigners applying for visas in their home countries were handled by the Beijing office, while the local Africans applied for visa renewal in Guangzhou. Due to differences in procedures and standards between the two places, the probability of failure of applications was high. In 2014, only 30-day visas were issued to Africans who wanted to live in Baohan Street Community. In the management office for foreigners at Baohan Street, only 60 queue numbers were issued, and numbers had to be obtained for visa application. Originally Baohan Street community had several thousand Africans staying temporarily, but the number dropped to a maximum of 1,300 at one time. In January 2015, the management office for foreigners at Baohan Street announced that those who apply for a 30-day visa could not apply for a residence permit, but could only stay in a hotel. To rent a house in China, they must first have a residence permit. That means all Africans in Baohan Street could no longer rent a house. Not all of the Africans made a lot of money from trade. They could not afford to live in the hotel every day. They were forced to leave. With many African traders leaving, Chinese business fell by one-third. Local governments were beginning to realize that this had a direct impact on China-Africa trade and ran counter to the strategic direction of the Central Government.

In 2015, the government started a comprehensive plan to reorganize the communities in Baohan Street. It was proposed to eliminate chaotic construction, disorganized selling stalls, and messy parking and put the district into a clean, safe and orderly environment. After a year of remediation, this street looked fresh. The local government accommodates foreigners who have obtained student and work visas in residential houses here. The procedures were also much simpler. Many African customers went to obtain the student visa to continue to live here.

In a stretch of less than 200 meters of the Baohan Street commercial district, there are two 300-square-meter supermarkets, one fish and meat market, and many open fruit stalls. There are about ten beauty salons run by local Chinese and African inhabitants in the street. The whole street is full of international telephone booths, laundry shops and broadband providers. It is like a village within the city, where people of different ethnicities live together. At an Internet kiosk, you can see a group of African men calling home and speaking in various tongues, while at another stall African man might be bargaining with a fruit stall owner in Chinese. A restaurant serving beef noodles from Northwest China might often be full of Africans.

Fewer foreigners resided in the Baohan Street neighborhood, but Africans, Pakistanis, Nepalese, Indians and Turks come there from all around the region in the evening to eat, meet, shop, trade and talk. There was also the housing with which they were familiar. An important place for them to socialize and exchange information.

Guangzhou has always wanted to create an international cosmopolitan city and continues to spend huge sums of money to build Guangzhou's CBD Zhujiang New Town. They planned to develop the Manhattan of China. However, it was hard to find the faces of Western people in the popular Tianhe Square. This is completely different from that of the CBDs in Paris, London, New York, Tokyo, Singapore and Hong Kong. Instead, the faces of all corners of the country are clearly identifiable. Intuitively, it can be concluded that Guangzhou is now only an urban high-rise. It is still far from internationalization. However, on Baohan Straight Street, one sees the opposite scene. Man Avenue has faces of Africans, Middle Easterners, Indians, and, occasionally, Europeans and Americans. People feel truly international in Guangzhou.

Itinerary

The tour starts at Exit D Line 5 Xiaobei Metro Station. You will see a McDonald's when you ride the elevator up to HUANSHI ZHONGLU. After this walk back and enter the tunnel which leads to the "African Street" in Guangzhou. The street named BAOHAN ZHIJIE is the main area of an urban village in Yuexiu district. On the other side of the tunnel, Africans and Muslims gather in the southernmost area of the Baohan Zhijie. Visit some trading malls along this street, it makes you feel like shopping in another country. Finish your trip at Xiaobei Metro Station.

Tips:

It is recommended to taste the authentic Arabian cuisine in Guangzhou. African cuisine and Xinjiang cuisine in northwestern China can also be found on this street. Most Han Chinese in modern times are businessmen who pursue their interests without any regard for others. But on this street, you do not have to worry too much about food safety. The restaurant's owner and chefs are Muslims, they observe halal food requirements, strict processing of ingredients and cooking oil. Cooking oil must be a particular brand, and to avoid the use of waste oil. The beef and lamb which one could eat there are authentic and without water processing, in Guangzhou. Many Chinese-run and joint venture supermarkets and vegetable markets sell beef and lamb are mostly water-injected.

Shek Pai Urban Village

HIGHLIGHT: Chinese Characteristics Slum
START POINT: Metro line 3 Gangding station Exit C
FINISH POINT: SHIPAI XILU
LENGTH: 1 hour (2 km)

A view over Shek Pai Urban Village, looking southeast

Historical Background

In Guangzhou, Shek Pai Village was one of the most populated urban villages with a long history. From the outskirts to the urban village in the city center, the village has a 20-year urban history in Guangzhou. At the beginning of the Republic, Shek Pai Village covered 14 square kilometers whereas today, its total area has reduced down to less than a one square kilometer. In the 1950s and 1960s, Tianhe District, which was 3 kilometers away from downtown, and was considered the outskirts of town with fields of mud and vegetable farms, in 1989, there were only two bus routes from Tianhe District to the city. After the implementation of the land contract system in 1984, Shek Pai village became the main provider of vegetables and poultry in Guangzhou. At that time, the greatest area of vegetable field in the whole town reached 2300 mu[1] and selling vegetables became the main source of family income for most villagers. In the early 1990s, Shek Pai Village had seized a market opportunity. It signed a cooperation agreement with the computer industry, granting the developers permission to invest in the interior computer center in Shek Pai West. With the vigorous and rapid development of the information technology market, the villagers gained a major increase on their year-end income. By 1996, when government had taken control of almost all of the lands in Shek Pai Village, the villagers constructed concrete and brick houses on top of old foundations on the land they were given in compensation for land taken away. During 1994-1995, with the prosperity of the businesses around Shek Pai Village, an increasing number of outsiders immigrated to this village, which brought along different accents from different places in China. As more and more tenants settled here, many villagers started to add floors onto the foundation of the original house so that they could use the house for more renters. The village became densely filled with houses, leading to the appearance of "Kissing House" and "Hand-shaking House". At that time, the average yearly individual bonus was about 10,000-20,000 Yuan, and the rent also increased up to the total amount of income, approximately 60,000-70,000 Yuan for one person. Since then the number of native villagers who live in Shek Pai Village has been declining. In 1998, Shek Pai Village raised funds for the construction of Anjufang[2] in Zhujiang New Town and the villagers of the new generation have been gradually moving out of the old village.

Shek Pai Village is the largest urban village in Guangzhou. With an area of only one square kilometer, it houses over 100,000 people who come from the rural areas to stay at Shek Pai Village. Urban villages are an unique phenomenon that formed part of China's urbanization efforts.

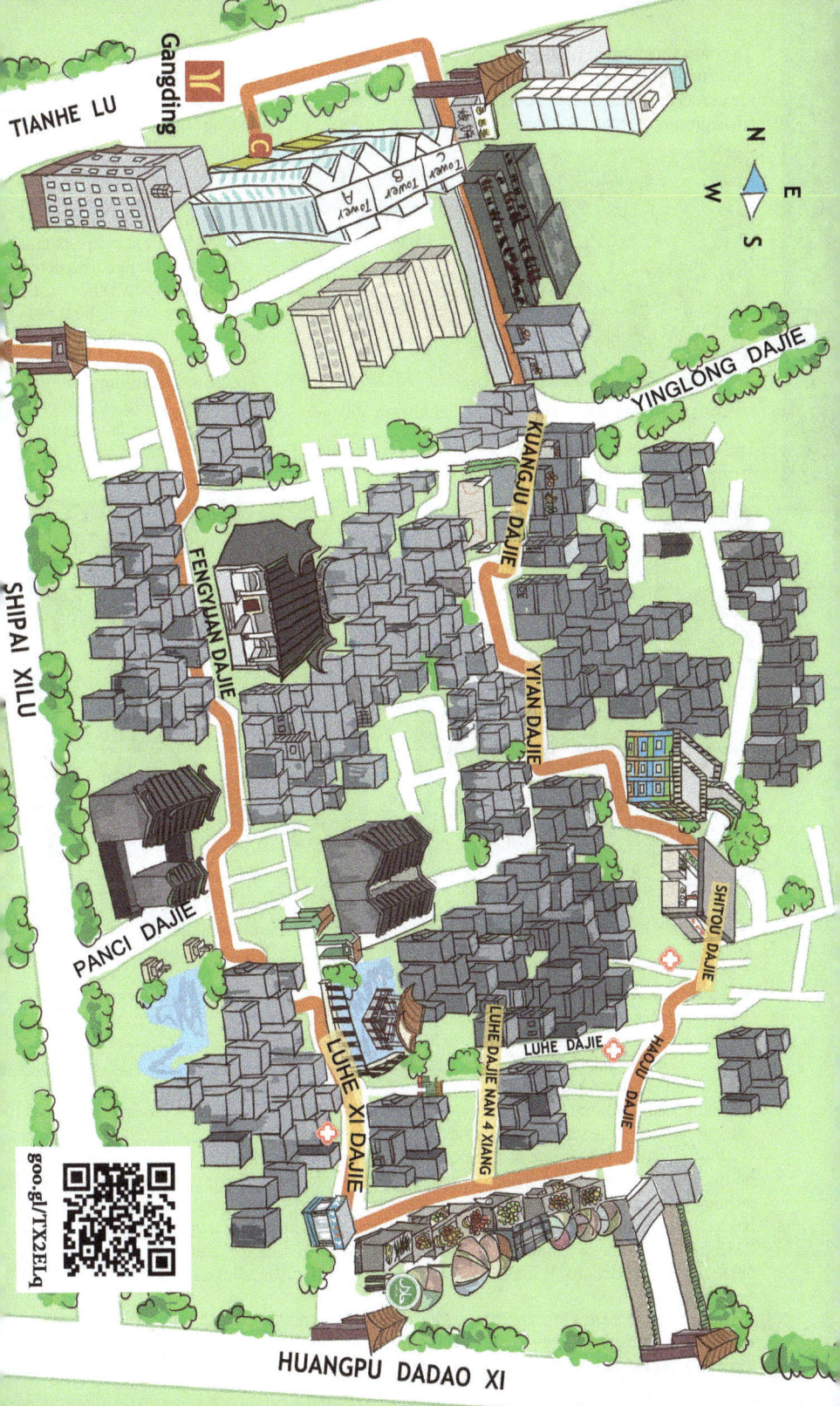

They are surrounded by skyscrapers, transportation infrastructures, and other modern urban constructions. Urban villages are commonly inhabited by the poor and transient and as such they are associated with squalor, overcrowding, and social problems. Thus sometimes you will see small groups of security officers dressed in green uniforms who go out on patrol.

The north entrance arch of Shek Pai Urban Village

Shek Pai Village is also famous for its countless confusing alleys and dense living conditions. Inside the village the surface of main streets and some of the alleys constructed with strips of slate. While exotic people are moving in, local residents are moving out. "One Line Sky" building was formed by two "Kissing Buildings" which were really close to each other in the Urban Village. Its super-high density, a tiny distance of about 50 cm between two facing balconies, caused the special light rhythm in Shek Pai's between-buildings space.

Disorderly wires

Various of Shops

Inside urban villages, a sense of clutter, tolerance, contrast, and multi-culture is felt everywhere, A porter with a pushcart, a cobbler, a little flower seller, erectors, rag pickers, writers, men in business suits, people from all walks of life live here. A variety of services are available, such as restaurants of different kinds, barber shops, massage parlors, make-up studios, and even hospitals. There are diverse people speaking different dialects with different styles of living You will see a vibrant scene with the hustle and bustle of daily life. Thousands of workers from other small cities or remote villages live here because the lower rents.

Playing mah-jongg is one of the most popular activities for villagers. Villagers rebuild their houses and rent them to outsiders who can only pay low rent, most of them are information technology employees and new graduates. The rental services have developed so rapidly that it has become the main source of villagers' income. The rental income of a villager is around 5,000 RMB per month for each building. Urban villages provide dwelling places for outside people to pursue their own dreams. Within the noisy and disorderly surroundings, dreams and ambitions never rest.

Urban villages are a form of slum with Chinese characteristics. If you want to see the developed side while catching sight of the wild and imaginary corner, your best choice is to take a walk through Shek Pai urban village.

Itinerary

Start from Exit C Gangding metro station, follow the route and finish your walks at Shipai Xilu.

- [1] A Chinese unit of area; 1 acre is approximately equal to 6.07 mu, and 1 mu is approximately equal to 667 m².
- [2] A kind of economical house in China, supported by the government and other concerning governmental organization.

Shiweitang Railway Station

HIGHLIGHT: The oldest railway station in Guangzhou
START POINT: Metro line 1 Fangcun station Exit C
FINISH POINT: SHIWEITANGT XIJIE
LENGTH: Approx. 2.5 hours (2.9 km)

Historical Background

Shiweitang Railway Station is one of the oldest railway stations in Guangzhou. It was the Guangzhou terminal of the Canton-Sam Shui Railway. Total length was 48.9 km. Sam Shui is located in 50 km west of Guangzhou.

Sam Shui is not the main railway in Guangzhou, but it was the first. It was built in September 1903 by American China Development Company. Initially it was only for passenger transport. The most prosperous period of this railway was in 1960s and 1970s, when a train ticket from Guangzhou to Foshan was ¥0.2 yuan. There was no bridge connected to the city center at that

Opening day on the Fatshan section of the Canton - Sam Shui Railway in 1903. A number of flat cars were converted temporarily to serve as passenger coaches until proper rolling stock could be acquired.

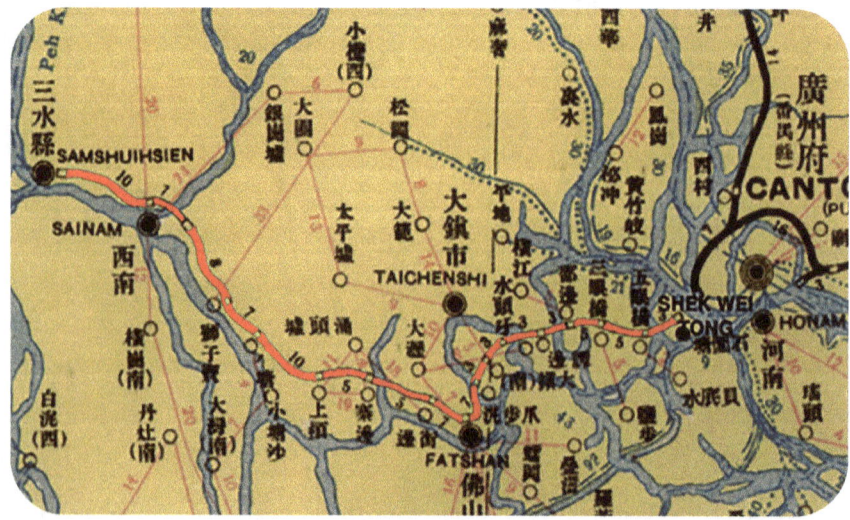

Map showing the route of the Canton to Sam Shui railway

time and passengers had to take a ferry to cross the Pearl River between Huangsha Dock and Shiweitang Dock. Passenger traffic at the Shiweitang Railway Station was more than half of that of the total traffic on all of Guangdong railways. It was the transport hub to the west and north of Guangdong. Daily passengers averaged more than ten thousand. With the rapid development of the highway between Guangzhou and Foshan, the railway became less important. The Shiweitang Railway stopped carrying passengers in 1992; before it stopped a train ticket to Sam Shui cost ¥1 yuan. Now this railway station is only used by Guangdong Sanmao Co., Ltd to transport goods to Guangzhou from all over the Pearl River delta. The goods are mainly are raw materials, including coal, coke and steel products for Guangzhou Zhujiang Steel Co. Ltd.

> **Travels From The Grandeurs of The West to Mysteries of The East, 1909, p. 274, CHARLTON B. PERKINGS**
>
> Fatshan-Samsui Line, leading from Shek Wai Tong to Samsui, a distance of 30 miles through the Canton delta. Trains every hour, return fare, $1.85. This section is the portion built by the world-famous "American Development Company," of New York City, J. P. Morgan, its backer, who sold out to the Chinese merchants of South China for seven and one half million dollars, and which will ever be remembered as a black page in the American commercial under takings in the Far East.

Itinerary

The tour begins at Exit C of Fangcun metro station. After exiting walk northwest on FANGCUN DADAO ZHONG and then you will pass **Zuiguan Park** (❶ ; page 141). Cross the bridge and turn right to get into SHANCUNTIE SANXIANG (SHANLAN SHANGJIE). This small alley will surprise you with black tiles, low walls and lush old trees. Originally it was the living quarters for station staff. Walk through the railway station until you see doorplate number 24, then turn right get into SHIWEITANG DONGJIE.

At the end you'll see six traditional Chinese Characters in red on a white wall. They mean "Welcome to Shiweitang". Diagonally on your right is Shiweitang Ferry Pier Wharf, you can come here by aquatic bus as well from Huangsha Dock.

Shiweitang Railway Station

You'll see 5 Chinese characters on a golden wall on you left hand side. This is the **Shiweitang Railway Station** ❷ . You can try to ask for permission to visit. After entering the station you will see on your right hand side an awning and baggage storage area 80 meters long with a yellow-colored wall and small orange-red window-shades. This is like many other administrative buildings built during the Soviet times.

After getting off the train people walked under the awning to the pier and took ferry crossing the river to Nan Fang Building. If you look further from the gate when entering, you can see several steel bars over the wall. To continue go back to the gate and walk round to SHIWEITANG BEIJIE to have a look at the old platform and railways. You will also see a group of old buildings down the road.

Make a U-turn before police station. Sometimes you can see piles of industrial salt waiting to be unloaded. At times temporary dock workers move the bags of salt from the railway carriages to trucks. There's a salt mine in Sam Shui. The dock workers could get ¥ 3 Yuan by moving a ton of salt, working more than 10 hours a day for a monthly income averaging ¥ 3000 Yuan. You could see mostly two types of people here: dock workers and shutterbugs.

Keep walking until you see a rail signal light beside the railway and a small path and then go along it. Then you can see a railway platform over one hundred years old. Walk along the railway line and you will see a blue locomotive which uses a 8240ZJ diesel engine as its power plant. It's for the railway shunting operation and has a maximum speed of 80km/h.

Finish your trip at Shiweitang Xijie. This is the oldest railway station and its surroundings will be torn down in 2017 to make way for high-rise buildings. If you would like to see the old parts of Guangzhou, don't miss it when you are here.

Points of Interest

Zuiguan Park (醉观公园)

Originally this was Zuiguan Garden, one of the eight gardens where it was possible to buy and appreciate the flowers and trees in the late Qing Dynasty. These gardens were destroyed during the Japanese war in 1938. After the war, it was neglected and became overgrown and now the botanical garden is not as beautiful as before. In 1984, it was rebuilt as a complex for entertainment and relaxation. The whole park is divided into four parts: Tree Garden, Flower Garden, Bonsai Garden and Amusement. There are six corridors and six pavilions, three man-made lakes and pools and more than a hundred kinds of trees and flowers.

Tairy Land was formerly located at Shang Shi Xin Long Sha Dong in Hua Di Street. It was relocated to Zuiguan Park following reconstruction work in 2002. It was initially constructed by the grandfather of Kang Youwei during the reign of the Emperor Daoguang during the Qing Dynasty. It is laid out in a triple structure, constructed by use of black bricks. It faces southwards and is composed of a main hall, small houses, a small garden, a pavilion, platform and artificial hill, etc. Unfortunately most of them have been destroyed. Kang Youwei once studied in here when he was a little boy, during the reign of the emperor Tongzhi during the Qing Dynasty.

- No.4 DONGJIAO BEILU
- Line 2, Exit D Fangcun metro station
- Free Admission
- 06:00~winter 17:00 / summer 19:00

Julong Ancient Village

HIGHLIGHT: The best preserved local style dwelling architectural complex in the late Qing dynasty
START POINT: Metro line 1 Fangcun station Exit B1 or Exit B2
FINISH POINT: Metro line 1 Huadiwan station Exit B
LENGTH: Approx. 4 hours (4.8 km)

Historical Background

The story begins in Taishan, a city that is over 100 kilometers away from Guangzhou. In the late Qing Dynasty, a clan from the Kuang family in Taishan fled abroad to make a living because of the discrimination they faced from within the clan. Later, this clan returned home with the fortune they earned overseas and searched for an area of land with a convenient geographical location and a business friendly atmosphere in the suburban area of Guangzhou.

In 1879, three elderly brothers from the Kuang clan (Kuang Jinghe, Kuang Jinggeng, and Kuang Jingji) purchased 200 Mu (a unit of area equal to 0.6667 hectare) of land in the Da Chong Kou (namely, a large stretch of land near a river). 100 Mu of land was used for building houses and the other 100 Mu for farm land. The time of establishing the Julong Village saw the impact and change imposed on Chinese traditional architectural style by the Western world. Combined with the fact that the owners of Dragon Den Village were a group of Chinese expatriates, this historical background inspired them to infuse Western architectural elements, such as multi-story structure, cathedral-like roof tops, etc., into the basics of Sai Kwan Ancient Mansion, creating a distinctive architectural feature. Some experts consider this feature as "the primitive way of developing real estate". The Kuangs hired specialists to plan and measure the area so that each of the 20 houses built faced south and occupied approximately 230 square meters. The next step was researching business plans and hiring construction workers who were responsible for building 3-meter tall buildings. Two porter lodges (where chime masters perform their duty) were situated in the eastern and western sides which were at least 20 meters in height. Apart from that, granite was laid on streets and alleys, trees planted along the roads, with stone chairs and tables being set up over the same time period. By 1889, twenty mansions with similar layouts were completed using black bricks as construction materials.

After being built, the mansions were then open to subscription by members of the Kuang clan, with houses in the first row each priced at 3,000 silver coin. For those in the two rows in the middle, the price was 2,500 silver coin per house and those in the back row, 2,800 silver coin each. To avoid disputes, the allocation of houses was determined by drawing lots after negotiation. The remaining arable land served as public farmland for the villagers. Tenants were invited to work on the field and the income earned was shared amongst the clan members.

At that time, each village would have one or more ancestral hall, but there was no ancestral hall in Julong Village. Collective donation was adopted when the clan members were planning to build the temple, as a large sum of money was needed to do so. The wealthiest man in the village, Kuang Mingjue, stated that he was willing to sponsor half of the money needed, but the inscribed board must be named after his father. Other clan members were against this proposal and believed that it should be named after their shared ancestor, so "The Ancestral Hall would be inscribed as Kuang Clan". The contention was long lasting and for this reason, the construction of the temple was delayed. After that warfare disturbed the village and the proposed ancestral hall was never built.

In 1937, the Anti-Japanese War was fought and before long, Guangzhou fell into enemy hands. Shops along the banks, which were near the entrance of the Julong Village, were burned down and travel by water was blocked. The Kuang clan fled to either Hong Kong or across the ocean to the United States, leaving their empty mansions behind.

Itinerary

Start from Exit B1 or B2 Fangcun metro station, walk to the main road and turn left. There is a **Sweet Garden Dessert Store** (①; page 146) in faint gold characters, that serves a traditional Cantonese dessert and snacks. Opposite the store is a blue archway, inside there is Guangzhou's folksiest beef offal street vendor owned by an old lady. Fill your stomach then keep walking down to the embankment of Pearl River where you will see Fangcun Dock and an abandoned Baie-Tan Bar Street. The architecture of these bars were built and decorated to imitate the European architecture style with belfry and windmill, area is quiet in the daytime. There is another route if you want to experience a ferry ride in Guangzhou. Take exit F in Huansha metro station and walk to Huangsha Dock, take a ferry across to Fangcun Dock, ¥1 per person).

From Fangcun metro station, walk toward northeast on LUJU LU, turn right and walk along the fading bar street on the way through Fangcun Dock. Walk ten minutes and you will see a very eye catching red brick building with a tile roof, which known as **Lutheran Hall** ①. Look carefully, not too far from here is a German Church, now in disrepair. At that time the church belief was Christian which is a branch of the Lutheran Church. In order to inherit the history, investors identified here called the Lutheran Church, Hall XinYi International Club. It was originally the workshop of Guangdong water conservancy hydroelectric power station. Nowadays rebuilt as a culture, business and exhibition place by several architectural backgrounds of the estate businessmen. It is also a popular location for wedding photographs besides Shamian Island. Continue walking southwest on BOCHANG HOUJIE, you will see the tree roots naturally growing on the tiled walls. Turn left at FANGCUN DADAO ZHONG, you will see **1850 Creative Park** ② beside the main road, it was originally an oxide factory, covers an area of 50,000 square meters and consist of 76 well proportioned buildings. By the use of reforming the old workshops, they create works of art, design exhibitions, and cultural exchange.

Continue walking towards and south on XINLIAN LU. This is a small alley full of local people sitting on the granite stones, chatting with each other under green trees that provide shade. Turn right to the main road and walk south on FANGCUN DADAO ZHONG until reach an arch with large white characters with the numbers 922 stand up among the flowers. Turn left and there is an ancient **Yuling Bridge** (③; page 145) which was built in middle of Qing Dynasty, at least 180 years old. The bridge was built with rocky construction materials, locals call it Qingyou granite. In the past this bridge was an important route and the main gateway of Fangcun, connecting the north and south Fangcun areas.

You will also see the former **Xietonghe Machinery Factory** (④; page 145). Take a walk along the creek and return to the main road. Across the road visit the **Julong Village** (⑤; page 145). Julong Village has the western style layout with grid like streets. Every family built their own house upon their lands with unified planning with the whole village arranged in three rows. The first row is a low level with front courtyard; the third row has two stories with a balcony. Note the bamboo shape drain pipes.

Curly Grass Pattern

There are black and white patterns on the interior and outer decoration of the eaves, that are called Curly Grass Pattern (卷草纹). It has aquatic weeds but look like a dragon and it reflects the water culture in Southern China. Finish your trip at exit B Huadiwan metro station line 1.

Tips:

On the day of the Dragon Boat Festival, there are dragon boat race activities on the creek which attracts many visitors.

Points of Interest

Yu Ling Bridge (毓灵桥)

This ancient bridge is located at the mouth of a branch of the Pearl River in Fangcun District is this ancient beam type bridge. Some say this bridge was erected in the Ming Dynasty, others believe in the Dao Guang Emperor period of Qing Dynasty. The bridge was named Yu Ling (which means a host of talented people), for the local region where many important dignitaries would meet.

Former Xietonghe Machinery Factory (协同和机械厂)

Xietonghe Machinery Factory was founded in 1912, formerly known as a rice milling factory in 1911. A partnership was formed with Mr. Ho and the factory specialized in the production of diesel engines. In 1915 the factory succeeded in producing a 44.3kw 4 cylinder two stroke hot bulb engine to become the first diesel engine in China. In 1918 a reversible two stroke diesel engine was manufactured and installed on a ship sailing on the Pearl River. In 1930 a branch was established in Hong Kong. Until 1937, the production of various specifications for diesel engine totaled 383 pieces and exported to Southeast Asia, Canada, and other areas. In 1956, 9 small sized machinery factories merged and in 1966, renamed to Guangzhou diesel engine factory and moved nearby. Now this former site has become the Machinery Factory Museum.

Julong Village (聚龙古村)

Julong Village is built near a creek. Currently there are 19 well-preserved two story mansions made of blue bricks and tiles. In 1879, during the 5 years of Guang Xu Emperor Reign during the Qing Dynasty, three brothers with the surname Kuang, from Guangdong's Taishan City, came to Guangzhou's wetlands to build houses. At that time a total of 20 families moved from Taishan to live in this village. This village was also named as 'Dragon Luck Village', because red water was exposed during excavation of the area. The workers nicknamed this water 'Blood of Dragon' and the village was eventually renamed Julong, which means 'Dragon Gathering'. The village has been the hometown of many distinguished people, such as the business tycoon Kuang Wuchen in the late period of the Qing Dynasty and Kuang Hengshi, a tycoon of gold supplies. Some old architectural features around town worth taking a closer look at are the communal well the various woodcarvings, murals, and the Manchurian style stained glass windows are well worth photographing. Once you enter this village the hustle and bustle of the city will instantly disappear.

Where to Eat

① Sweet Garden Dessert Store (甜园甜品店)

People who live around Fangcun area often eat desserts at this small shop. The small shop only has 7 small tables so sometimes you need to eat with strangers at the same table. Prices are cheaper than downtown and they mainly serve local desserts with a few snacks. There are a variety desserts on the menu but I only recommend some typical desserts to you. How many servings you should be eating? Order one of the sweet desserts listed for each person in addition to one of the snacks. Scrambled egg white with milk and egg yolk is recommended.

Menus

Sweet Desserts:

双皮奶	Double-skin Milk
姜撞奶	Ginger Milk Pudding
炒蛋奶	Scrambled Egg with Milk
绿豆沙	Sweet Mung Bean Puree
红豆沙	Sweet Red Bean Puree
芝麻糊	Sesame Paste
椰汁香芋西米露	Sweet Sago Syrup with Taro and Coconut Juice
杏仁炒奶糊	Scrambled Egg White with Milk and Almond
风栗炒蛋奶	Scrambled Egg with Milk and Wind Chestnut
凤凰炒奶糊	Scrambled Egg White with Milk and Egg Yolk
椰汁西米露	Sweet Sago Syrup with Coconut Juice

Snacks:

黄金糕	Pan-Fried Sponge Cakes
鱼蛋	Curry Fish Balls
鸡翅	Braised Chicken Wings
番薯饼	Pan-fried Sweet Potato Cakes
玉米饼	Pan-fried Corn Cakes
煎饺	Slightly Fried Dumplings with Pork

📍 No.38 Luju Road (陆居路38号)　　🕗 8am-1am

Tips:

How to eat Scrambled Egg White with Milk and Egg Yolk?

The egg yolk is complete sink in the bottom of the bowl, use spoon mix it with the milk and stir well, it looks like the phoenix graphic, hence it also called scrambled egg white with milk and phoenix.

② Ching Sum Chicken and Sha Tin Roast Pigeon Restaurant
(广州清心鸡沙田乳鸽店)

This restaurant serves Cantonese cuisine primarily with open air tables along the street. The roast squab is a must try, the skin is crispy and the meat is tasty. They charge 3 RMB each person for the tea and water.

Menus

红烧乳鸽	Roast Squab
土猪大包	Steamed BBQ Pork Bun
凉拌鱼皮	Cold and Dressed with Sauce Crispy Fish Skin with Peanuts
荷叶蒸田鸡	Steamed Frog on Lotus leaf

📍 No.20 Huadi Avenue North (花地大道北20号)
🕐 11:00-23:45

Huangpu

HIGHLIGHT: The first Seaport for European traders in Ancient China
START POINT: Bus No.229 Shiji Bus Terminal
FINISH POINT: Northern Entrance Memorial Archway
LENGTH: Approx. 4 hours (2.7 km)

Historical Background

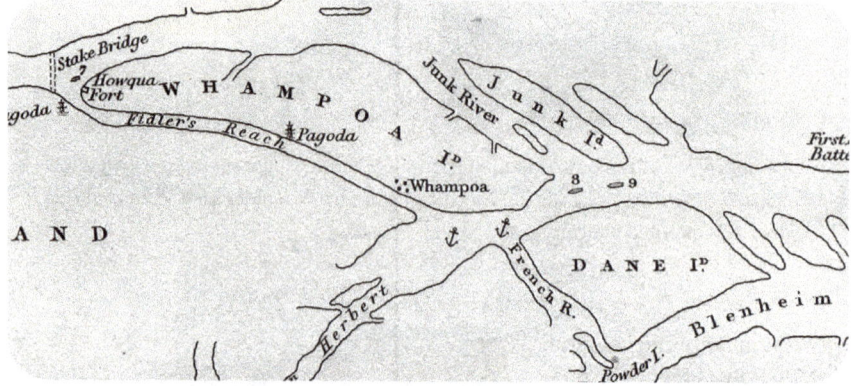

Map of Whampoa Island and Dane Island, 1841

Huangpu, formerly known as Whampoa. It's located in Pazhou in present day, an island known historically as Whampoa Island. Whampoa anchorage is 10 miles beyond Bocca Tigris and 10–16 miles from Canton. Here the merchants hired a Chinese agent, or comprador, to manage the needs of the ship and crew, and paid the customary taxes and bribes. Western sailing ships could not go beyond this area because the water was too shallow, so sampans and other small craft ferried goods to Canton, 10 to 16 miles farther up the river. At the height of the seasons in 1820s and 1830s, there were as many as 100 sailing vessels laying at Whampoa anchorage for three months or more, awaiting their cargoes of tea. This area became one of the primary scenes of inspiration for artist. Artists often combined the most prominent features of the Whampoa anchorage, such as the nine-story pagoda (present Pazhou Pagoda), the junks, sampans, and Dane's Island (present Changzhou Island).

View into Whampoa Island & Whampoa Pagoda.
A view from Danes Island in 1850

Itinerary

Take exit B of metro line 4 Wangshengwei Station. Transfer bus 229 to the last stop, Shiji bus terminal (石基总站). When you get off the bus the first thing you see is a local market on both side of Shiji Lu. That sells fresh farm products that are grown by the local people. If you walk straight ahead you would see the **Museum of Ancient Whampoa Sea Port** (**1**; page 152). Whampoa Ancient Seaport was the first port of call for many $17^{th}/18^{th}$ century European traders. Today you can visit the first customs house built in China which has exhibits in both Chinese and English. The seaport also has a small renovated village

Monument of Ancient Huangpu Seaport

close-by. Wander up and down the alleyways of these older villages where you can grab a local snack, such as the **Ginger Milk Dessert Store** (**2**; Page 156), and **Mau Kee Congee Store** (**1**, Page 155), famous for its traditional sampan congee. You must try the Ginger Milk Pudding where the merchant blows the aroma at you as you walk by the store.

Walk towards the north across a small bridge over the river to reach the **Memorial Gateway of Fengpu** **2**. You can see two Chinese characters in red color "鳳浦" (Fung Pou) on the memorial gateway; Whampoa Village was originally called Fung Pou. Since the Song Dynasty (960~1279), Fung Pou Village has played an important role in trading with foreign countries. During the time of South Song (1127~1279), it had become "A place where ships converge". In the later Ming and Qing Dynasties, Fung Pou Village gradually developed into a harbor for foreign trade. Due to foreigner's mis-pronunciation, the name has changed from the local pronunciation of Fung Pou; as time passed, Fung Pou Village became known as Whampoa Village.

Due to the increased deposition over the years after the opium war, adverse to vessel berthed, this seaport eventually became obsolete. During emperor Tongzhi reign of Qing Dynasty (1862~1874), the seaport moved to Changzhou Island but still used "Whampoa" as the name of new seaport.

Walking towards Whampoa Park you will arrive at **the Culture and History Museum Of Ancient Huangpu Village** **3**, take a visit and learn about its culture and history.

Oyster shell wall

As you approach **4**, there's an oyster shell wall between two traditional dwelling houses. With hundreds of years of history, construction by poor fishermen who couldn't afford to buy traditional materials to build their houses. Whampoa village ancestors used local materials such as a large number of oyster shells from Sandbar to build with. This style of house was built with oyster shells and yellow mud, keeping the inside warm in the winter and cool in the summer, no hydrops and prevents from damaged by insects. Oyster shell houses were very suitable for the climate of the Guangdong area. The wall thickness is around 60~100 centimeters and tens of thousands oyster shells were used to build one house. Villagers built over a hundred Oyster shell houses in the past, most of them have been destroyed. It's an art of the Pearl River delta region people's labor.

Keep walking to **Hu's Ancestral Hall** (**5**; page 153), it was built in Qing Dynasty. There are two stone flagpoles in front of the Ancestral Hall that are believed to be ancient scholars, "certificate of honor" during Ming and Qing Dynasties. It was engraved with who, when, and what kind of officer on the stone, so that the clan could show off their glory and educated to their descendants. From a cultural point of view the stone was made to illustrate

Stone Flagpoles and Stone Drums in front of Hu's Ancestral Hall

how distinguished one's ancestors once was, this has become the ancient imperial cultural monument, the amount of prominence can be seen in a local cultural civilized level. The more stone flagpoles, the more talents and outstanding achievements. On both sides of the entrance stand a pair of stone drums, which is only allowed to build when someone in the family received scholarly honors by special authorization from the emperor. The ancient building had a strict hierarchy in decorations because they reflect feudal hierarchical distinctions. In the middle of the Ancestral Hall is a gathering Hall once a place for meeting and discussing event. The Back Hall is a worship place for their ancestors; The Back Hall in **Feng's Ancestral Hall** (6 ; open every day from 9 am to 4 pm) is more magnificent, Feng is the dominant family name of Whampoa village. Every clan set up an ancestral temple where their ancestors were enshrined and worshipped. Door Gods are painted on the gate, which is a Chinese decoration placed on each side of an entrance of temple, home, etc, believed to keep evil spirits from entering.

Back Hall in Feng's Ancestral Hall

Diagonally opposite of Feng's Ancestral Hall you can stop to enjoy a moment of the **Traditional Art Studio** 7 , which is set up in the ancestral hall, the owner has a large collection of basic household items in the period of Canton System. He will happily show you around once you enter into the ancestral hall.

Walking towards Whampoa primary school, you will enter SHENMING St which one of the oldest parts of Whampoa Village, the main focus here are the various ancient ancestral halls and buildings. Take a look at one of the local celebrity's family temples, **Ancestral Hall of Huangting Liang's Family** (8 ; page 154)

Continue walking to SHASHI St., Further along on DUNYONG JIE, you can see a **Building of Overseas Chinese from Japan** (9 ; page 153), diagonally opposite is **Spinster's House** (10 ; page 153). Neither building is open to the public but one can still see and appreciate the exterior architecture.

Lastly visit the **Pak Tai Temple** 11 , this temple is the same as Renwei Temple (page 51), which is dedicated to water god. Almost each village in south China has its own temple for the worship of Water God. Finish your trip at the north memorial archway of Whampoa Village. You can take a double-decker sightseeing bus No.1 back to the city center.

The return bus is between the Pearl River Swimming Pool (珠江泳场) and Huangpu Village (黄埔村), and departs every half hour from 7:00 to 21:00, fare is RMB 3. During pub-

Traditional Art Studio

Pak Tai Temple

lic holidays, you can expect long queues to guarantee a seat on the upper level, so try to avoid coming here on weekends or public holidays.

Regretfully most of the buildings are not open to the public, only Museum of Ancient Huangpu Seaport, Hu's Ancestral Hall, Feng's Ancestral Hall and, Private Resident Garden. In general, residents haven't developed much of a tourist trade so the village has a mellow, quiet feel.

Connecting The Bike Tour

If you haven't fulfilled your sightseeing desires, turn right at the memorial archway and walk a few minutes further to a bus stop. Take bus No. 262 to Xinzhou Dock (新洲码头), then take ferry to Shenjing Dock (深井码头) to begin a bike tour on **Changzhou Island** (page 172).

Points of Interest

Museum of Ancient Huangpu Seaport (黄埔古港博物馆)

Construction of the village started in the 22nd year of the reign of Emperor Qianlong of the Qing Dynasty and used to have the only Customs House in China at that time. The Yue (Guangdong) Customs House was set up as a registration office and a tariff section in Huangpu Village. In the 22nd year of Qianlong's Reign (1757) in Qing Dynasty, the royal court cancelled the other three Customs houses, kept only Yue, and appointed Guangzhou as the only port for foreign trade. According to records of "The History of Huangpu Port", during the 80 years from the 23rd year of Qianlong to the 17th year of Daoguang (1837), 5,107 foreign ships were anchored at Huangpu Port, making it the only anchoring place for the foreign business ships. The Swedish business ship "Gotheborg" visited the port three times over a period of 10 years, laying a firm foundation for the Sino-Sweden trade links. The port now consists of a commemorative exhibition area, the park of the ancient port, ancient docks and plank roadways. The commemorative exhibition is comprised of the Huangpu Tax Office, Yongjing Military Barracks, Comprador Office, and Foreign Affairs Office, with the Huangpu Tax Office being the center of the building complex, featuring a historic architectural style with green bricks and grey tiles. The ancient port park serves as a supporting park for the commemorative exhibition area while the Gotheborg commemorative sculpture is the biggest tourist attraction in the park.

- Huangpu Village Station, Bus No. 137 , 229 and 262 stop at Shiji bus terminal
- Xingang Dong Road
- 9:00-17:00
- Free Admission

Spinster's House (姑婆屋)

The Gu Po house also known as spinster's house which is built in the Qing Dynasty, it was inhabited by girls never get married in their life. There were many separate rooms in the house, which was the particular construction style of the Qing Dynasty. In feudal society, some girls were not willing to be constrained to feudal ethics, so they live by themselves and never married, they were called 'Zishu Girl' or 'Gu Po' in Chinese.

Zishu Girls were not allowed to die in their parents or relative house. The body could not be buried next to their parents but next to a sister who lived in the Gu Po House. If there is no Zishu sister, the body would be thrown into the river by villagers. Thus, Zishu Girls saved their money and lived together to buy a Gu Po House in order to take care of each other. Zishu Girl is a type of women culture in ancient Pearl River Delta since late Ming and early Qing dynasties.

📍 No.1 LIUTANG DAJIE

Building of Overseas Chinese from Japan (旅日华侨楼)

It was also called 'Japan Building'. In 1900, there was a Whampoa villager named Feng Zuobing who studied in Japan and married a Japanese woman named Ping Mei Ai Zi, She was Japanese Emperor Hirohito's niece, Emperor Hirohito gave a Japanese sword as wedding gift to them when married. They came back to village in 1924 and to comfort his wife's homesickness for Japan, Feng Zuobing built this Japanese style building in 1925. During the Anti-Japanese War, she saved the Whampoa village by showing her Japanese saber when Japanese aggressors came to destroy the village. The nearby villagers heard the news and came into Huagpu Village to take refuge. During the Japanese aggression period, Whampoa Village was a rare village which was not destroyed by the Japanese troops.

📍 Opposite side of No.9 DUNYONG JIE

Ancestral Hall of Hu's Family (胡氏大宗祠)

Ancestral Hall of Hu's family is the pioneer ancestral hall of the Surname Hu which moved in. The ancestry of Surname Hu is from Fujian, with ancestors moved from Shaoguan to Guangzhou Haopan Street during the period of Southern Song Dynasty, later moved to Whampoa Village. The character whom the villagers took pride of was Hu Xuanze with the Surname Hu. He was the re-

Hanging Plaque Awarded by the Emperor

nowned overseas Chinese leader from Singapore in the late 19th century, the first Chinese foreign consul, and also the first diplomat who held consul post of three countries in the history of international diplomacy. He has been bestowed by Australia as baron, was granted by the British of CMG and the other Orion Belt's titles. Due to his outstanding contribution, he was known as "Mr. Whampoa." Now the Hu family reconstructed "An Edict by Emperor as Singapore Consul Hu Xuan Ze" plaque hanging on the lintel of the ancestral hall. In 1830, the 15 year-old Hu Xuanze went to Singapore from Whampoa Village and studied business with his father. The company he runs is named Whampoa Company.

There are now Whampoa River, Whampoa Road, Whampoa School and so on in Singapore, to commemorate him. Hu Xuanze has run plantations, founded the ice plant, and later served as a member of the Legislative Council. He was passionate about charity, benefiting the Chinese community, donating and repairing the Fuk Tak Chi Temple on the Telok Ayer Street - where overseas Chinese came ashore in Singapore - and also founded Panyu Hall in Singapore. He with the identity of leader of overseas Chinese, mediated dispute and promoted unity. Together with other leaders of the Chinese community, he also advocated the implementation of Chinese syllabus in Singapore's school education and personally couched the teaching. In 1877, Hu Xuanze was appointed by the Qing court as a consul in Singapore and became first Chinese who took consular's post. Before and after that, he was also appointed as a consul in Singapore by Russia and Japan and was a consul of the three countries. After his death in 1880 due to ill, his remains were transported back to his hometown by steam boat and buried on Danes Island across from Whampoa Island, which is today's Changzhou Island.

No.8 BU XIANG LI

Ancestral Hall of Huangting Liang's Family (晃亭梁公祠)

Huangting is the courtesy name of Liang Guochi, he is the fourteenth generation of Liang's family in Whampoa, who used to work as a shop assistant in Tian Bao Factory of Thirteen Hongs of Canton. He is kindhearted and enjoys helping others. Under the influence of the foreign trade, Liang Guochi decided to go abroad to break through. After Liang Guochi left home and went abroad, the epidemic began to prevail in the country. In the absence of drug cure, smallpox like a scourge of flood attacked the lives of Chinese people, countless lives were lost.

Liang Guochi spent millions to buy a lot of western vaccination, the methods to cure smallpox, and learned about it. After returning home, he had that as his business and could settled his family, to get rich as well. Ancestral Hall of

No.6 RONG XI LI

Huangting Liang's family was built after he became rich. In the rear hall, there are two pictures of Liang Cheng, a great-grandson of Huangting and a patriotic diplomat. In 1875, Liang Cheng who was just 12 years old, admitted as one of the fourth group of students studying in the United States with the sponsorship of his family. At the age of 18 after returning to China, he was assigned to work in the Qing government's diplomatic system. From 1903 to 1908, he served as minister to the late Qing Dynasty in the United States of America and on behalf of the Qing government to visit many countries in the America.

He had fought for part of the "boxer indemnity" for education use in China, part of it was used to send Chinese students to study in the United States and part of it was used to establish Qinghua University (Formerly known as Tsinghua School). He also helped Zhang Zhidong, the Viceroy of

Liangguang fight back the right of road construction of the Guangzhou-Hankou Railway from the United States.

Where to Eat

 Mau Kee Sampan Congee Store
（猫记艇仔粥）

The store is near the Whampoa Ancient Port. The most authentic and cheapest sampan congee in Guangzhou. There are lots of tasty local snacks, at very affordable prices. The store has simple decorations like most of the local stores. When you come here in the summer when the weather is hot it is still worth to try. There is an outdoor dining area with fans when the indoor room is filled with people. A waitress will carry a tray that holds some dishes, walk around every table and cry out the name of the dish, get what looks interesting to you. When you pay the bill they charge based on number of dishes, shape of dish, and residues. You also can order before you eat.

Menus

Pan-fried Lotus Root Pie	Fried Rice-flour Noodles
莲藕饼	炒米粉
Fried Ipomoea Seedlings	Fried Pearl Clams
炒番薯苗	炒珍珠蚬
Pan-fried Turnip Pie	Sampan Congee
萝卜饼	艇仔粥
Fried Gourd	Marinated Cold Cucumber
炒丝瓜	凉拌黄瓜
Garlic Fried Lettuce	Hushpuppy
炒生菜	玉米饼
Pan-fried Taro Pie	Fried Wonton
香芋饼	炸云吞
Garlic Fried Rapeseed	Pig Trotter Marinated with Vinegar and Sugar
炒油菜	和味猪手
Pan-fried Pumpkin Pie	Pan-fried Kumara Pie with Almond Flavored
香煎南瓜饼	番薯饼
Fried Dumplings	Fried Whelks Tops with Vegetable
香煎饺子	炒螺肉
Fried Wheat Noodles	Congee with Taro Whelks Tops
炒面	香芋螺肉粥
Fried Rice Noodles	White Radish and Beef Brisket
炒河粉	牛腩萝卜
Fried Clams with Soybean Sauce	Garlic Fried Choy Sum
炒皇沙蚬	炒菜心

Huangpu

155

📍 No.1/2 Xidi, Shiji village（石基村西堤 2-1 号）
🕗 8:00-18:30（Holidays and weekend till 19:30）

②Nai Po Ginger Milk Dessert Store
（古港奶婆姜撞奶）

The most authentic ginger milk custard in Guangzhou. The waitress is very skilled at pouring the water milk into the bowl of ginger juice in front of you, then tells you to wait one minute to give the creamery time to solidify. All dairy products in this store are fresh and tasty, such as home made yogurt and bovine colostrum. It is known for the Xinzhou farm where milk is guaranteed to be fresh. In the 1950s until 2000s, this area was used to breed the Dutch dairy cows and Xinzhou had one of the largest stock yards. After 2000 the Xinzhou stock yard moved to Panyu area but dairy products are still supplied by the Pearl River milk company from the Xinzhou stock yard.

📍 No.14 Punan Street（浦南直街14号）
🕗 8:00-20:30

Lung Dou Mei

HIGHLIGHT: Experience the local daily life in full swing
START POINT: Metro line 8 Fenghuang Xincun Station Exit B
FINISH POINT: Hongde Road Bus Stop
LENGTH: Approx. 3 hours (3 km)

General Information

In spite of rapid development in Guangzhou and environment changes, the way of local life may not necessarily change. Lung Dou Mei is an area that has retained some original character and way of life. Experience the endless forks and the many alleys. You can make a turn whenever you want, you won't run into a blind alley but one can easy get lost. There are granite streets and grey brick houses with typical Cantonese residential style entry. Entrances usually consist of 3 parts, the 2-leaf thick wooden doors, the sliding rail door, and the foot door. Similar 3 door systems can be seen in the Sai Kwan area. But when you look at the street nameplates, most of the alleys are named '龙' as the first Chinese characters of the street name, in English means 'Dragon'. The local annals call this area Lung Dou Mei (龙导尾), but the local people call this area is lóng dù wěi (龙肚尾) via word of mouth, means the dragon's tail. This name has almost 1400 years history.

Historical Background

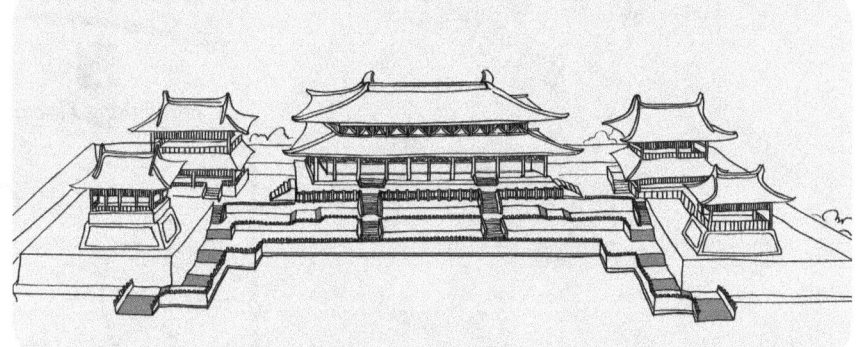

Dragon tail passage of imperial palace

The king of Southern Han Dynasty, Liu Yan, built a temporary imperial palace complex on Honam Island two-thousand-year ago. This palace actually imitated from the Daming Palace of Tang Dynasty in Chang'an, the capital city of the Tang dynasty (618-907 AD). There was a passage at the front of the palace, with seven turnings in total and bluestones on both sides. The passage was just like a dragon tail down on the floor, thus it is called "Lung Mei Dou" (meaning "Dragon Tail Passage" in English). Before long, Song Dynasty unified China and the temporary imperial palace of Southern Han Dynasty gradually turned into dwellings. However, the name of Dragon Tail Passage was passed down. In the early Qing Dynasty, it was also called "Lung Dou Mei" (referring to "Dragon - Tail Controller" in English), because the Chinese character, "Dou", of the name was once mistaken to be the other Chinese character with similar pronunciation but different writing.

Lung Dou Mei is like a maze. Though you would not come across a dead end, you might be coming back to where you were after taking a few turns. Lung Dou Mei was a village which was very large, however, after several administrative planning over a few years, the words "Lung Dou Mei" disappeared from the map. Today the only thing remaining that is related to those words is the Long Dao Wei Market, which sells fish, vegetables, Chinese herbal tea, clothes, and big flow-

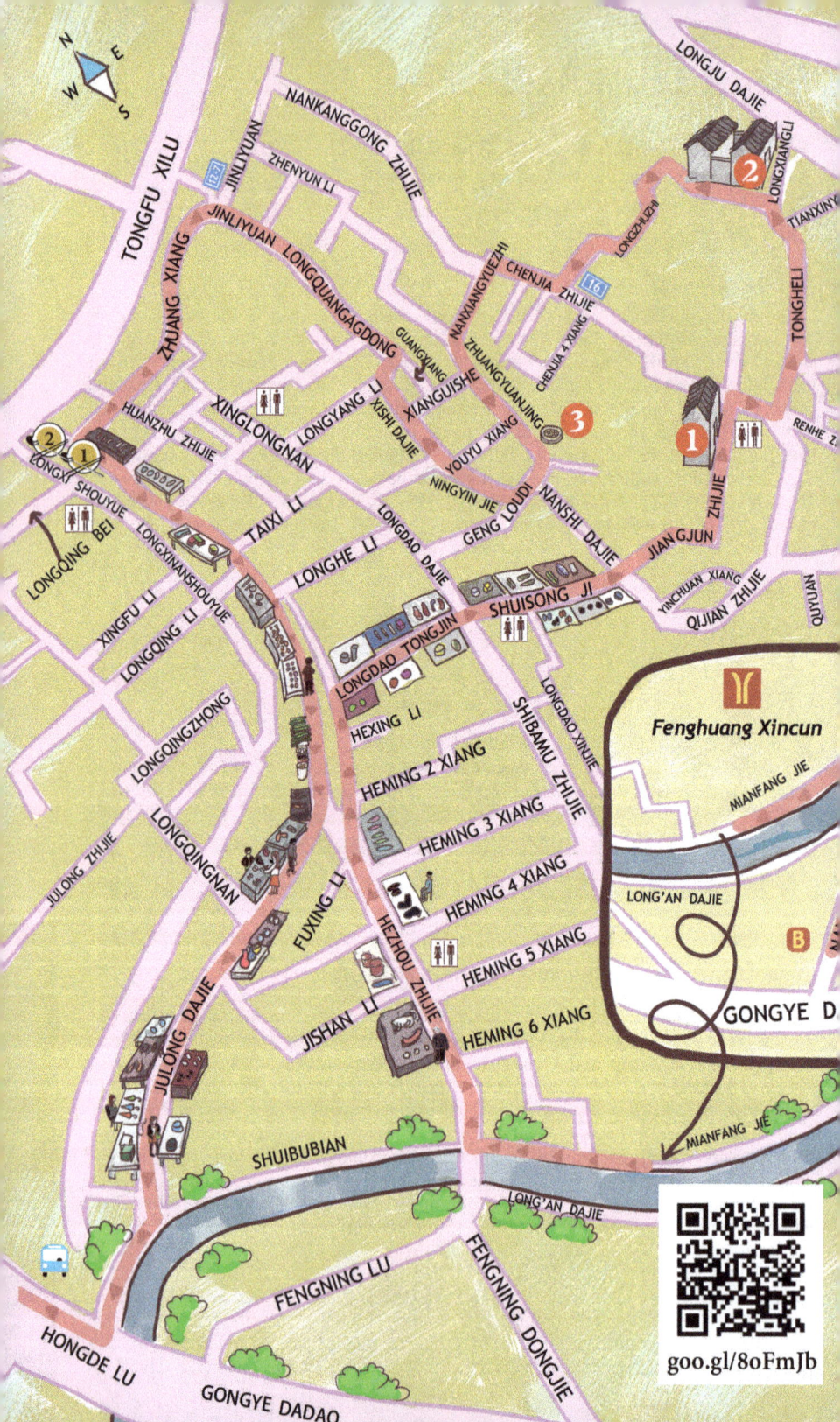

ered shorts. Lung Dou Mei, is comprised of two of historical sites, which are Zhuangyuan Well and the Former Residence of Deng Shichang. Zhuangyuan Well, which is not only the name of a well but also the name of the street where the well is located. "Zhuanyuan" was the title given to the scholar who achieved the highest score on highest level of the Chinese imperial examinations. Zhuangyuan Well is in remembrance of the top scorer in the Song Dynasty's, Zhang Zhensun.

Itinerary

Begin at Exit B from metro line 8 Fenghuang Xincun station, go straight on NANTIAN LU until you reach river, walk down the stairs and walk along the river until you reach a small bridge on HEZHOU ZHIJIE, turn right, there are lots of delicious local food stores hiding in the alley.

Temple of General

The Well of Number One Scholar

Stay on HEZHOU ZHIJIE and walk north up to LONGDAO TONGJIN, walk east to JIANGJUN ZHIJIE, there's a small temple opposite the public toilets, locals call the **Temple of General** ❶ , known as the sacrificial General because he was not conferred by the emperor. The temple was built in the middle of the Ming Dynasty and rebuilt in 1904. Legend says there was a watchman in charge of security in this area who lost his life while fighting with a thief. Villagers had a high regard for him because of his unselfish dedication and bravery, so he was respectfully called the General by local folks who built the General Temple where he was once stationed.

Walk along TONGHELI to **The Memorial Hall of General Deng Shichang** (❷; page 160), he was a national hero and military officer in the late Qing Dynasty Military of China.

Continue walking until ZHUANGYUANJING, sometimes you will see locals set up tables outside and play Mahjong along this alley. According to legend the great-grandson of Zhang Zhensun established the village in Lung Dou Mei, drilled a well naming it and the alley as Zhuang Yuan Jing, the meaning in English is the **Well of Number One Scholar** ❸ , in memory of his great-grandfather. The well has been blocked by villagers because during the Anti-Japanese war people who felt desperate ended their lives by jumping into the well. There is another archway leading to an area known as shopping alley called Zhuang Yuan Fang Alley (next to No.168 Renmin Road South) in memory of Zhang Zhensun (1235~1278).

Follow this route and this brings you to the local daily market, which is a long street (JULONG DAJIE) that takes you to the end of the road. Various kinds of goods are displayed in front of local doorsteps, the owners peddle their goods in the hustle and bustle of large crowds along the street. Most of the people who live in this area are traditional Guangzhou locals, few people are non-local, unlike **Shek Pai Urban Village** (page 134). People here enjoy the small businesses and life style, the local activity brings vitality and the most humane to this city.

If you are adventurous to know how delicious the beef offal is then go to **Chan Chiu Kee Snack Store** (❶; page 161) and try the Beef Offal in Stock (page 162).

Both sides of the street are filled with market stalls selling cooked food, meat, vegetables, fruit, shoes and clothes, and general merchandise, even the funeral items. There are also tailor shops, electrical appliance repair shops, general repair shops, Chinese medicine cupping therapy shop,

Wet market in LUNG DOU MEI

etc. Practically everything you could ever think of.

You can often see the elder people send greetings to each other in the alley or chatting while sitting on the granite stone benches. When you ask for directions, people will cheerfully tell you the way. This area reflects the life style in which local people live and is the most deeply felt of local life in Guangzhou. Finish your trip in HONGDE LU.

Points of Interest

The Memorial Hall of General Deng Shichang (邓世昌纪念馆)

Built in 1994 in commemoration of the 100th anniversary of national hero Deng Shichang's death for his country. The memorial hall is based in the Deng Clan Hall, where Deng Shichang was born and covers an area of 4700 square meters. It features exhibitions commemorating General Deng Shichang and the Naval Battle of 1894, and contains a noble bottle tree planted by Deng Shichang and the Shichang Well, which was once used by Deng Shichang.

In 1999, the Haizhu District government established the Haizhu Museum on the site of the Memorial Hall of General Deng Shichang. The hall displays exhibitions about the Sino-Japanese War and presents many heroic stories. The museum is an integrated museum displaying local features, collections, and showcasing historic artifacts relating to Haizhu. It presents an exhibition of significant historic objects in its collection and exhibits a show of potted landscapes and exquisite stones.

- No.2 LONGXIAN LI
- 7:00-19:20
- Free Admission

Where to Eat

Chan Chiu Kee Snack Store (陈超记美食店)

It is more than 20 years old with antique flavor tables and stools. Customers are mainly students and neighbors. The signature snack is Beef offal in soup stock which is tasty and refreshing, all dishes are served in huge portions. Feel free to ask for a refill of the Cantonese Style Pickled Radish.

📍 No.34 LONGXI SHOUYUE (龙溪首约34号)
🕐 7:00-19:20

Menus

牛三星汤	Beef Offal in Stock
牛三星河粉	Rice Noodles with Beef Offal in Stock
云吞面加菜	Vegetables with Wonton Noodles
牛脷河粉	Rice Noodles with Beef Tongue
排骨河粉	Rice Noodles with Spareribs

For Vegetarian:

净河粉加菜	Rice Noodles with vegetables
炒油菜	Fried Oilseed Rape Crops

Lam's Herbal Tea Store (林氏凉茶)

This is a traditional style herbal tea store and quite small. They mainly sell different herbal teas relieving different symptoms, such as the syndrome of cold, moisturizing dry-heat, and clearing away dampness. The introduction of different herbal teas and their various treatments are written on a chart hanging on the wall. Dozens of clay pots are placed on the counter. ¥8 for each cup, ¥16 for per bottle. Customers can consult with the vendor on which kind of herbal tea to drink according to their health disorder by sticking tongue out, or just come for a drink and a break. Since herbal tea tastes bitter, some herbal stores offer sweet preserved orange peel to customers for free to ease the bitter flavor. A small bag of preserved sweet orange peel also available in the store, ¥4.5 for each small package, good choice of leisure food for travel.

📍 No.34 LONGXI SHOUYUE (龙溪首约34号)
🕐 9:30-21:30

Lung Dou Mei

Featured Food

Beef Offal in Stock (牛三星汤)

Offal dishes are particularly popular in the southern region of Guangdong and its culinary capital of Hong Kong. In the more pragmatic folksy eateries, maximum utilization of the food resource is the traditional wisdom so the use of beef organs is classically represented in noodle shops here. Contrary to a common Westerners' distaste for these dishes due to cultural unfamiliarity and sanitary concerns, these offal items are very well cleaned. OX-heart, tripe and loin are preserved in ginger juice and rice wine before boiling, then added to soup and garnished with green onions and Cantonese style pickled radish on top. Locals believe it has the function of improving a persons body resistance to disease, and particularly suitable for nourishing spleen and stomach.

Bike Trails

Ersha Island

HIGHLIGHT: An oasis in a bustling city.
START POINT: Metro Line 6 Donghu station Exit A (Donghu Lu)
FINISH POINT: North Bank of Haiyin Bridge
LENGTH: Approx. 2.5 hours (9.5 km)

Historical Background

Overlooking Er'sha Island from Canton Tower

Ersha Island's former name was Ersha Village. 30 years ago it was just a little village with farmlands, ponds, swamps, and streams. In 1985, when the local residents still lived in the village, the government started to fill this island with sand on vast scale. The level of sand rose to greater than the height of a man. The sand fill lasted more than one year and didn't stop for a single day. In order to meet the needs of urban planning in Guangzhou, the purpose of which was to build up a senior citizen residential area in Ersha Village, this village's name was officially changed into Ersha Island in the late 80s. Since then the name of Ersha Village has slowly faded out from Guangzhou people's memory.

At that time, China didn't have a factory producing furniture like cabinets, pedestal toilets, or wood flooring. Almost all of the finishing materials and crafts of the sample villas in Ersha Island needed to be imported. On September the 21st, 1994, the first house in "Cloud Shadow Garden" was completed and offered for sale. This also marked the official opening of Ersha Island. The home buyers in Cloud Shadow Garden were mostly from Hong Kong, as well as some foreigners and local Guangzhou people. Until 2000, Ersha Island established its benchmark status in the Guangzhou property market, just like the Upper East Side in New York City. The original sales slogan of the villas in Ersha Island, "The China's first pure upper crust area", had become a reality. The average price for a condo is US$23,600 per square meter.

Ersha Island has been a sports training base of the State since the founding of New China. China's first world men's singles champion of table tennis, Mr. Rong Guotuan, and the world's gold medalist for weightlifting, Mr. Chen Jingkai, were trained here. In the 1990s, many other structures have been erected in the island, such as the Xinghai Concert Hall, the Guangdong Institute of Fine Arts, the Guangdong Overseas Chinese Museum and several hundred luxury residential houses.

Itinerary

The tour begins in line 6 Donghu Metro Station Exit A. It takes you about 5 minutes to walk towards the pathway on the edge of the river. The pathway has a very pleasant environment and is not too crowded. More importantly, the deck of Haiyin Bridge is utilized ingeniously as a natural barrier against bad weather. The municipal and district governments, and the sub-district office invested a total of over RMB ¥500,000 in the square during 2003-2005 in order to build a place for community culture and sports. Thanks to the advantages of the square, the sub-district office organizes diversified activities here on holidays including some which take into account traditional customs. The riverfront fitness area is nearly 1,000 square meters in size, and a wide range of fitness apparatus is available, making it an attractive scene on the north bank of the Pearl River.

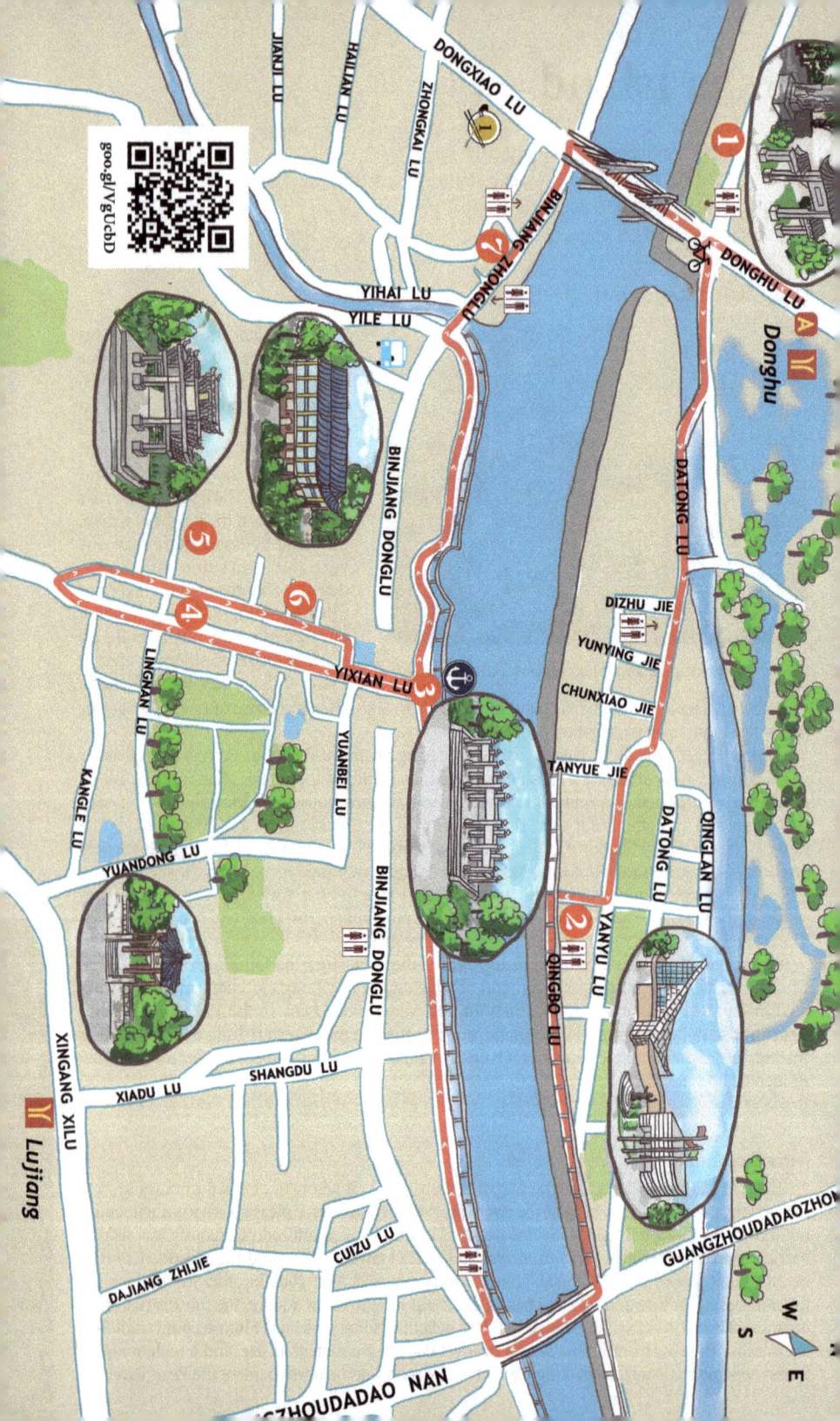

Lin Zexu Memorial Park

Lin Zexu Memorial Park ❶ is located on the right hand side of the Haiyin Bridge (The double tower single plain cable-stayed bridge). The wire slings stretching over it look just like the strings of a harp and the tops of the towers resemble the heads of goats, implying the City of the Goat. Lin Zexu was an official from the Qing dynasty known for his role in the events which led to the first Opium War (1839-1842) and in particular to the destruction of large quantities of opium on Haiyin Sizhou beach, today the location of Haiyin Square.

Rent a bike next to the bridge and ride toward Er'sha Island. Looking ahead, you will see the high-rise **Canton Tower** (page 168) and the new CBD area. On the north bank of the river is the Zhujiang New Town, which is a new city quarter within the jurisdiction of the Tianhe District. Twenty years ago this area was farmland, but now it has become a new financial, cultural and recreational center of the city, with all kinds of modern conveniences and facilities, such as gymnasiums, shopping centers, office buildings and subways.

Going on, head for the Guangzhou development park, where you will find a quiet park in the center of the island. This is a great place for people to relax or do some exercise. The park runs almost the entire length of the island and there is a bike rental stand there as well. It's good for quiet walks where one can enjoy a green environment, with trees and park areas over majority of the island. It is clean and somewhat unspoiled and has an opera theater house, an art gallery, and a couple of coffee shops to sit and have a rest. Turn right at HAISHAN JIE and ride up to **The Xinghai Concert Hall** ❷. This is the best concert venue in Guangzhou. In front of the hall, there is a statue of China's famous musician Xian Xinghai.

Xinghai Concert Hall

Ride along QINGBO LU and cross the Guangzhou Bridge. This was completed in 1985, and was the third to be built across the Pearl River in Guangzhou. On the other side of the river the second tallest building is the Guangzhou International Finance Center. In front of it is Haixinsha Island which has a temporary stand, seating 35,000 in three tiers. The opening and closing ceremonies of Asian Games in 2010 were held here at a cost of about USD $53 million. Now it as a free park open to the public. At the time the Guangzhou Government seized the opportunity to reform the whole city and changed it into a modern metropolis. Zhujiang New Town and Haixinsha form the new center of the City creating new city landmarks as well as becoming the cultural and financial hub. The new landmarks include the Canton Tower, the Guangdong Provincial Museum, the Guangzhou Opera House, and the Guangzhou New Library.

Ride west along the riverbank and you will reach the **Northern Gate of Sun Yat-sen University** ❸. Go into the campus through the north gate. You will see lush trees and green grass all around the campus. There are many beautiful old buildings. When you walk through the university, not only can you see the beautiful scenic spots but also enjoy the academic feel and long history of the renowned institution of higher learning. If you wish you can have a coffee inside the campus restaurant. There are two buildings designed by Henry K. Murphy who was an American Architect in China a hundred years ago. They are **Zhesheng Hall** (❻ ; page 169) and **Xingting Bower** (❹ ; page 168). Opposite is the **Yi Chou Jinshi Memorial Archway** (❺ ; page 169) which for more than three hundred years.

After leaving Sun Yat-sen University get back onto the riverside pathway visit the **Haiyin Park** (7 ; page 170), try the local favorite dishes in **Bing Shing Restaurant** (1 ; page 171) to finish your pleasant cycling journey.

Tips:
1. The charge of public bicycle rental is ¥ 200 deposit, ¥ 3 per hour.
2. If you are a foreigner traveling in Guangzhou then you must have seen long line of orange minion-looking bicycles waiting for people to take a ride. MoBike is one of the popular bike sharing services in China. You can install and activate from your smart phone, it's widely available in the city.

Points of Interest

Canton Tower (广州塔)

Standing gracefully in the heart of the Pearl River landscape axis, it is also known as the Guangzhou TV & Sightseeing Tower and nicknamed "Supermodel". It offers an awe-inspiring experience for it visitors with its unique design and a variety of excellent facilities. Over 600m in height, the Canton Tower first attracts visitors with its enchanting exterior. It is different from other "male-like" skyscrapers, which are introverted, strong, straight, rectangular and based on repetition. The Canton Tower has a female–like form, being complex, transparent, curvy and gracious. It is the world's highest TV tower and is a new landmark of Guangzhou. It is also one of the most energy-saving and environmentally friendly buildings in the world.

- No.222 YUEJIANG XILU, Haizhu District
- 9:00-23:00
- CNY ¥150 - ¥398

Xingting Bower (惺亭)

Xingting Bower was built with the donations of Lingnan university students in 1928. It was designed by Henry K.Murphy and located in Sun Yat-sen University. It commemorates three teachers and students: Shi Jian-ru, Ou Li-zhou and Xu Yao-zhang who sacrificed themselves during the republican revolution. Shi Jian-ru, in order to help the Huizhou uprising in 1900, dug a tunnel and attempted to kill the Viceroy of Guangdong and Guangxi Province with explosives, but he failed because they did not detonate. He was captured, killed and became a martyr. Ou Li-zhou was a teacher and Xu Yao-zhang was a student of Lingnan University. They died in the Shaji Massacre in 1925.

📍 On the campus of Sun Yat-sen University

Yi Chou Jinshi Memorial Archway (乙丑進士)

YiChou Jinshi Memorial Archway was built in 1635 by the Chongzhen Emperor in the late Ming Dynasty in order to reward seven Scholars of Guangdong province in 1625. The first two Chinese characters '乙丑' were one of the Chinese sexagenary cycles, it is a cycle of sixty terms used for recording days or years in ancient times. They translate as the year of 1625. '進士' means the former third degree candidate in the final imperial examination.

The original Memorial Arch was located in Liberation Middle road, and in 1947, the municipal government widened the road and moved the Memorial Arch to Zhongshan University. During the Cultural Revolution it was destroyed, but most of the stone components were preserved and the arch rebuilt by the Lingnan university alumni association in 1999 at a cost of RMB ￥700,000.

📍 On the campus of Sun Yat-sen University

Zhesheng Hall (哲生堂)

Zhesheng Hall has classical Chinese architecture but features a combination of Western styles. It was designed by Henry K.Murphy, an American Architect in China, from 1914 to 1935.

It has a roof style which is ancient Chinese: there are five ridges with six porcelain beasts sitting at each of the four diagonal ridges. This roof style was usually seen in magnificent palaces during imperial times. Each end of the main ridge is decorated with a beast called "A swallowing beast" (吞兽).

The decorative tile or earthenware beasts placed on the ridges of ancient Chinese buildings are called "ridge beasts" (脊兽). However, other than for palaces and temples, it was forbidden to put beasts on the roofs. They could, however be placed on civilian residences if the emperor issued a special edict to grant permission.

On the four diagonal ridges line five beasts called "crouching beasts" (蹲兽), usually to the odd number (singular). Fairy riding the Phoenix, followed by: Dragon, Phoenix, Lion, Pegasus, Hippocampus. The maximum number is nine. All the beasts are supposed to have three functions: praying for good fortune, serving as a decoration and protecting buildings. Because the roof has a certain inclination, to stop the tiles falling, a cross beam with multiple nails needs to be fixed. In order to cover up the nails and protect it from the rain, it was decorated with the glazed small beasts.

Murphy had lived in the Forbidden City in 1914 when he first arrived in China, but he didn't know the Chinese legends about the beasts and Chinese culture, thus the beasts on the ridge of

Zhesheng Hall are a little bit different from the traditional ones. There is a young man with a cap riding a cock, but traditionally this should be an old man without cap riding the Phoenix; also what should have been a lion turned out to be a dog, etc.

Squat beasts on the roof of Zhesheng Hall   Traditional immortal riding the Phoenix

📍 On the campus of Sun Yat-sen University

Haiyin Park (海印公园)

Haiyin Park is located on the Guangzhou River south of Binjiang Road on the southeast side of Haiyin Bridge. The park is bordered by the East Binjiang Road. It is divided into the North and South Park areas. The North Park area is mainly filled by a river. The park has a total area of 35,500 square meters. Building the park started in April 1991, and was basically completed in November of the same year and opened to tourists. The garden is planted to banyan, kapok, Araucaria, palm and a number of other tropical trees, along with azaleas, wine Jinrong ornamental flowers and other trees. Overall the garden is dominated by tropical and subtropical species. The area across the Binjiang road pedestrian bridge, connecting the north and south park has a number of sculptures, landscaped areas, beaches, flower and other pavilions, and other attractions and facilities like restaurants and other food service points.

📍 Near No.466 YANJIANG DONGLU, Yuexiu District

Where to Eat

 Bing Shing Restaurant
(炳胜品味)

A local Cantonese favorite, Bingsheng is most famous for its best BBQ Pork/Char Siu and the Fish Sashimi. Some of their dishes come with awards and recognition. The restaurant provides picture menu with English description. Must try their signature dishes.

People come here for lively, family-style atmosphere and excellent local food. Make sure that you reserve a table in advance and arrive early, because the signature dishes will sell out early. Avoid the rush by getting in line by 6 pm or after 8:30 pm.

- No.33 Dongxiao Road（东晓路 33 号）
- (020)34286910
- 11am-4am

Changzhou Island

HIGHLIGHT: The island bear witness to the old China trade and rich in historical culture, natural scenery and modern revolution
START / FINISH POINTS: Bus No.262 Xinzhou bus terminal
LENGTH: Approx. 4 hours (10 km)

Historical Background

View of foreign cemetery on Danes Island, c. 1840

Changzhou Island formerly known as Danes Island (see picture page 148) by the westerners in the 18th and 19th centuries, it is an island in the Whampoa District at the mouth of the Pearl River in East Guangzhou.

When the imperial government of Qing Dynasty decided to close all Chinese ports except Guangzhou to foreign ships, the "Thirteen-Trades Monopoly" was developed. The Hong (see picture page 74), a kind of Cantonese chamber of commerce established in 1720, managed all contacts between the foreign merchants, the Chinese authorities, and local merchants. A set of rules made the whole process very clear to all foreign ships anchored in the Pearl River at the Whampoa Reach. At the height of trade in the late 19th century, there could be as many as 100 foreign ships at Whampoa. Traditionally the Danish and French ships were close to two adjacent islands, which were given the names Danes Island (present day Changzhou Island) and French Island (present day Guangzhou Higher Education Mega Center) by the foreign visitors. For many years Dane Island served as a dry dock for boat repair and a burial ground for all foreign sailors and merchants who died while staying in this area. In 1924, Dr Sun set up the Republic of China Military Academy on Changzhou Island of Whampoa district. The historic Whampoa Military Academy supplied many outstanding military commanders for both the KMT and CCP. Changzhou Island plays an important role in Whampoa military area since then.

Itinerary

Take Bus No.262 to terminal Xinzhou Dock, then take the cross-river ferry to Shenjing Dock (深井码头, ¥1), the ferry departs every 30 minutes from 06:00 to 22:00; Look for a shared bike on the sidewalk near the dock, and then ride northwest on AN'XIN LU. The first stop is the **Christian Foreign Cemetery** ❶ at Whampoa. There is also a Muslim burial ground which is a testament to the dangers of living in south China's extreme tropical climate. The cemetery dates back to the 17th century, a period during the Canton System. Living at Whampoa, where foreigners resided for several months each year, involved many hardships. The high heat and humidity was a climate to which northern Europeans were not accustomed, and the weather weakened many men's health; crews were constantly stricken by typhus and other fevers. The foreign cemeteries were sober testimony to these dangers and the lists of ship crews routinely described sailors who fell overboard, died of disease, or were killed by pirates. Unaccustomed to the extremes of hot and

The Christian foreign cemetery at Danes Island

cold, often drunk, and poorly nourished, the foreign sailors did not last long in Asia.

Pass by the **Whampoa Military Theme Park** ❷, where during the summer vacation, you will see some children dressed in green camouflage uniforms to experience life in the barracks over half month or a summer holiday. China's current generation of children are known as the "little emperors." The government's one child limit for most couples means millions of kids have six adults, their parents and two sets of grandparents, caring for them. Military training try's to reinforce the concept of teamwork, with emphasis on discipline, self-reliance, and respect for others. It will help prevent these children from being too selfish and arrogant as their parents spoil them. Thus many parents enroll their children in boot camps during their holiday. In addition, Chinese students require mandatory military training when they graduate to a higher level of schooling, such as Junior high school, senior high school, and university. The new policy allowing Chinese couples to have two children came into effect in March 2016 in order to help increase the number of births in the country.

After cycling past huts and a section of uphill areas, there is an opera stage at the bottom of **Dafei Hillock** ❸, Cantonese Opera is performed to the villagers when important festivals approach.

Lookout Point from Dafei Hillock

You can lock your bike at the end of the path, then take the stairs up to the top of hill, from the lookout pavilion you can see the view of Whampoa Shipyard. Compare the view with that of 1850 and you can see how Canton has changed over the past 165 years. You will see the entire skyline of Whampoa Dockyard and part of Changzhou Island in a single view. The shipyard built in 1851, was the earliest dockyard in Guangzhou area, when major manufacturing was for military use and civilian ships were secondary. During the reign of Yongzheng in Qing Dynasty, there was a formal decree on foreign merchants where they could only stay in Whampoa and could not arbitrarily move into town. In order to prevent foreigners from entering into Guangzhou, the Qing Government required that foreign ships could only anchor at Changzhou or Shenjing. Therefore China's modern shipbuilding industry began from here. Take your time to let this picture imprint itself in your memory, or at least in your camera.

Ride into Shenjing Village along ZHENGJI DAJIE, it is said that the aborigines from Fujian Province moved here in 1295, to flee from the horrors of war during the late Southern Song Dynasty. According to historical records, Changzhou was the distributing center of foreign trade in the past. Most of the Shenjing villagers were engaged in dock work, ship building, and businesses. Villages were fairly rich, the blue brick houses and the granite streets form a beautiful landscape of the village. Apart from the village ancient dwellings, the villages had the same layout as Sai Kwan residences, and absorbed the architectural features of Hakka style and Western style, such as the stone pillars and arch over a gate, and the patterns. Many villagers still live in hundred year-old houses, some of the houses were abandoned by owners who moved abroad to live. There is an ancestral temple in the village where the villagers are invited to come and have a great banquet during festivals. This is a place for those who appreciate ancient buildings. It has never been developed, no souvenir shops, no annoying motor bicycle drivers to entwine you.

Ahead you will see the abandoned wok-ear gable houses, the big ear-shape gables are symbol of the wealthy. Most of these houses were built by merchants, the narrow windows have the function of protecting the occupants. The owners have moved overseas.

Keep cycling, a little bit ahead on your left hand side (CONGGUI DONGJIE), you will see a mud-brick archway with two traditional Chinese characters "扶輪" (Fu Lun). This was the original entrance into the village, when foreign merchant arrived at Shenjing Village they used this entrance when they came ashore.

Plantation of Night blooming cereus

Fu Lun archway

In Shenjing Village where you can see the night blooming cereus covered with thorns, hang thickly all over the walls of the village in summer, the general reaction of plants is to climb higher to get to the sunlight, particular on the walls of abandoned houses. There's a large **plantation for night blooming cereus** ④ in the village, it has more than 100 years of cultivated history in the village. The night blooming cereus has a rich nutritional value and valued for medicinal purposes. It alleviates fever, eliminates phlegm build-up to relieve coughing, and is extremely good for soup seasoning (it makes it clear). The Cantonese are familiar with its use in hot-pot pig bone soup. It is especially beneficial to long term smokers or those who consume large amounts of alcohol.

Continue to move forward, you will see a **Tomb of the First Ancestor of Ling Family** ⑥ who lived in this village 700 years ago. It was founded in late Ming and early Qing dynasties, this is the site where the body of the earliest ancestor - Ling Song, his son and his grandson were buried from left to right respectively. Ling Song is worshiped by his descendants in the **Ancestral Temple of Ling Family**(⑤ ; page 177).

Enter into JINZHOU NANLU, a few hundred meters you will see the **Literature Pagoda** (⑦ ; page 177), which opens on the 1st and 15th of the each lunar month calendar to worship.

Keep cycling towards GUANNAN LU, you will pass by **Zhongshan Park** (⑧ ; page 178) and **Museum of 1911 Revolution** (⑨ ; page 177). In the Zhongshan Park, there's an isolated island in the middle of the lake, there is no shortage of wading birds on the island. Egrets and Grey Herons are probably the most photographed & painted birds in the park. The stunning lake of lotus flowers peaks in late June and lasts until mid August, with the peak bloom in early July around the time many people come and take photos.

When you reach XISHEFANG DAJIE you will pass through vegetable market, winding roads, pond and small alley. Continue along JINZHOU BEILU, if you are reading this a few days before the seventeenth day of the fourth lunar month, you should be visiting the **Ancient Temple of Kamfa** (⑩ ; page 179). There is a big celebration of Kamfa Festival (page 35) that is held in front of the temple between 8:30 a.m. and 11:00 a.m., it is a traditional event that has been held in Guangzhou for over 600 years.

Have a lunch at **Ren Ren Restaurant** (⑪ , page 179) and try the Shenjing Roast Goose before heading to the next destination. Shenjing Roast Goose is well known throughout Hong Kong and it is also a traditional Guangzhou cuisine. Guangzhou and Hong Kong both have the same names of Shenjing and Changzhou. The origin of the name Shenjing Roast Goose is not because the goose are produced from Shenjing. Shenjing literally means "deep well", actually it is a special form of oven where people dig a dry well in the ground, place a pile of charcoal at the bottom of the well, and put an iron bars above the mouth of a well. The goose with hooks are hanging in the middle of iron bars and placed into the well to roast.

If you are interested in the history of Kuomintang-Communist cooperation, stop for a while and visit the **Memorial of Whampoa Military Academy** (⑪; page 176) and **Monument of Premier Sun Yat-sen** (⑫; page 176). Some businesses send their staff to Whampoa Military Academy for short term Military training in order to improve their attitude, obedience, and discipline.

Finish your trip at Junxiao Dock, take the ferry from Junxiao Dock back to Xinzhou Dock, the boat departs every hour at :40 min from 07:20 to 19:20.

Tips:

1. Down at the pier of Xinzhou dock and Shenjing Dock, you can see fishing boat that are anchored next to the dock, it is a charming alternative to cross the river by a small fishing boat, ¥15 per boat.
2. Sometimes there is ship repair and building operations off the river of Whampoa Shipyard, so the Shengjing Dock moves forward near the big river temporarily.
3. Using a bike-share will be a good option for this trip without return route. Bicycles are not allowed to enter into Whampoa Military Academy.

Points of Interest

Monument of Premier Sun Yat-sen (孙总理纪念碑)

It was built in September 1930 on the Bagua Hill in the Sun Yat-sen Park. Its height is about 40 meters and its shape looks like the Chinese character Wen (文). The copper statue of Sun Yat-sen, standing on top of the monument, is 2.6 meters in height and over 1000 kg in weight. It was one of four copper statues sponsored by Umeya Shokichi, a Japanese friend of Sun Yat-sen University in Guangzhou and Memorial of the Founder of Nation in Macau.

- 📍 Inside the Memorial of the Whampoa Military Academy
- 🕘 9:00-16:30, Closed on Monday
- 💰 Free Admission

Memorial of the Whampoa Military Academy (黄埔军校旧址)

The original Military Academy was founded in 1924 by Sun Yat-sen, with support from the Chinese Communist Party and the Soviet Union. The mission of the Academy was to create an officer corps for the new Chinese Republic, many famous Chinese war heroes were trained here. The original site was destroyed by Japanese troops in 1938. Two exhibition halls on the Campus of the Academy cover the History of the Academy with English translations. Unfortunately the other exhibition halls, such as Heroes of the Academy, do not have English translations. The site is far from the city center.

9:00-16:30, closed on Monday   Free Admission

Metro Line 5 Yuzhu station Exit D, take 431 bus get off at Yuzhu pier, and then take ferry from Yuzhu Pier to Junxiao Pier or Changzhou Pier

Museum of 1911 Revolution (辛亥革命纪念馆)

South China's Guangdong province was one of the most important provinces during the 1911 Revolution, which finally led to the overthrow of China's last imperial dynasty, the Qing. Through historic photos, documents, and original artifacts, the exhibition demonstrates that overseas Chinese established revolutionary organizations, published newspapers and magazines, collected money for the revolution, and joined the uprisings during the 1911 Revolution. First, they were the revolution's direct organizers; many revolutionary organizations including the Revive China Society and the Revolutionary Alliance were founded outside China. Then overseas Chinese were the revolution's direct supporters. In 1911 the revolution leader Sun Yat-sen considered Chinese citizens living overseas as the mother of the revolution because they were the individuals who provided much of the financing. It is believed that overseas Chinese donated around ten million Hong Kong dollars to the revolution. In addition to this, many overseas Chinese were direct participants in the revolution. Many overseas Chinese returned to China to join the revolution, for example, among the 72 Martyrs of Huanghuagang Uprising, there were more than 20 overseas Chinese.

- No. 563 JINZHOU BEILU
- 9:00-16:15 close on Monday
- Free Admission (need a passport to exchange the free entrance ticket)

Literature Pagoda (深井文塔)

Literature Pagoda is built in 1895. It is a hexagonal tower constructed of brick and timbers. There are three floors inside which are separated by planks. This pagoda is similar to the 'Pagoda of Fame and Success' (page 51) in Sai Kwan walking tour. Literature Pagoda is considered to be the most important treasure in Shenjing Village.

- Wenta Park, Changzhou Island, Huangpu District
- On the 1st and 15th of every lunar month
- Free Admission

Ancestral Temple of Ling Family (凌氏宗祠)

Ancestral Temple of Ling Family is built in late Ming Dynasty and it has been expanded and rebuilt in 1846. There are a pair of small drum stones on both sides of the stone steps in front of the door that symbolize good fortune, blessings, and ward off evil spirits. They are an indispensable feature of traditional houses and are also a sign of rank and status of the house owner in feudal China. There is a golden statue that is enshrined and worshipped at the back hall. It is the first ancestor Ling Song (凌嵩) who came from Putian of Fukien Province, moved here and settled down in Shenjing Village in 1295. His father (凌震) was commanding officer in Southern Song Dynasty and was a hero against the Yuan Dynasty. So far this clan has 30 generations in this village and his descendants are throughout China and even overseas. There is a historical culture exhibition about Shenjing Village inside the ancestral temple.

- Beside No. 2 Conggui Street West
- 7:30-11:30 & 13:30-17:30
- Free Admission

Zhongshan Park (中山公园)

Zhongshan Park was built with the theme of commemorating Mr. Sun Yat-sen and ecological recreation. There is a 5 meter high bronze statue of Mr. Sun Yat-sen built in the main square. After setting up the National Revolutionary Government in Guangdong, Sun Yat-sen was ready to take part in the Northern Expedition and unify China. Chen Jiongming rebelled against the Revolution and attacked the Presidential House. This forced Sun Yat-sen to take the Yongfeng warship to break through the blockade of the rebel forces and arrived at Changzhou Island to defend his position and wait for help. However, Chen Jiongming was not reconciled to giving up. He used the Xieshan Fort on the west side of Changzhou Island and the Fish Bead Fort on the east side to bombard the Yongfeng warship and block the sea port in an attempt to kill Sun Yat-sen. Sun Yat-sen called all the captains for a meeting and pointed out that heading southwards was the only escape route. He spread out the admiralty charts, then selected the Shenjing Reach between Changzhou Island and Shenjing Island as the escape route of the fleet. On June 16th, 1922, with the support of the local people, and taking the advantage of high tide, the fleet miraculously passed through the Shenjing Reach through which no warships had passed before. In order to commemorate this incident, a park was built on the north side of Shenjing Reach and named Zhongshan Park. There is a bicycle track along the lake in the park for visitors to cycle around and sightsee. There is an island in the heart of the lake. The island is full of egrets. It is a good place for bird watching.

- Intersection of Jinzhou Road North and Guanxi Road
- 24 hours
- Free Admission

The Ancient Temple of Kamfa
(金花古庙)

The Ancient Temple of Kamfa is built in Hongwu period of Ming dynasty. The temple has a history of 600 years and is a very popular temple in ancient Canton area. It is enshrined and worships Madame Kamfa who is responsible for people on earth giving birth. People come here to pray for pregnancy and children. This temple is the only well-preserved Kamfa temple in Guangzhou. There is a wishing tree in front of the temple where people place pieces of cloth with wishes and are tied to the tree.

📍 No.26 Fujufang Street, Huangpu District
🕐 8:00-17:00
💲 Free Admission

Where to Eat

Ren Ren Restaurant
(人人菜馆)

This place isn't like 5-star decoration, it is not a romantic date spot for sure. But if you want no frills, just good Chinese eats, you need to go here. One of their specialties here is the Cantonese roast goose, which uses age-appropriate black mane goose. The goose Cooked in a traditional way, the taste here is moist, meaty, flavorful and was served with the plum (light yellow in color) dipping sauce. Blindfold yourself and pick something off the menu, you'll still most certainly end up with a great choice! You may notice that at around 12:30 pm or so, the restaurant starts to get relatively crowded.

📍 No. 45 Jinzhou Road North, Changzhou Island, Whampoa District
(长洲金州北路45号)
🕐 11:00-14:00 & 17:00-20:00

Menus
Spit-roasted Suckling Pig	Whampoa Stir-fried Egg
烧肉	黄埔炒蛋
Shenjing Roast Goose	Mung Beans Stuffed Lotus Root
深井烧鹅	绿豆酿莲藕

Changzhou Island

Dawen Agricultural Village

HIGHLIGHT: Leisure and sightseeing agriculture village, home to boat people.
START POINT: Dongchong Hospital Bus Stop
FINISH POINT: Dawen Village Bus Stop
LENGTH: Approx. 2.5 hours (10 km)

Historical Background

Dongchong water town, the Exhibition Hall of Farming and Fishing is on the right

  Villagers are living on both side of the watercourse, their pole houses are made from Sugarcane leaves. Before the 1980s each family had small boats they used to transport grains and sugarcane across the river. Most of the villagers learned how to row boat before they were 10 years old. Pole houses were built before brick houses on both sides of the river in villages of the Panyu district since the 1960s. Villagers had a variety of surnames and they didn't have ancestral temples. Before the movement of land reform (1950) and the people's commune (1958), villagers in the movement lived on boats as a family or individuals, they didn't have a place to build their homes. If they rented farmland to grow crops, they would build a grass hut beside the fields to live in when ashore. They did not have the common community and collective ritual activities in this village, thus people around this area would not have formed a village and ancestral temple, they did not have the society of a traditional village.
  Many people in this village lived by fishing and growing fruits and vegetables in the past 30 years. As a result of pollution and petrol getting more expensive, individual fishermen found it increasingly difficult to make a living by fishing, Fishermen were forced to settle on land. Their fishing boats are berthed along river banks in front of their houses and they don't know when they will ever fish for a living again. Most of the young people leave the village to work in factories, elderly people live in the village and take care of their small vegetable gardens in the daytime, and some of them have jobs as porters in the nearby restaurants at night.
  Every year during the Dragon Boat Festival, villagers are hired by Shunde Dragon Boat Teams from other provinces who are competing in the dragon boat races. Middle aged people who live in this village are good candidates, since they have been rowing since they were very young. Shunde is the hometown of Chinese dragon boats in China, they could find rowers in their village in 1980s, however, as the previous generation are slowly getting old, the younger generation are quickly transforming into the industrialized era. Due to the limited source of participants, rowing teams are not capable as previous generations, teams have to go out and seek those residents who live on the river since they were young, as a source of athletes. A villager can win ¥ 20,000 prize money if they win and become the champion in the race, when the daily salary is only ¥ 100.

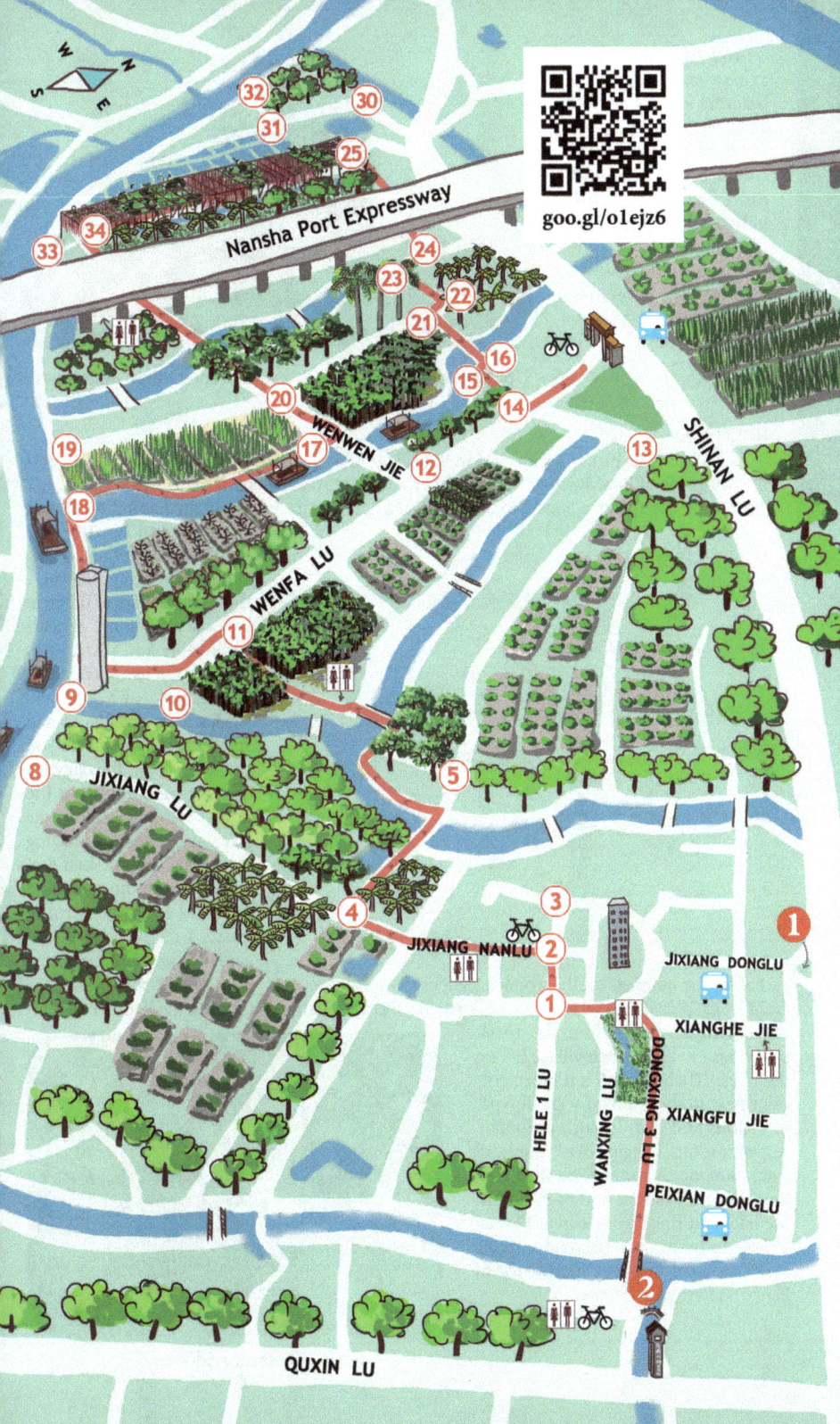

You can take a boat cruise experience the beautiful scenery on both sides of the river in this water village, or you can ride a bicycle through these fields and breathe in the cool and fresh air that mixes with the vegetable and fruit fragrances. Comfortable is the first impression of this village.

Sculpture of Boat Racing, a sign of the Dongchong town

Itinerary

Take Exit A of Panyu Square and walk to Pan Yu Square bus stop, take Bus 11, it will pass the **Sculpture of Boat Racing** ①, then after 2 stops get off at Dongchong Hospital (东涌医院站, 14 stops from Panyu Square in total). Walk back across the river, visit the **Exhibition Hall of Farming and Fishing** ②, the first floor is the farming culture exhibition hall, where there are displays of different types of traditional agricultural tools and pictures of farming. On the second floor, are displays of a thatched shed, stream pole house, and small fishing boat. Here you can learn about the daily life of fishermen and what the houses looked like along the river in the past by viewing the virtual shows. Then rent a bike next to the exhibition hall and follow the route paths that will take you across villages and farms.

Follow the numbers on the wooden signpost: 1-> 2 -> 4 -> 11 -> 9 -> 18-> 17-> 20-> 34 -> 25 -> 24 -> 23 -> 22-> 21 -> 16 -> 15 -> 14 -> 1; Try the farm-flavored cuisine at the Yun Kee Restaurant or take a little boat from the stream pole house to experience village life on the river. There is a 1.5 km green corridor next to the toll road with all types of melons and gourds, such as loofah, serpent melons, hanging over your head from bamboo in a shed. The shed is so long you can't see the end of it. Return the bike and finish your trip at Dawen Village Archway. Cross the road and take No.11 (toward west direction) back to Panyu Square Metro Station.

Green corridor ㉞

SURVIVAL GUIDE

This guide will help you to get around like a local and give you the information you need for a smoother and more enjoyable trip.

Mosques in Guangzhou

Tomb of Ancient Sages Mosque (先贤古墓)

Tomb of Ancient Sages Mosque is the largest worship building for Muslim people in Guangzhou. It was first built in the 3rd year (629) of Zhenguan, Tang Dynasty (618-907). The Mosque covers an area of about 1,860 square meters including the building which is of about 1077 square meters. The Mosque is a garden style cemetery which was built to honor 40 famous Arabic Muslim missionaries. The major architectural features are the prayer hall, pavilion, wing-room, and other facilities. The prayer hall is a two level building which has capacity for 3,000 people to pray. Most of the existing buildings in the temple are the architectural style of the Ming Dynasty.

- Huanshi West Road (环市西路)
- Free Admission

Guangzhou Xiaodongying Mosque (小东营清真寺)

This mosque was first built in the Chenghua Period, Ming Dynasty(1368-1644). The mosque has a long history and has a fine cultural tradition. It has served as a place for church education and has set up the "Guangzhou Muslim YMCA", which provides for funeral ceremonies. The temple covers an area of 600 square meters including a building of 462 square meters. The prayer hall is a Chinese palace style building which covers an area of 153 square meters. The mosque houses 100 Muslim people and has a total population of about 300 people who are are Hui people and follow the Gedi tradition.

- No.1 Xiaodongying, Yuehua Road (越华路小东营1号)
- Free Admission

Haopan Mosque (濠畔清真寺)

This mosque was recorded to have built in the Ming Dynasty (1368-1644) and covers an area of 1,491 square meters. The temple architecture is of Southern garden style. The major existing buildings are the main hall and the gate. The gate faces south; the main hall is 18.8 meters wide and 19.6 meters long, is located at the west end.

📍 No.378 Haopan Street (濠畔街378号)
💲 Free Admission

Huaisheng Mosque (怀圣寺)

Built in 627, this is one of the oldest Muslim mosques in China and has a history of more than 1,500 years. The temple covers a total area of 3,000 square meters, including the building which is 1,553 square meters and 400 square meters of main hall. The major architectural features are the main hall, moon building, east and west galleries, scripture-stored room, pavilion, minaret, and other facilities. The main hall is located in the center of the courtyard and has classical architecture with brackets. In the bright hall, the decor is simple and the floor is very clean. The minaret is a cylindrical shape and Arabic style tower is 36 meters high. The mosque is open to Muslims only, not the general public but you can take a peek outside.

📍 No.56 Guangta Road (光塔路56号)
💲 Open to Muslims only

Where to eat Halal food in Guangzhou

Lanzhou stretched noodles (兰州拉面)

Islamic/Halal restaurants are very limited in most major eastern and southern cities in China, which are typically run by migrants from Western China such as Lanzhou; they primarily offer inexpensive noodle soups. Northern Chinese Islamic cuisine rely heavily on beef and rarely use duck, geese, shrimp, or seafood, while southern Islamic cuisine is the reverse. Remember the four Chinese characters, you can see everywhere. Noodle is generally made as a bowl of Lanzhou Beef Noodles and takes less than two minutes to prepare. You can see how hand-pulled noodles are made by watching trained cooks at work through the restaurant windows. They don't have English menus.

Sunrise and Sunset for Ramadan

Month	Sunrise	Sunset	Month	Sunrise	Sunset
1st Jan	7:08	17:53	1st July	5:45	19:17
1st Feb	7:07	18:15	1st Aug	5:58	19:09
1st Mar	6:49	18:30	1st Sep	6:09	18:45
1st Apr	6:20	18:43	1st Oct	6:19	18:15
1st May	5:54	18:54	1st Nov	6:32	17:49
1st June	5:41	19:08	1st Dec	6:51	17:41

Getting Around

As a well known transportation hub and tourist city, Guangzhou is famous for its extensive transportation system as it is the communication junction of Southwest China and the gateway to Tibet. Conveniently connected to over 100 domestic and international airports. If you intend to stay in Guangzhou for longer than a few days, purchase a Ling Nan Tong or Yang Cheng Tong (岭南通-羊城通) stored value card, which can be used to pay fares in metro, bus, taxi and ferries and used at many convenience stores and vending machines. After 15 uses of your Ling Nan Tong or Yang Cheng Tong you will receive a 40% discount on all fares. If you only stay less than 3 days or a stopover in Guangzhou, Metro One Day Pass and Metro Three Day Pass also available to purchase at any metro service window, so you can make as many metro journeys as you want within 24 hours or 72 hours for a set charge.

Authorities in Guangzhou have launched a tourist travel card for all public transport in 2018. The Guangzhou Travel Card is owned and operated by Guangzhou Yangchengtong Co. Ltd. Travel cards are valid on all public buses, trams, metro, ferries services and offers discounts at about 100 tourist attractions, hotels, restaurants and travel agencies. Travel cards are available for 1 day, 2 days and 3 days, the price are CNY ¥36, CNY ¥56 and CNY ¥76 respectively. You can buy Travel cards at Yangchengtong customer service centers, tourist information center, bus terminals, metro stations, rail stations, airports, tourist attractions and hotels.

Metro One Day Pass

Yang Cheng Tong

Guangzhou Travel Card

By Metro

Taking the metro would be the best and the easiest means to get around the city. Although the first metro line of Guangzhou was only opened in 1997, the city now has 15 lines and 10 more lines are under construction. Stations are regularly added, occasionally move, and sometimes change names, so maps are often out of date. Explore Guangzhou has interactive maps of the metro network as well as a Metropedia, which lists businesses and places of interest close to every station. It can be really crowded in rush hours especially in Line 3.

By Taxi/ Ride Sharing Apps

The drivers are always happy to give advice to visitors. Visitors do not need to worry about not being able to get back to their hotel, because every hotel will offer its guests a business card written in Chinese and English that will instruct taxi drivers how to take you back to your hotel. Be aware of taxi scam, see page 189.

Uber sold its China operations to Didi, and the merger was completed late 2016. Its interface will look fairly familiar to anyone who has used Uber. Users from most foreign countries will be able to register for a Didi account with their mobile numbers. Didi will also accept payments using major international credit cards as well as Chinese mobile wallet payments such as WeChat Wallet or Alipay. Drivers don't speak much English, but the in-app text messaging translation service facilitates communication between driver and user. There are some sites such as the airport, and railway station where pickup at curb side is difficult, passengers/travelers are required to be picked up at parking garage, drivers will always call you before hand asking for your location, which makes it slightly challenging since users don't know the layout, this will probably work better for people who can read and talk in Chinese.

Ride price is about the same as taxi fare. It depends on what kind of car you request, whether you are sharing with other passengers, the time of day, and on other factors such as weather. If you lack a bank card you will only be able to call taxis and pay in cash. If you are getting a ride from a random driver or taxi on the street, the estimated fare given at the beginning of the trip is a basis for negotiation of the taxi fare when your taxi driver doesn't use his meter.

By Public Bus, or Sightseeing Bus

There are public buses that travel throughout Guangzhou City. The buses charge only ¥2 RMB. Most bus routes run from around 6am to 10:30 pm, after which there are night buses with the prefix Ye (夜, night). The night route numbers are not related to the normal route numbers. The fare is usually ¥3. Virtually all night buses stop running around 1 or 2am, and some start again around 5am. In most cases, taking a taxi at night is a better idea.

The new city sightseeing buses have ticket takers who speak both Chinese and English and also have multimedia systems for foreigners who speak other languages. As their 3 bus routes cover most of the famous and interesting tourist attractions in Guangzhou City. 1 day pass ¥30 for each person, 2 day pass ¥50 for each person. Ticket is valid for all the routs.

City sightseeing 48-hour bus ticket

Route Blue is Sai Kwan Line, a double-decker open sightseeing bus, operates 8:30–18:00 with an interval less than 30 minutes, and the main tourist sites it stops at include: Beijing Road Pedestrian Street (Lido hotel), Chenghuang Temple, Six Banyan Temple, Guangxiao Temple, Chen Clan Temple, Litchi Bay, Liwan Museum, Cantonese Opera Art Museum, Shangxiajiu Pedestrian Street, Shamian West, Shamian East, Xidi Wharf, Shishi Sacred Heart Cathedral, Haizhu Square.

Route Red is A Thousand-year-old Ancient City Line operates 9:30–18:00 with an interval less than 30 minutes. The main tourist site stops include: Baiyun Mountain, Luhu Lake, Guangzhou Art Museum, Sun Yat-sen Memorial Hall, Museum of the Mausoleum of the Nanyue King, Beijing Road Pedestrian Street (Lido hotel), Tianzi Wharf, Dashatou Wharf.

Route Yellow is New Urban Central Axis. Line operates 9:30–19:00 with an interval less than 30 minutes. The main tourist site stops include: Canton Tower, Sun Yat-Sen University, Dashatou Wharf, Xinghai Concert Hall, Haixinsha Asian Games Park, International Finance Centre (Four Seasons Hotel), Tee Mall.

By Ferry

The ferries are the cheapest way of crossing the Pearl River (Zhujiang). They were very popular in the 1980s and early 90s, carrying tens of thousands of people across the river each day. Nowadays its popularity declines greatly, mostly because of the construction of many bridges along the Pearl River and the availability of other public transportation.

Rent a Bicycle or Car

Bikes-sharing getting popular in Guangzhou in 2016. It's a perfect way to discover more places far from the subway station. Mobike and ofo are the two of bike-sharing companies in China. Download the Shared bike applications from Apple Store or Google Play, then register on the mobile phone number. You can find the bikes easily and pay about ¥1/30 minutes(deposit of the bike is ¥299). After finish riding, you can just lock and leave it on the sidewalk.

For visitors who are not using a tour company to visit Guangzhou and can't walk for a long period of time, a car rental would be a good option. Car rentals begin at 650 RMB for an 8 hour day in the city range.

Tips, Secrets & Tricks

Shopping

There are many "tourists traps" targeting the western tourist, so watch out for counterfeits and be careful of scams. When you walk along Beijing Lu Pedestrian Street and Shang Xia Jiu Pedestrian Street, there are many street frauds & crooks who will ask if you want to buy the Brand watches and follow them to somewhere to have a look. Do not be tempted to buy those fashion brand products for 10% of the cost you pay in Europe or the USD; they are sure to be fake products. Do not trust anyone who gets close to you on purpose.

Massages

Scams include extra charges for use of a room or a change of price at the end because of "some misunderstanding". Make sure the price is clear at the start. To avoid embarrassment don't order a massage from a hotel, especially of the type where the masseuse comes to your room, as most hotels have massages with a sexual nature and you may be forced to pay if they start. Most massage shops are genuine, honest, and very good value for the money but beware of places with private rooms, often found on bar streets. If you are unsure you can ask your guide or contact us and we can advise or arrange a suitable genuine massage.

Retail at Tourist Attractions

"Tourist traps" could also take the form of shops or lone hawkers found at legitimate tourist attractions or other tourist-frequented locations, selling over-priced goods to a captive or possibly unsuspecting market. Some of these places include airports, railway stations, bus stations, Hotels, Tours, Restaurants, Shops, etc. offering overpriced hotels or on an overpriced ride or tour. There will often be a difference of opinion on what is a fair price. The "local price", the "tourist price," and the "foreigner price" are a hard to distinguish in the minds of many vendors. Food and drink sold at remote locations, e.g. on mountains, may reasonably expected to be a bit more expensive due to the cost of transporting goods there.

Commission Shopping Tours

A normal part of tourism in China is for travel agencies to make money on commissions when their tourists shop. This cannot be done in normal markets, the travel agencies have contracts with tourist markets which record who buys what and pays a 30% or 40% commission to the travel agency, guide, and driver. Often a tour guide is paid zero per day and relies solely on commission charges to pay their salary. Common commission shopping markets include tea and tea sets, pearls, jade, Chinese paintings and calligraphy, traditional calligraphy sets, silk, rugs, and other more localized specialties.

Fake Liquor and other Scams by Liquor Stores

There are many fraudulent liquor stores that would sell you liquor which many turn out to be fake. Real bottle labels on the outside but altered wine inside, so be careful about different liquor scams such as these. To be safe, it is better buy your liquor at big large supermarkets.

Always Bargain with the Treacherous Trader

When buying goods (the exception being food and big shopping centers), look around at other shops before purchasing. Chances are you will be able to find the same item offered for a lower price. And always remember to bargain, especially since you are obviously not Chinese (identified by accent or skin color). More often than not you will be able to buy the item for

30-40% less than the quoted price. Don't trust the salesman in the shops, especially souvenirs shops in Shangxiajiu and Beijing road pedestrian street, no matter how they describe the products such as, you will regret it if you lose this chance to buy.

Thieves and Pickpockets

Make sure you stay with your group, if alone try to hook up with a buddy or make it look like you're with another group of people. Thieves are everywhere and blend in with the local people, they know already you are tourist no matter how well you blend in, they can tell from your clothing, posture, speech, and the way you carry yourself.

Pick pocket thieves work in pairs or groups and will try to separate you from your group by cutting in and creating distance between you and your group. They will follow you for a long ways, another clue is that they will watch you and stalk you. They will stop when you stop and they will be a few stalls away pretending to browse. They will follow you into stores and come up very close pretending they are shopping for the same items as you. This is especially true in those busy street markets.

Others will come up to you and try to whisper in your ear whatever they are selling, maybe even touch you by the arm to pull you the direction they want you to go. This a problem in the City of Guangzhou, even though there are many public security officers around, but this is not the case local villages. Don't keep all your cash in one spot. Carry your backpack in the front of your body, if you have to carry one. Do not count your money in front of the ATM machines, just put it in your pocket quickly and leave immediately. Use ATM's that have security guards if possible and go when it is daylight. Be extra cautious on those crowded buses.

Common Sense and Caution Crossing Streets

As with any other large city in China, one should use caution when crossing the streets of Guangzhou. Not all crosswalks have "Walk" and "Don't Walk" signals, so you must be alert and cross the street at your own discretion. Yet even when a "Walk" signal is shown and gives you the green light, you still have to be cautious of vehicles making right turns. At a crosswalk, never assume that pedestrians have the right of way anywhere in Guangzhou and even throughout China.

Cell Phones for Sale

At the Metro stations and on the streets especially around China plaza, people will come up to you with phones. Some of them are fake phones that will work, some of the phones will be real, so just make sure of what is being sold. They sell the phone in their jacket, show you that it works and the cam as well, the person will walk a couple more meters switch phones and sell you a toy phone. Quickly tell them to put the phone away because of cops and the guy.

Hotels Crazy Prices Increase Their Prices During Apr ~ May & Oct ~ Nov

Be forewarned when coming to Guangzhou from April 15th through May 5th every year there is an annual trading fair and meeting in the city of Guangzhou during this time of year. It is believe (according to what local peoples told me) that an estimated 10,000+ of representatives and traders come from all over the world gather at Guangzhou and therefore hotel prices are increased up by 200% – 300% during this period. Budget hotels also grab this opportunity to increase their prices. Even taking a city bus or a Metro can be difficult and stressful during this period because you will have to fight for a place at anytime.

Beware of Taxi Scam

When you pay for a taxi ride, the driver may not accept the money(Normally ¥100) because it was trimmed in the corner, which is an excuse for the driver to return the bill to you in exchange of another one, check the money carefully. The driver may have already switched a fake bill to you. I recommend that you try to remember the last 4 digits of your notes when you pay the taxi fare while you are sitting in the front passenger seat beside the driver. Don't give him ample time to fish out a fake note to exchange for authentic money.

Avoid Visiting Guangzhou During National Holidays

National holidays are the worst time to travel in China. A week before and after the Chinese New Year billed as the world's largest annual human migration. For many people from white collar to migrant worker in China, it is the only time of year that they can be together with their families. The experience is always a difficult one for people making the trip because airports, roads and trains are overcrowded and uncomfortable. Most businesses are on holiday and your options for eating and shopping also become severely limited. But if your scope of activity is only limited in Guangzhou during the Chinese New Year, the city is much less crowded than usual, you can enjoy this empty and beautiful city.

Avoid visiting those popular tourist attractions in Labor Day (May 1st) and National Day (starts Oct 1st), also avoid being in transit during this time. If you can't avoid traveling during these times, you should consider visiting less popular tourist destinations and make all arrangements and reservations well in advance.

A massive traffic jam on highway a week before Chinese New Year

Sexual Service

Picking up girls on the streets to have a few brief moments of sexual pleasure, male customers sometimes get more than what they have bargained for. As some men are getting ready in the toilet, the girls disappear from the hotel, together with their client's wallets, money, and cell phones. Sometimes the prostitutes are working with mafia gangs, beat up their customers and rob them of all their money. The women normally offer massage services in customer's hotel rooms besides offering sex services. Don't be seduced by their soft-spoken poor English and bringing them to your hotel room, it may end up to be a scheme to steal money or a worst incident if you refuse to give the girls what they are asking from you. Robbery cases have been reported by tourist who use this service, which results with loosing money, camera, electronics, and many other valuable items.

Fake Money in Circulation Everywhere

You might have heard about how extensive fake money is circulating in China. Don't trust ATM machines, you could be getting fake money from big bank's ATM machines. Once you leave the ATM, there is no proof of you obtaining the fake note from that bank's ATM and you can't ask for a "refund". If this happens, contact the bank at once. Suggestions: Arm yourself with a UV-enable pen. We got ours at a figurine shop at 5-10RMB. It shines UV light so you can use it to check the 100 dollar notes. If you don't have the pen, another way to check the note is the shirt of the President. The color can be rubbed off if it is real money. Turn the note over and rub his shirt on a piece of paper, red ink can be rubbed onto the paper. Also, the shirt is supposed to have some texture, so feel for it. If not, check the watermark, through careful inspection, if it can't be seen the bill is a fake.

Motorbikes

Outside of Guangzhou city center you can see motorbikes everywhere. It is the most common mode of transportation and most of the drivers don't have a motorcycle driver license. Some teenagers hide from their parents to ride a motorcycle. Be careful when you cross the road, look out so you won't be knocked down.

End of Year, Up in Crime Rates

The crime rate will rise at the end of each year. With the year coming to an end and Chinese New Year approaching, there may be an increase in crime rates in Guangzhou, like many other countries. It is always good to be cautious and have an awareness of your surroundings. In some cases, robbers open the taxi door and try to snatch hand phones. And beware of motorcycle robbers outside the city.

1) Lock the taxi doors when you take a cab.

2) Try not to use cell phones along the streets as you are become easy prey while you are preoccupied in your conversations. If we have to answer a call or make an urgent call, find a nearby place like, standing with a wall behind you, so that people cannot attack you from your back.

3) Motorcycles had been banned in Guangzhou, because riders steal bags and purses and drive off. So if you hear the sound of a motorcycle near you, be alert! Of course, it may be those motorcycle for the handicapped, which are still permitted in Guangzhou, but it is better to be more careful.

Bring the Thumb Size Portable Wi-Fi Router with You

When you are on the road traveling and you want to comfortably use your laptop and/or tablet or smart phone in the hotel, but for some reason there is just one wired Ethernet connection for Internet access. If you want to break free of the desk and work comfortably from another area or share that connection with other devices (like your smart phone or tablet) or your co-workers, a wireless travel router (also known as a pocket router) is a great mobile accessory to have. Price is around ¥65 - ¥95 in the computer market.

Laundry

Few lower end hotels and hostels have coin-operated self-service laundry rooms. Self-service laundromats are not available on the streets, although dry clean and laundry stores are available to clean your clothes. Normally you can drop your clothes off and pick them up the next day. One laundry chain is Tiantian (天天洗衣), which is conveniently located in most Metro stations. There are many stores on Shamian Island that have laundry service. An average load of laundry costs about ¥100.

In other parts of the city, there are laundry and dry clean shops sprinkled throughout neighborhoods. An average load should cost no more than ¥40. If you are doing sheets and blankets, they should charge no more than ¥10 for a blanket, ¥30 for a quilt. Dry-cleaning a sweater is about ¥8.

Television

Guangzhou Television (GZTV) has an "English" channel, now called Guangzhou I Channel (still "English" according to the Chinese name), offering entertainment and cultural programs from around the world, mostly dubbed in Mandarin and subtitled in Chinese. Hong Kong's international channels, TVB Pearl and ATV World, are available in most hotels, have a great selection of programs from the UK and US plus news at 7:30 pm and late (11 pm or later) every day.

Medical Treatment

Hotels usually have access to a doctor. The major cities of Beijing, Shanghai, Shenzhen, and Guangzhou have hospitals that will reach the standards of foreign hospitals, however the hospital systems differ considerably. Hospitals in other cities may not offer the same standards of hospitals as foreign countries.

Upon entering a hospital all patients are required to pay a substantial deposit before any treatment will be administered. Nursing care in hospitals is strictly limited to medical treatments so some patients will require another person who can assist with all other activities. No food is supplied. We highly recommend that all travelers buy comprehensive travel insurance in their home country before departure.

Newspapers and Magazines

The China Daily and/or Global Times are the two only English language newspapers available in Guangzhou (unless you go to a library), and both can be found on newsstands throughout the city. There are several bookstores throughout the city that sell current English and Foreign periodicals. The South China Morning Post from Hong Kong is also available by subscription only. South China TALK is a monthly English-language magazine based in Guangzhou.

Foreign Currency Exchange

If you come to Guangzhou from Hong Kong by the express train, which mean you arrive at the East Railway Station. Make sure you have exchanged your money for RMB (Chinese Yuan) before you leave Hong Kong. There is no foreign exchange counter at the railway station.

Changing Money can be done in a number of ways. Most hotels will have a foreign exchange service and will exchange cash and travelers checks. As with hotels everywhere, the exchange rate will not be the official bank rate. Most large banks will exchange money and travelers checks. It is a requirement that you produce your passport to complete the transaction. Banks will only accept foreign bank notes that are undamaged. Notes that are even slightly torn will be rejected. Travelers Checks can be a secure solution if you are traveling for a longer period of time. It is not advisable to go to the currency exchange desk at the airport because they will charge you high commission fees on each transaction. One suggestion is to exchange cash by using the currency exchange machine located at the lobby of Shifu Holiday Inn.

Electric Current

China uses a 220 volt 50 Hz cycle system so electric appliances from countries that use 220/240 will operate without any adapter. Appliances requiring 110 volts will need a adapter to operate. Hotels will not always have these, so we recommend that you bring a transformer with you. Chinese hotels provide for most plug types.

Taking Pictures

There is no problem in taking photos in most areas. Please refrain from taking pictures of the armed forces when they are training on the Shamian Island. At some tourist areas you may have to pay for the privilege of taking a photo.

Using the Telephone

Phone booths are rare in China but you can use a public phone at most kiosks instead. Cellular phones from other countries work in China. These calls can be expensive so it would be wise to talk to your local provider before leaving your home country. International phone calls can be made from most hotels but be aware that the call rates may be expensive. In China, some mobile shops will have difficulty selling you a normal SIM card if you aren't a Chinese citizen or resident permit holder, but you still can get the Chinese SIM card with your passport information by triple as much as the original cost and different mobile plan for foreigners. Many mobile phones have global roaming which will allow calls to be made as if you are at home. Please check your phone service provider to obtain call rates. To make an international call from China use the following procedure:

E.g. to dial New Zealand: 00 (to get an international line) 64 (country code) 6 (then area code without any zeros) 8709111 (then ph number);

Domestic calls: 0773(area code) 999 9999 (phone number)

Email facilities are available in most hotels and many have Wi-Fi connections in the rooms. Internet cafes are plentiful and inexpensive in China.

Post Office

China Post, the official post office is your best bet for regular letters and postcards. For sending packages other than the post office, there are many shipping centers around the city that are agents for DHL, FedEx, UPS, TNT, and EMS. There are usually shipping counters at higher-end hotels, ask your hotel concierge for the nearest shipping locations.

Facebook in China

For Westerners in China not being able to access your Facebook account basically cripples your ability to keep in touch with the outside world. Great Firewall(Internet censorship system of Chinese government) use DNS hijacking, IP blocking, and keyword IDS (Intrusion Detect System) to prevent you accessing Facebook, twitter, YouTube, and more. Chinese government wants to control the Chinese speech on the Internet, if it considers something "harmful", someone will call the webmaster to delete the contents, or they will just disconnect the power. For a website with a server located overseas like Facebook, the only thing the government does is block it. However, there is an exception, Wikipedia, which is not entirely blocked is sensitive to entries. Use GoAgent or prepare your VPN before enter China.

Meet Locals

If you are a foreigner travelling in Guangzhou and want to talk to local people in English, you can go to the English Corner at Xingting Bower (page 168) on every Wednesday between 19:30-21:30.

A few years back, people started to show up at the English Corner around 7 am but people are getting lazier these days, you are well advised to go there after 8 pm if you want to see more people. Don't worry, no one will try to get money from you, people go there mainly to practice their English and meet new friends. Their English levels vary greatly, some of them can keep a conversation going for some time. Please be warned that a foreigner will attract a lot of attention at the English Corner and will be surrounded by a crowd of people. It is difficult to leave English Corner because more and more people would surround you and want to talk to you and ask more questions. Each foreigner probably has anywhere from 5 to 12 Chinese people surrounding you the whole time you are there.

Some of the English-Corner-goers are very enthusiastic about practicing their English. They can stand and talk for hours on end without a stop! Ladies are advised against wearing high heeled shoes, as the few benches near the English Corner are always occupied.

Free Accommodations for Layover Passengers

Passengers flying with China Southern Airlines and have a layover in Guangzhou with connecting time between 8 hours and 48 hours are able to get a free accommodation. After acquiring free transit visa at the customs, go to the transit accommodation counter of Gate 20 in departure hall of Bai Yun airport and show your passport and boarding passes to book a hotel. You also can visit China Southern Airlines website (www.csair.com) and book your transfer hotel.

If passengers' layover duration is under the minimum 12 hours before boarding time of their connecting flights, passengers are very likely not able to get the free transit visa through the customs. If you would like to get a flavor of what Guangzhou has to offer or get quick look, schedule a mini tour with us, or plan to extend your layover time and enjoy one of our local tours.

China's Bar Culture

The bars in western countries are places where friends come out to chat, meet, and visit sometimes watch a sports event together, watch the football matches. However, in China, the bar represents a trend. They are the places of entertainment where the rich young generation and young girls meet and find friends. It is a place with high spending and a small target group of the society. The wine served in the bars are all known as western wines, but many of them are fake. There is no way to purchase the real wines without knowing the right people. Most of the bars in China set a minimum purchase amount. One is not allowed to take away unfinished drinks. If you are going to the bars in Guangzhou, the Party Pier and the Bar Street at Xingsheng Road and Jianshe 6th Road are relatively formal. Avoid going to the Bar Street at Yanjiang Road. Guangzhou neighborhood's convenience store and late-night street food peddler are closer to the Western bar culture. The bar is synonymous with decadent life for most decent Chinese people.

1. Neighborhood's Convenience Store

Guangzhou may not have the outdoor cafe culture of Europe or nearly the number of small street side stalls as Southeast Asia, but the neighborhood's convenience store is one part of Guangzhou cultures. There are many foods and drinks sold in stores which can easily be found near schools or even in some corners in quiet crooked lanes that could bring childhood memories to local people, such as Five Rams Ice Cream, Sarsi soft drink, Asian soft drink, Chinchin soft drink and Meichin soft drink etc. There are always a few plastic short legged stools and small tables in front of stores. The local people, especially workers and students, often come here to rest and take a break after an exhausting work day, gathering around and waiting for friends. A bottle of Sarsi soft drink or a bottle of Pearl River beer and a small dish of snack, are enough for everybody to have a great time at a very low price. If you are lucky, you will find a can of Pearl River Draft Beer containing a prize-winning ring pull. "1元换壹罐" means you win 1 can with extra ¥1 yuan exchange at the convenience store. This is a chance to have a closer look at daily life of young Cantonese, listen to their conversations about all the hottest events, fashion vogue, technology, and any gossip that one can think of.

Pearl River Draft Beer

A prize-winning ring pull

2. ShaoKao (BBQ) on Street Peddler

Sometimes you may want to try a variety of foods. One great option is Chinese barbecue. Try one of those street side eateries that openly display all their available types of food. You simply select your items and they grill it for you. They offer all sorts of meat and vegetables on skewers, which you could then pick out for eating. Some of the selections include bacon, octopus, chicken hearts, chicken feet, lotus root, green onions, eggplant, beef, lamb, quail egg, the list goes on. Everything is spiced with a delicious mix of cumin, chili powder, and flower pepper. Squatting down on stools with a Tsingtao or Pearl River beer, this snack is the perfect nightcap after a day of biking around to various villages. You can even get oysters! If you go to Guangzhou, don't spend all your time in fancy restaurants, make sure to experience food from street peddlers. You won't regret it, unless you get really sick.

The Spa Clubs in China

In China, spas and bars are not places for decent people to go. There are many spas that have a signs advertising beauty and wellness, yet, in fact, offering sexual services, or having healthcare services coexist with sexual services. Many of these spas adopt a membership system. Strangers are only offered massage services. If they see a familiar face, they will immediately provide an exclusive lounge and arrange for somebody to provide service. It is a well-paid business so some young women take the initiative to join the men's spa club to pursue a luxurious and comfortable life, and get engaged in covert pornographic activities. If a tourist would like to enjoy a regular and affordable massage services, it is advised to go to the foot massage parlours in the old town. There are many small foot spa parlours in the old town, usually with glass doors. The tourists could see many people lying on the reclining chairs for massages. The price is about $10 US dollars per hour. There are also Chinese medicine therapies such as cupping jar, scraping therapy, etc. In the Haizhu Square walking tour, you will find a couple of such traditional massage parlours.

INDEX

A

A Bite of China 67
African Town 130
American Southern Baptist 73, 128
Ancient Temple of Kamfa 175, 179
Antique curio 107
Autumn China Import and Export Fair 14
Aw Boon-Haw 91, 92

B

Baiyun Mountain 42, 106, 187
Battle of Canton 61
Beijing Road Ancient Path 109, 115
Beijing Road pedestrian street 187, 189
Bingsheng Restaurant 168, 171
British and French Colonies 61
Bronze Statue Square 170
Buddha Ancient Temple 104, 109, 116
Building of Overseas Chinese from Japan 151, 153

C

Canton Baptist academy 122, 127
Canton Fair 13, 14, 76, 82, 87, 88
Canton Hospital 78
Canton Tower 165, 167, 168, 187
Cantonese architecture 23
Cantonese cuisine 19
Cantonese culture 19, 25
Cantonese dialect 17, 19, 20
Cantonese embroidery 20, 27
Cantonese opera 19, 25, 35, 47, 49, 50, 51, 52, 53, 81, 174, 187
Cantonese opera art museum 49, 187
Central Bank Building 89
Chan Chiu Kee Snack Store 161
Chan Tim Kee Fish Skin Store 57
Changdi 69
Changzhou Island 36, 119, 148, 150, 152, 154, 172, 174, 177, 178, 179
Chen Clan Academy 26, 27, 98
Chen Shuren memorial hall 124, 125
Chenghuang temple 23, 108, 113
Chinese calendar 34
Chinese herbal medicine 19
Chinese Medicine 59, 66, 102, 120, 129, 159, 195
Chinese New Year 29, 35, 190, 191

Ching Choi Hin Restaurant 103
Cho Temple 33
Choi Fook Noodles Store 117
Chong Yang Festival 41
Chunyuan Villa 124, 125
Copper shop 49
Culture Park 31, 69, 74, 81, 82
Cultural Revolution 88, 92, 106, 127, 128, 169
Customs House 64, 74, 80, 152

D

Dafei Hillock 174
Dafo Buddhist Temple 116
Daming Palace 157
Dane's Island 148
Daughter's festival 31, 37
Dawen Agricultural Village 180
Dongping Pawnshop Museum 106, 111
Dong Zhi 42
Donghao Moat 106, 112
Dongshan Christian Church 125, 128
Dongshankou 122, 124
Dragon boat 36, 37, 113, 144, 180
Dragon Boat Festival 36, 37, 144, 180
Dui Shan Yuan Garden 50

E

Eng Aun Tong 86, 91, 92
English Bridge 61, 63, 64
English Corner 193
Erawan Shrine 49, 52
Ersha Island 165
Examination hall 106, 107
Execution ground 84, 85
Exhibition Hall of Farming and Fishing 180, 182

F

Fan Fong Desserts and Snacks Store 128
Fangcun Dock 66, 144
Father of China's Railroad 51
Feng's Ancestral Hall 151, 152
Fengshui 21
Fire Dragon Dance 40
First Ancestor of Ling Family 175
First Opium War 61, 80, 167

Five-Genii Gate Power Station 82, 86, 90
Flower city 13
Flower fair 29
Flower Pagoda 31, 97, 100
Foreign cemetery 172
French Bridge 61

G

General Temple 159
Ghost Festival 38, 39
Ghost Market 98
Ginger Milk Pudding Store 150, 156
God of Wealth 112, 113
Goddess Mazu's Birthday 34, 37
Goddess of Mercy 31
Golden Voice Cinema 49
Guangdong Foreign Affairs Museum 65, 66
Guangdong Guest House 96
Guangdong Institute of Fine Art 165
Guangdong Overseas Chinese Museum 165
Guangdong Provincial Museum 27, 167,
Guangdong Puppet Theater 24
Guangxiao Temple 5, 100, 187
Guangzhou Baiyun Airport 195
Guangzhou Bonsai 24, 63
Guangzhou Children's Library 106
Guangzhou Development Park 167
Guangzhou Hotel 84,88
Guangzhou International Finance Center 167
Guangzhou Liberation Monument 84, 87,89
Guangzhou Opera House 27,167

H

Haixinsha Island 167
Haiyin Bridge 165, 167, 171
Haiyin Square 167
Haizhu Bridge 69, 82, 86, 89, 90
Haizhu Square 65, 82, 84, 88, 92, 187, 195
Hakka 18, 20, 21, 174
Halal Restaurant 97,185
Haopan Mosque 184
Herbal tea 19, 157, 161
Higher Education Mega Center 172
Honam Island 61, 157
Hospital Franco-Chinois Paul Doumer 86, 91
Hotel Landmark Canton 88
Hu's Ancestral Hall 150, 151, 152
Huaisheng Mosque 96,97,185
Huangsha 47,52,61,65,66,74,82,140,144
Huangpu Port 152
Huangpu Village 150,151,152

Huangsha Dock 61,65,66,140,144
Huangsha seafood wholesale market 65

I

Imperial examination 106, 107, 112, 113, 159, 169
In-town Da Sun Co. Ltd 109, 114

J

Jade Emperor 37, 113
Japan Building 153
Jianyuan Villa 124, 126
Jiefang Bridge 86
Joss paper 33, 38
Jook Yuen Bamboo-pressed Noodles 63, 67
Julong Ancient Village 110, 131, 167
Junxiao Dock 176

K

Kamfa Festival 35, 36, 175
Kang Youwei 113, 141
Kapok 13, 171
Kuiyuan Villa 124, 126
Kwan-yin Temple 32
Kwang Dung 17
Kwang Nam Dung Lou 17

L

Labor Day 190
Lantern Festival 30, 31
Lettuce Fair 31, 32
Liang's Ancestral Hall 47
Lin Zexu Memorial Park 167
Lingnan Architecture 22
Lingnan Art 23
Lingnan Garden 23
Lingnan Painting 24, 125
Lion dance 24, 25, 50, 51
Litchi Bay 47, 50, 187
Little Sun Yat-sen Memorial Hall 56
Liurong Temple 95, 96, 100
Liwan Lake Park 56
Liwan Museum 47, 187
LongHu Walls 107, 112
Longtan village 34, 35, 37
Lung Dou Mei 157, 159, 60

INDEX

M

Mandarin 17, 20, 104, 191
Marriage 20, 49, 54, 129
Martyrs' Park 31
Mau Kee Sampan Congee Store 155
Mid-autumn Festival 40
Mingyuan Villa 124, 126
Museum of 1911 Revolution 175, 177
Museum of Ancient Huangpu Seaport 152
Museum of Donghao Moat 102, 116

N

Nai Po Ginger Milk Pudding Store 156
Nan Fang Building 140
Nan Guan Cinema 85, 86
Nanhai God Temple 32
Nanhai Prefecture 16
Nanyue Kingdom 16, 100, 108, 114, 115
National Day 14, 79, 190
Night Blooming Cereus 175

O

Oi Kwan Hotel 76, 81
Oriental Hotel 75
Oyster shell 150

P

Panyu Square 182
Party Pier 193
Pat WO Wui Kun Association 49, 52
Pawnshop 93, 106, 111, 112
Pazhou 38, 148, 156
Pearl Island 73, 76
Pearl River
17, 18, 22, 31, 32, 36, 37, 50, 61, 69, 71, 73, 76, 81, 82, 84, 86, 89, 90, 106, 113, 140, 144, 150, 151, 153, 156, 165, 167, 168, 172, 187, 194

Pearl River Draft Beer 194
Peasant Movement Institute 104, 106, 110
Polo Birth 32
Pooi To Academy 65, 122, 124, 128
Puppet Troupe 24
Purnell 65

Q

Qi Qiao 37
Qing government 91, 113, 114, 127, 154
Qingping Market 66
Qu Yuan 37

R

Relic of West Gate Barbican 93
Renwei Temple 34, 40, 41, 47, 50, 51, 151
Revolution of 1911 Museum 98
Rose Desserts and Snacks 116

S

Sai Kwan
22, 47, 49, 50, 51, 52, 53, 54, 55, 60, 117, 177, 187
Second Opium War 61, 71, 73, 92
Shaji Massacre 63, 64, 168
Shamian 25, 61, 63, 64, 65, 66, 69, 4, 75, 144, 191, 192
Shangxiajiu pedestrian street 187
Shek Pai 134, 136
Shenjing Dock 152, 172, 176
Shenjing Village 174, 175, 177, 178
Shiji village 156
Shipai 134, 137, 159
Shishi Sacred Heart Catholic Cathedral 86, 92
SHIWEITANG 25, 66, 138, 140, 141
Shiweitang Dock 140
Shiweitang Railway Station 25, 66, 138, 140, 141
Shun Homg Fung Stewed Soup Store 95, 102
Shun Kee Dessert Store 57
Six Banyan Temple 31, 100, 187
Spinster's House 153
Spring China Import and Export Fair 13
Spring Festival 29, 40

T

Taoist 34, 38, 39, 49, 51, 58, 113
Temple of General 159
Thirteen Factories 61, 74
Three-ply Door 24
Tianzi Dock 86
Tiger Balm 86, 91
Tomb Sweeping Day 33, 41

U

U.S. 67, 77, 89
United Kingdom 80
United States 67, 74, 75, 99, 137, 154, 155
Urban village 133, 134, 159

V

Victory hotel 64
Viceroy 84, 85, 92, 154, 168
Vietnam 16, 34
Xi Men Kou 93, 97

W

Wanmu School 108, 113
Water-dropping clock 109
West Bund 69
Whampoa anchorage 148
Whampoa Island 148, 154, 172
Whampoa Military Academy 172, 176
Whampoa Military Theme Park 174
Whampoa Pagoda 148
Whampoa Shipyard 174, 176
Whampoa village 10, 150, 151, 153, 154
White Swan Hotel 65, 67
Winter Solstice 42

X

Xi Guan Ancient Mansion 142
Xiaobei 130, 133
Xiaodongying Mosque 184
Xidi 74, 79, 81, 114, 115, 156, 186
Xiguan 47
Ximenkou 93, 100
Xinghai Concert Hall 165, 167, 187
Xingting Bower 167, 168, 193
Xinzhou Dock 152, 172, 176

Y

Yang Cheng Tong 186
YiChou Jinshi Memorial Archway 169
Yuexiu Park 31, 195
Yuling Bridge 144
Yuyin Garden 23
Yuyuan Villa 122, 125, 127

Z

Zen Buddhism 16, 100
Zhan Tianyou Memorial Hall 47, 49, 51
Zhesheng Hall 167, 169, 170
Zhongshan Park 175, 178
Zhongshan University 169
Zhu Village 30, 31, 37, 38
Zhuangyuan Well 159
Zhujiang New Town 92, 133, 134, 167
Zuiguan Park 25, 140, 141

www.ingramcontent.com/pod-product-compliance
Lightning Source LLC
Chambersburg PA
CBHW072044160426
43197CB00014B/2620